ROUTLEDGE LIBRARY EDITIONS:
PUBLIC POLICY

Volume 6

PUBLIC POLICY AND ECONOMIC THEORY

PUBLIC POLICY AND ECONOMIC THEORY

J. M. OLIVER
AND
G. H. WEBSTER

Routledge
Taylor & Francis Group
LONDON AND NEW YORK

First published in 1970 by Hutchinson Educational Ltd.

This edition first published in 2026
by Routledge
4 Park Square, Milton Park, Abingdon, Oxon OX14 4RN

and by Routledge
605 Third Avenue, New York, NY 10158

Routledge is an imprint of the Taylor & Francis Group, an informa business

British Library Cataloguing in Publication Data
A catalogue record for this book is available from the British Library

ISBN: 978-1-041-10085-0 (Set)
ISBN: 978-1-041-08421-1 (Volume 6) (hbk)
ISBN: 978-1-041-08422-8 (Volume 6) (pbk)
ISBN: 978-1-003-64530-6 (Volume 6) (ebk)

DOI: 10.4324/9781003645306

Publisher's Note
The publisher has gone to great lengths to ensure the quality of this reprint but points out that some imperfections in the original copies may be apparent.

Disclaimer
The publisher has made every effort to trace copyright holders and would welcome correspondence from those they have been unable to trace.

PUBLIC POLICY AND ECONOMIC THEORY

J. M. Oliver and G. H. Webster

HUTCHINSON EDUCATIONAL

HUTCHINSON EDUCATIONAL LTD
178–202 Great Portland Street, London W1

London Melbourne Sydney
Auckland Johannesburg Cape Town
and agencies throughout the world

First published 1970

This book has been set in Imprint type, printed in Great Britain on smooth wove paper by Anchor Press, and bound by Wm. Brendon, both of Tiptree, Essex

ISBN 0 09 101010 1 (paper)
0 09 101000 4 (cased)

Contents

To the memory of E. A. Bingham
For J.M.W. and O.G.W.

Preface

This is yet another textbook of applied economics. Since it is a textbook the reader will discover no theory and no facts which are not available elsewhere. Since it deals with applied economics the description of policies and the examples quoted will be superseded by events and replaceable by new examples.

This is exactly how it should be. It is important that a textbook should give a reliable guide to the present state of theory; we have given an account of those parts of theory, which are reasonably agreed among economists, relevant to our purpose. We have tried to make clear where economists disagree or can make little contribution to policy-problems. We have tried to avoid the more descriptive kinds of applied economics and to make some use of theory—partly because the only worthwhile applied economics is that which is informed by theory and partly because mainly factual accounts soon become obsolete and of no value to the student.

What we believe it has to offer is a coherent treatment of the subject at a particular level. The subject is the application of economic theory to government intervention in the economy. Part One of the book deals with the techniques and size of such intervention and the accepted objectives. It also uses economic analysis to show that the goals of government policy will not be produced by a free market mechanism and so the government is obliged to intervene in the economy once it has chosen particular policy aims. Part Two is largely concerned with analysis of specific examples of intervention, classified by the techniques used.

The level of treatment is appropriate for a final year student in HND/HNC in Business Studies, first or second year students in Business Studies or Economics degrees and for D.M.S. students. Put more generally, it is for students who have done a reasonable amount of serious economics but who find most textbooks of applied economics now available too descriptive or too advanced for them. It is a pity that so many students now study economics within their curriculum without ever seeing it put to much use.

We believe that its major virtue lies in providing at an all-inclusive price a treatment at this level of both theory and its application. We are not suggesting that Chapters 3, 4 and 5 would teach a reader innocent of economic theory; they should organise the thoughts of one who has followed one of the books mentioned in the bibliographies. All books reflect the prejudices of their authors in terms of emphasis, inclusions and exclusions; we have emphasised welfare economics (e.g. the Theory of the Second Best) and the distinction between positive and normative judgements. The emphasis on nationalised industries is placed on pricing and investment rather than structure. We have included concepts which are at present not always treated at this level (e.g. The I.S.L.M. model, discounting techniques, regional analysis). The exclusions follow from our objective of dealing with a number of examples in some depth, thus intervention by legislation in the labour market and in the reform of the international monetary system is ignored. We are not concerned with applied economics in general but specifically with the theory and its application to government intervention.

We have used references to journal articles liberally, hopeful that they may encourage the student with a particular interest in some part of our field and mindful that some students are required to submit an extended essay.

It is with pleasure that we are able to record the assistance which we have received. First from M. A. Pocock, Head of the School of Business, Ealing Technical College, for his continued encouragement and resourceful help in our hour of need. Secondly to the I.R.C., I.C.F.C., F.C.I., A.M.C. and N.R.D.C. for material used in Chapter 9 and, thirdly, to authors who have allowed us to quote them; all are acknowledged individually in the text and we now thank them collectively. Fourthly, to our colleagues who have read and criticised so helpfully our work in draft form; Mrs. R. R. Taylor, Messrs D. A. Chatterton, B. Harris, J. H. Lloyd, F. J. Rendall, M. F. J. Simpson and A. Smith.

We have found this invaluable; errors of theory and fact however remain our own, for although the authors have practised division of labour, with Oliver mainly responsible for theoretical content and Webster mainly for the applied content, they now practise collective responsibility. Lastly we are indebted to Jean Browne and Una Walker for coping with the incomprehensible in typing for us.

J.M.O.
G.H.W.

PART ONE

Chapter 1

A CLASSIFICATION OF GOVERNMENT ECONOMIC INTERVENTION

This chapter has three purposes. Firstly, it categorises government intervention in the forms used in the rest of the book. Secondly, it gives some statistics concerning the measurement of total intervention. Thirdly, it refers briefly to the difficulties in the notion that there is a proper relationship between private and public enterprise.

If information is grouped under various headings it is normally no more than a matter of convenience—that is, the classification has no explanatory power at all. Unfortunately, students sometimes mistakenly think that they have *understood* something if they have done no more than remember it because of the manner in which it was presented to them. The main purpose of the categorisation is simply to arrange the material in a pattern that can be remembered.

The following classification of economic policies may help the student to remember the data but it can give him no training as an economist—that is, it provides the reader with a mental filing cabinet and not with comprehension.

Our classification groups together items which have a common characteristic, although, of course, the items in one group may, nevertheless, have many similarities with those in another. The range of economic techniques available to the government is categorised either according to the nature of the policy or to the arm of the government which exercises the policy. The following merely describes quite briefly the various kinds of policy to make clear the sense in which the terms are used later. A working knowledge of the institutions, like the Bank of England, and of the mechanism of the policies, such as how the Bank Rate affects other interest rates, is assumed throughout the book. The efficacy and rationale of these techniques are discussed in Chapter 6.

MONETARY POLICY This is a battery of techniques the common feature of which is that they are operated by the Bank of England.

Policies are conveniently analysed into their effects on the *whole* economy and their effects on *sectors* of the economy—that is, their impact on, say, total spending and also on, say, spending on a particular industry. Like most policies, monetary policy operates on the total level of spending because *aggregate* spending is itself significant for some problems such as the price level; it also operates on particular *components* of total spending. This is partly because altering spending in a sector is a convenient way of altering total spending and partly because some sectors of the economy have their *own* significance for certain problems, such as economic growth or foreign trade. Thus, if it could be shown that agricultural spending was sensitive to monetary policy then that might be an effective technique for manipulating agriculture if this is important for the Balance of Payments.

The Bank of England has some control over the *availability* of cash, bank deposits and hire-purchase credit. It alters the volume of cash in the economy by buying or selling securities and so the public's holdings of cash decrease while those of paper assets increase, or vice versa. Through the mechanism of the cash-liquidity ratios, a change in cash provokes a larger change in the quantity of credit available from hire-purchase houses and other similar institutions.

Hire-purchase control is sometimes regarded as part of fiscal policy—this example illustrates the arbitrary nature of our classifying system. A theoretical distinction between monetary and fiscal policy is advanced in Chapter 5. Generally there is no such thing as 'pure' monetary or 'pure' fiscal policy.

The government is concerned with the volume of cash in the economy as it is held that there is some relationship between the cash base and the total volume of money. Unfortunately, the nature of this relationship is by no means clear. It was once thought that since a bank's deposits equal the value of its assets and its cash is in the ratio to total assets £8:100 that any change in the volume of cash generated a total change in the volume of money twelve and a half times greater. This view is too naive in fact, simply because not all cash is held by the banks. A second view is that it is the banks' liquidity base, £28:100 in ratio, that is vital, thus giving a much smaller multiplier effect. A further problem is the significance—if any—of the forms of money in the secondary banking system. These and other difficulties confuse the size of the effect on the total supply of money of a change in the cash base.[1] There is no question that there is some relationship between the two and so that the Bank of England can influence the money supply—especially if it also issues directives to the joint-stock banks about their credit policy.

The purpose of all this is that it is hoped that the availability of cash and credit can influence total spending and that, in consequence, to take only two examples for the moment, the restriction of total spending may limit both inflationary pressure and the growth of imports. The reverse of the coin is that the expansion of aggregate spending may alleviate unemployment and promote economic growth.[2] These latter purposes might also be served by expanding certain forms of spending and restraining others so that aggregate spending remains constant.

Monetary policy is concerned not only with the supply of various forms of money and credit but also with the *cost* of credit, that is with the rates of interest current in the economy. They, too, are thought to be relevant to the level of spending in the economy. The Bank of England can exercise some influence over the general level of interest rates by changing the Bank Rate, which is the rate at which it re-discounts first-class bills for the discount houses.

BUDGETARY (OR FISCAL) POLICY This is a group of control weapons in the hands of the Chancellor of the Exchequer. They used to come into play only at the Annual Budget but most of them may now be used at other times during the year and there have occasionally been two budgets in a year so that budgetary policy is now a more flexible technique than it once was due to the introduction of the 'regulator'—the government power to vary certain indirect taxes between budgets. However, our prejudices remain; we still expect one budget a year and regard the introduction of a second budget as a sign of failure while regarding two or more Bank Rate changes as quite a different matter.

The first aspect of budgetary policy is that the Chancellor can alter the volume of spending power in the hands of the public by raising more in taxes than the government spends in the same year, or the reverse. A budget surplus diminishes spending and a budget deficit can do the reverse and, as will be seen, they also have monetary effects. This relationship between government spending and tax revenue is intended to serve the same purposes as the bank's attempts to vary the volume of money in the economy. This is not, of course, the sole purpose of taxation.

The *form*, rather than the level of taxes and subsidies, is a second weapon of budgetary policy. Taxes, or subsidies, on goods or services will alter their prices and thus influence the pattern of spending and, also, its level. A wide range of consequences are possible. They might affect the total value of imports by changing the manner in which people spend their money, the size of exports by altering the attractiveness of the domestic market to producers, employment in the affected industries or the prosperity of industries relevant to economic growth. Taxes, or subsidies, on incomes are more likely to influence the level of aggregate spending than the structure of its component parts. This assumes that the government does not spend the tax revenue; if it does, there is no change in the level of expenditure[3] but there is a change in its structure. Any such changes in the structure of spending might ameliorate unemployment, stimulate economic growth or influence the Balance of Payments. The form of income taxes and subsidies, that is their progressiveness or regressiveness, may lead to some redistribution of income and so, too, in the pattern of spending. So those taxes falling on goods have most of their effect on the components of total spending and those falling on incomes have their impact largely on the level of spending.

The third major form of budgetary policy is the nature of the government expenditure arising from the tax revenue. Different industries will be stimulated according to the manner in which the government spends the money. Alternative effects are possible on employment, exports, imports or economic growth depending on the industry benefiting from the government spending; again it might be the economic growth of another country if the expenditure takes the form of development aid and there may be 'feed-back' effect benefiting the donor country.

There is a collection of other devices such as National Insurance contributions, Selective Employment Tax and others, not currently used in Britain, like Payroll and Value-Added Taxes, which may affect resource-use according to the precise way in which they are administered.[4]

EXHORTATORY POLICY The distinguishing characteristic of this group of control methods lies in their nature rather than in the arm of the government that exercises them. They attempt to influence economic activity by propaganda and the pressure of public opinion. Examples are savings campaigns, National Productivity Year and the Council on Prices, Productivity and Incomes. By changing the community's knowledge, or attitudes, they hope to have some effect on the performance of the economy.

PHYSICAL POLICY This is the use of the law to achieve particular economic patterns. Some of the other policies also resort to the use of legal processes but only as sanctions to achieve their purpose; the defining characteristic of physical policy is that it relies *solely* on the law for its effects rather than in changing prices, the supply of money or the rates of interest. Examples of physical policy are price control, as an anti-inflationary device, and rationing which can influence the consumption pattern and so, in turn, the production pattern and possibly the foreign-trade pattern. The Town and Country Planning Acts govern the use of one scarce resource in the general public interest accommodating the rival claims of local employment, investment and amenity standards. Exchange-control regulations are designed to protect the official I.M.F. exchange rates. By these and similar techniques the government hopes to achieve a resource-use quite different from that which would result without state intervention and which is felt to warrant, or need, the sanction of the law rather than the use of other policies.

The policies so far might be conveniently summarised by saying that if the government wishes to protect the domestic car industry, or the Balance of Payments, it may restrict the imports of foreign cars by a propaganda campaign, by changing the cars' price by means of a tax, by restricting the supply of money, by raising the cost of credit or by simply making such imports illegal. Economic theory can help to distinguish the effectiveness of these different techniques.

PRICES AND INCOMES POLICY This is a collection of methods used by the government through the National Board for Prices and Incomes and the National Economic Development Council mainly to control inflation and promote economic growth. Some of their work, like that of the various Economic Development Committees, is a form of exhortatory policy, while the Prices and Incomes Act, 1966, used the courts to enforce its provisions.

These five kinds of economic policy are the conventional subdivisions and it is convenient for the words to carry these meanings in this book. This convenience seems to be self-justifying; to declare the term 'Prices and Incomes Policy' redundant and distribute its parts under exhortatory or physical policy flies in the face of common usage without any gain in clarity.

The terms 'economic planning' and 'economic policy' are sometimes used as though they are synonyms; ambiguity results from the fact that they are also occasionally used so that 'planning' focuses on the long-run rather more than does 'policy'. In this book 'planning' will have this more positive connotation, meaning attempts to predict and achieve a given future performance from the economy, while 'policy' will carry a more negative emphasis in that it is rather more concerned with preventing undesirable results than with achieving desirable ones.

Economic planning and economic policy both concentrate on the whole environment of the economy, but the government may also intervene at a particular level as well as a general one. Apart from the five kinds of policy already noted, there are three other forms of intervention which operate at this particular level instead of generally on the economic environment.

CONTROL OF FIRMS' ACTIVITIES By means of such methods as location of industry policy and monopoly policy the government seeks to influence the decisions of individual firms in what it takes to be the public interest.

PROVISION OF FINANCE The government may feel that in particular circumstances state finance should be used without the government taking over complete control of the firm. Examples are provided by the Industrial and Commercial Finance Corporation and the Agricultural Mortgage Corporation. The purposes are either to promote a particular industry or a kind of firm that it is felt deserves public support.

GOVERNMENT PRODUCTION OF GOODS AND SERVICES The chief examples are provided by the nationalised industries and the welfare services. Once the government has chosen this form of intervention it has three courses open to it. The service or product may be provided free and financed out of taxation; this means that the consumer pays roughly according to his ability to pay and not according to the use he makes—London Bridge is an example. Secondly, the consumer may pay according to the use he makes and not according to his ability to pay. The Forth Road Bridge (a toll bridge) is an example. The third course is for everybody to pay the same, irrespective of either the use they make or their ability to pay. This is the case with insurance-financed welfare services.

The government has to choose from a range of competing goals and from a number of techniques for reaching these goals. These choices are made partly against a background of economic theory which can vary from a sophisticated model to something that is no more than an informed awareness of the relevant factors, which can shade, in its turn, into economic superstition.[5]

This book is concerned with the relationship between economic theory and government policy. It is a fair generalisation that there are now few supporters of complete *laissez-faire*, although there is a well-established hostility to detailed forms of state intervention such as nationalisation; the main political problem concerns the nature of the intervention rather than the principle of intervention; the main dividing line is between those for whom state action is mainly defensive in nature and those for whom it is also positive in character, that is it is between those who accept economic policy and those who also accept economic planning. However, it is worth considering in Chapter 3 the economic reasons for minimising government intervention in the economy and allowing, as far as possible, the price mechanism to govern the use of resources.

This section of the chapter is intended to give some idea of the nature and scale of government intervention.

The analysis of expenditure in Table 1 is intended to show the relative size of government spending in different fields. It is a very imperfect measurement of the importance of government intervention for two different sets of reasons.

Firstly, there are many cases where the money value of expenditure cannot represent the importance of the intervention, e.g. the budget of the National Board for Prices and Incomes does not measure the importance of the Board's work.

Secondly, the data in Table 1 may mislead the reader not familiar with the definitions and assumptions on which the figures are based. Thus 'public expenditure', as defined in the Blue Book,[6] includes not only the purchases of goods and services in the period but also purchases of capital items (gross domestic fixed-capital formation) and increases in the value of stocks. The last two items would not be called (revenue) expenditure in the case of a trading company.

Table 1 shows $\dfrac{\text{Total public expenditure}}{\text{Gross national product at factor cost}} \times 100$ as 52·1%. It should be noted that this value is lowered by the inclusion of 'public corporations' in total public expenditure, not in terms of expenditure or turnover, but only by gross fixed-capital formation and any increases in the value of their stocks. On the other hand, another *equally* valid proportion would be much lower if it excluded that part of public expenditure which represents transfers of income from one sector of the community to another[7] on the grounds that it did not affect the size of G.N.P. We have included such items because we wish to show the relative importance of classes of expenditure. If

TABLE 1. *An Analysis of public expenditure 1968*

Type of expenditure	*£ Million*	*£ Million*
(1) *Collective services provided by the state*		
Defence and external relations	2,776	
Education	2,176	
National Health services (including local welfare, child care, etc.)	1,999	
Social facilities (including water, sewerage, refuse disposal, parks, libraries, fire service and employment exchanges, roads and public lighting, transport and communication)	2,709	
Law and order	424	
Finance and tax collection	223	10,307
2) *National insurance and pensions*		3,344
(3) *Direct government intervention*		
Housing	1,115	
Other industry and trade (including investment by public corporations)	1,863	
Agriculture	400	
Research	178	3,556
(4) *Debt interest*		
Central government	1,249	
Local authorities	543	
Public corporations	123	1,995
TOTAL PUBLIC EXPENDITURE (A)		£19,122
Gross national product (B)		£36,686
% Total public expenditure ($\frac{A}{B} \times 100$)		52·1%

SOURCE *Blue Book*, National Income and Expenditure (1969). Tables 1, 49 and 50.

we wish to show 'public expenditure' in this manner we should include transfer payments in the private sector—which also do not affect the total G.N.P. and for which no figures are available. Thus Table 1 simply indicates that magnitude of different forms of government expenditure. 'Public expenditure' and 'gross national product' are, as it were, balloons which are inflated or deflated by including or excluding particular items. International comparisons can only be made if the same statistical conventions are used in both countries and comparisons within a nation of public and private expenditure are only meaningful if both balloons were similarly inflated, that is transfers, for instance, must be similarly treated in both sectors of the economy. Propagandists have not been above including them in the public sector and not in the private in order to magnify the extent of the government in the economy. Figures are often produced purporting to show the share of G.N.P. in the hands of the government. They should be treated with reserve that borders on scepticism.

Table 2 below makes international comparisons possible with other countries using one particular measure of government intervention, *viz.* the proportions of G.N.P. at market prices devoted to government current revenue and current expenditure. Using either measurement, the U.K. ranks *sixth* out of the eight countries for which figures are shown. The U.K. figures are much lower than in Table 1, since G.N.P. is now measured at market price, rather than factor cost, and transfer items are now shown separately, counted as either revenue or expenditure.

In terms of revenue, the U.K. is distinguished by having, apart from Switzerland, the *lowest* proportion of G.N.P. devoted to 'Direct taxes on persons'. By either measurement social security is low for the U.K., particularly compared to France, Netherlands and Germany.

Measured by expenditure the U.K. ranks *second* to the U.S. in terms of the proportion of G.N.P. spent on 'Defence expenditures and the National Debt'.[8] As already mentioned these two items are dissimilar in nature, interest on the National Debt being a transfer payment. Great Britain has the *third* highest proportion in indirect taxation. The significance of government current saving is examined in Chapter 5.

The reader may well come across 'measures' of government expenditure quite different from these two tables. Every such measure can be arithmetically correct and also conceptually correct in the limited sense of being consistent within its own definitions. The user of such tables must be sceptical of any claims for superiority made on behalf of a given set of figures by its compiler; he needs to satisfy himself only on two points, that the table is designed to meet the particular purpose he himself has in mind and that it is technically consistent in meeting that purpose. In other words, there is no true measure, but only a particular measure to answer a particular question.

Not only is there no given 'true' measure of the size of government intervention in the economy, there is also no clear set of principles

TABLE 2. *Government current revenue and expenditure in relation to national product (percentages of G.N.P. at market prices)*

	United Kingdom	*France*	*West Germany*	*Netherlands*	*Norway*	*Sweden*	*Switzerland*	*United States*
	1967	*1967*	*1967*	*1967*	*1967*	*1966*	*1966*	*1967*
Direct taxes on persons	15·1	19·2	18·5	23·9	20·8	24·9	12·3	15·2
Personal income taxes	10·3	4·4	8·2	11·3	12·0	18·4	7·6	10·0
Social Security contributions	4·8	14·8	10·3	12·6	8·8	6·5	4·7	5·2
Direct taxes on corporations	2·6	2·0	2·2	2·5	1·5	2·1	2·3	4·2
Indirect taxes	15·1	17·5	14·6	10·7	15·5	14·1	7·1	8·9
TOTAL TAXES	32·8	38·7	35·3	37·1	37·8	41·1	21·7	28·3
Other current revenue	2·7	0·7	2·2	2·9	3·2	5·2	3·7	0·0
TOTAL CURRENT REVENUE	35·5	39·4	37·5	40·0	41·0	46·3	25·4	28·3
Consumption of goods and services	17·9	13·5	16·7	16·2	16·9	20·9	11·8	20·7
Defence	5·8	4·1	3·9	3·7	3·5	4·5	2·5	9·3
Civil consumption	12·1	9·4	12·8	12·5	13·4	16·4	9·3	11·4
Subsidies	2·0	2·2	0·8	0·7	4·5	1·7	1·0	0·2
Social Security benefits and other transfers to persons	8·5	17·6	14·7	15·5	11·1	10·9	7·2	5·8
Interest on the National Debt	4·0	1·2	0·9	2·8	1·2	1·5	1·3	1·3
Foreign aid	0·5	1·0	0·5	0·2	0·2	0·3	0·2	0·3
TOTAL CURRENT EXPENDITURE	32·9	35·5	33·6	35·4	33·9	35·3	21·5	28·3
Civil consumption, subsidies and Social Security benefits	22·6	29·2	28·3	28·7	29·0	29·0	17·5	17·4
Defence expenditures and interest on the National Debt	9·8	5·3	4·8	6·5	4·7	6·0	3·8	10·6
Government saving: current revenue les current expenditure	2·6	3·9	3·9	4·6	7·1	11·0	3·9	0·0

SOURCES O.E.C.D.'s National Accounts Statistics—quoted in T. H. Hill, 'Too Much Consumption', *National Westminster Bank Quarterly Review*, 1969, Table 2.

governing it.[9] There is some public debate concerning the role of the government in the economy with the implication that there is some discoverable correct size for government expenditure. There has been an erudite discussion among economists concerning the form and the magnitude of the role of the state in the economy. It will serve our present purpose to indicate briefly the trickiness of this apparently simple matter.

An obvious principle in discovering what the public wants is to resort to the democratic processes of voting and to say that the proper role for the government within the economy is that for which the public votes. This may well seem straightforward, obvious and 'fair'; but in fact ambiguities immediately arise.

The first difficulty concerns consistency and transitivity. It is an idea familiar in elementary algebra that if *A* is preferable to *B*, and *B* is preferable to *C*, then *A* must also be preferable to *C*. A perfectly plausible voting pattern by a group of people can breach this simple condition and provide our first anomaly in trying to identify the wishes of the majority about economic policy. If three persons, *A*, *B* and *C* are asked to rank three alternative government policies *X*, *Y* and *Z*, it could happen that *A* ranks the policies in the order *X*, *Y* and *Z*, that *B* prefers the order *Y*, *Z* and *X* and that *C* prefers *Z*, *X* and *Y*. Now this means a majority, *A* and *B*, prefer *Y* to *Z*, that a majority, *B* and *C*, prefers *Z* to *X*, so that by the transitivity rule *Y* should be preferred to *X* but in fact a majority, *A* and *C*, prefer *X* to *Y*! Thus simple voting can provide meaningless majorities and does not necessarily provide a clear guide for a government choosing between policies.[10]

A quite different difficulty arises when trying to compare the different consequences of a proposed economic policy. A rich man might say that the amenities of his estate were worth £½ million to him (and be prepared to pay this to stop the building of council housing). A hundred poor people might be willing to pay £2 per week rent for twenty years to give £208,000 (interest and discounting ignored). Few people would find any such facts a convincing reason for not building the houses. And the reason is that a given sum of money means different things to different people according to tastes, habits and, particularly, existing wealth and income; that is money does not have a constant marginal utility. This assumption—that the significance of a given sum of money varies between persons, and that its legal tender is objective but that its economic value is subjective—brings us to the central problem of welfare economics. People can have an opinion about government policy and they can point to, and sometimes quantify, its consequences but what they cannot do is scientifically measure its economic value. Inter-personal comparisons of welfare are unscientific. This is not to say that we can escape the necessity for such comparisons or cannot measure, in some way, costs and benefits. It is to say that we should know the limit of what we are doing when we make such comparisons. It was on this difficulty, among others, of inter-personal comparisons, that the Compensation Test failed. This was the idea that a policy, say not building the council estate, is a gain if those who benefit, in this example the landowner, place a higher value on their gain than the losers, the potential council tenants, place on their loss.[11] The subjectivity of money as a measuring rod of value ended this technique for evaluating policies.

Having failed to overcome the voting paradox, or the difficulties of inter-personal comparisons of utility, economists have met yet other difficulties when turning to a third construct to discover a criterion for judging government economic policies; Buchanan and Tullock[12] have investigated some of the problems in identifying the public will. Let us postulate the comparative costs and benefits of the provisions of a road system by private enterprise and by government action, from the point of view of a particular individual. We may take as our base that position in which his costs equal his benefits and this is represented by the origin of the *Y* axis in Figure 1. The *X* axis shows differing proportions of votes necessary, according to the political system, to gain *his* ideal level of road-building in which the individual gets that proportion of road-building which satisfies his clear need for roads near to him and that proportion which meets his smaller need for roads further away.

Now if the roads are provided by private enterprise (toll roads) there will be too few roads from the individual's viewpoint so that the 'costs' to him are *OA* in this sense of sub-optimal provision, of divergence from his ideal pattern. But if any one individual can by his one vote initiate a road building programme then many individuals will do so and too many roads will be built *from the viewpoint of our one individual* so that the 'costs' are now *OB* which exceeds *OA*. If the percentage of votes necessary for any road-building scheme is increased then road-building will be less over-expanded and his costs fall, say, to *C* or *D*. But this process will not continue indefinitely. As greater and greater proportions of votes are necessary, 'costs', in this sense, will rise as awkward individuals demand more than their share of the benefits as their votes become significant. It is clearly to the advantage of the individual to transfer road-building from the

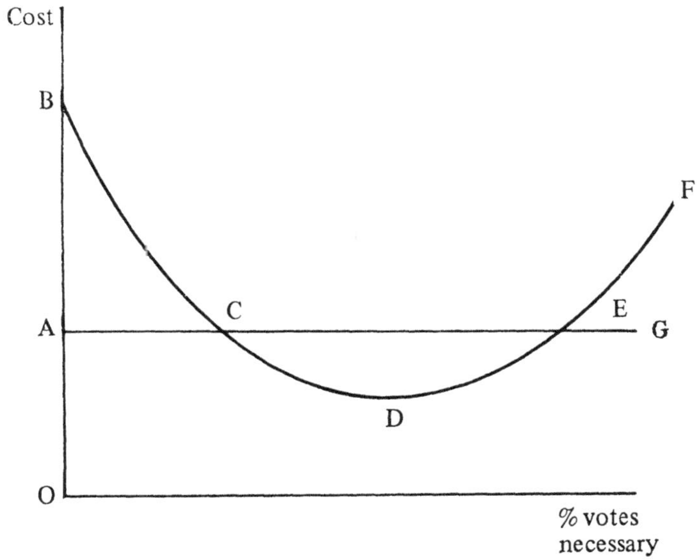

Figure 1

private to the public sector as long as the electoral system puts him on the *C*, *D*, *E* segment of the cost function where *his* 'costs' are lower.

Now this construction is ingenious, but what it tells us is that government intervention may or may not be advantageous and that it depends on the 'costs' of private provision, the attractions of the private enterprise road pattern (the *A*, *C*, *G* function) and those of public provision (the *B*, *C*, *D*, *E*, *F* function) which vary with the proportion of votes necessary to complete a road programme. Now 'costs' in this sense are departures from cost-benefit equality and are largely generated by externalities.[13] This is one reason why so much attention is now correctly paid to the measurement of externalities.

However, although some progress is being made, it is easy to see that the detailed knowledge required of the functions, in order to determine whether or not an activity should be within the public sector, is just not available.[14]

Any reader unaware of the narcissistic discussions among economists about methodology might conclude that the lack of success of these three approaches, especially the difficulties of inter-personal comparisons, reduces economics to an empty box. In fact, as later chapters will show, there is a great deal of activity which, even if it cannot satisfy the strictures of the purist, is beginning to make economics an operational science.

An extremely hard line 'hawk' position is that the whole notion of positive economics is a snare and delusion, that value-judgements are inescapable in the economic analysis of government policy and that the role of the economist is to analyse value-judgements.[15] A more philistine approach regards welfare economics as a waste of time and gets cheerfully down to the business of economic prognostication.

The present purpose is not to demolish either of these aforesaid positions but to clarify some difficulties in the course of discussing some of the applications of economics to government policy. It is certainly important to know exactly what is being done, and what assumptions made, so that the appropriate scepticism can be directed to the work of economists.

Notes

1 A further explanation is offered in the appropriate section of Chapter 6.

2 The fact that a given change in spending can promote some goals and block others is an example of the inconsistency of government economic goals, given present techniques. See Chapter 3.

3 The facts of the matter are not quite so simple as this implies due to the possibility of a Balanced Budget Multiplier. See Chapter 6.

4 See Chapter 6.

5 For example, the widely held belief that investment is greatly dependent on interest rates.

6 Central Statistical Office, *National Income Statistics—Sources and Methods*, Chapter VIII, H.M.S.O. (1956), as amended by: *Blue Book*, National Income and Expenditure, Section XIV *Notes*, p. 118 (1966). Superseded by *National Income Accounts*, ed. by Rita Maurice, H.M.S.O. (1969).

7 For example, interest on national debt, old-age pensions, sickness benefits and scholarships.

8 It can be shown that the U.S.A. figure is greater than, and the German figure less than, U.K. largely as a result of big differences in the importance of military expenditure.

9 See Chapter 6.

10 For a detailed analysis of these problems see *Social Choice and Individual Values* by Arrow, K. J., Wiley (1951).

11 'A Note on Tariffs and the Terms of Trade', Kaldor, N., *Economica* (1940).

12 Buchanan, J. M. and Tullock, G., *The Calculus of Consent*, University of Michigan Press (1962).

13 See Chapter 3 for a fuller account of externalities.

14 Apart from our present innocence, other objections are made on grounds of practice, rather than principle, to this approach. It seems, for example, inappropriate for 'once and for all' decisions such as joining the Common Market.

15 See Hutchinson, T. W., *Positive Economics and Policy Objectives*, Allen and Unwin (1964).

Bibliography

This is a book about applied economics and therefore gives greater attention to the use of theoretical ideas than it does to deducing them. Only the briefest explanations are given of the theoretical concepts. It is assumed throughout that the reader is following, or has followed, some systematic course in economic theory using such books as:

STURMEY, S. G. and PEARCE, D. W., *Economic Analysis*, McGraw-Hill, 1966

SAMUELSON, P. A., *Economics* (7th edition), McGraw-Hill, 1967

LIPSEY, R. G., *An Introduction to Positive Economics* (2nd Edition), Weidenfeld and Nicolson, 1966

DORFMAN, R., *Prices and Markets*, Prentice-Hall, 1967

Accounts of government policy after 1945 are to be found in:

DOW, J. C. R., *The Management of the British Economy 1945–60*, Cambridge University Press, 1964

SHONFIELD, A., *British Economic Policy Since the War*, Penguin, 1958

BRITTAN, S., *The Treasury Under The Tories*, Penguin, 1965

CAVES, R. E. and Associates, *Britain's Economic Prospects*, Brookings Institution, Allen and Unwin, 1968

HACKETT, J. and A.-M., *British Economy : Problems and Prospects*, Allen and Unwin, 1967

Further details and explanations of the growth in government expenditure to its present size and composition can be found in:

PEACOCK, A. T. and WISEMAN, J., *The Growth of Public Expenditure in the United Kingdom*, N.B.E.R., Oxford, 1961

VEVERKA, J., 'The Growth of Government Expenditure in the United Kingdom since 1790', *Scottish Journal of Political Economy*, 10, pp. 111–27 (1963)

Chapter 2

AIMS OF GOVERNMENT POLICY

It is sometimes thought that government intervention in the economy is based on relatively modern attitudes. In fact, many of the ideas central to this kind of government action are much older than the practices at present based upon them. The growing importance of the state in the economy is due less to new ideas than to new uses of old ideas. It is a routine idea, for instance, that there is a category of goods and services which it is rather impractical for the individual to provide for himself but which can be conveniently provided by the government or one of its agencies. Military defence and sewerage have long been seen in this way. In a sense, the growth of government intervention in the economy is simply a process in which other goods and services are re-classified into this list as the various difficulties of private provision are recognised.

Many of the apparently 'economic' problems in the political arena are really this kind of classificatory dispute. Technically, they are problems to which the economist can bring only limited expertise. The person who thinks that a given service, say medical care, has more difficulties if provided privately than if provided by the state is engaged solely in a value-judgement.[1]

The economist cannot claim to the layman that he can solve these classificatory problems by the techniques of scientific analysis.

This chapter concerns the economic goals of government economic policy. This only seems tautologous; the goals of government economic policy are subject to political appraisal as well as the economic appraisal. Thus the role of the economist is to analyse the economic content of the goals, to predict the economic consequences of choosing these goals rather than any other economic goals and also to assess the effectiveness of the various techniques available to the government. In selecting both the goals and the policy methods to obtain them, the government may call on the expertise not only of economists but also of many other scientists. The government is thus put into a position where it can choose a goal, and the policy corresponding to that goal, fully aware of the likely implications, only some of which are of an economic nature; the final decision is always political in nature, that is, it involves the qualitative assessment of priorities. The control of inflation, for instance, is a government economic policy; the economist can point out the implications of achieving this goal and of not achieving this goal, but it is for the government to rank one set of implications as more important than the other.

Many of these goals have an outwardly economic appearance and seem to be based on economic considerations; but this is a surface delusion. They are, in fact, all well within the political arena. Government economists, along with other advisers, can certainly make the choice a knowledgeable one but they cannot make it a scientific one; it will inescapably remain a value-judgement.

The classic statement of the purposes of a modern government in the economy is given in the Radcliffe Report[2] which listed full employment, price stability, economic growth, aid to under-developed countries and a surplus in the Balance of Payments. This report was concerned with monetary policy, which is only a part of economic policy, and many people would add to this list 'a fixed and stable exchange rate'.[3] Others might also add the redistribution of income, thus making a list of seven aims of government policy.

Three things need to be said about this roll call. Firstly, they are all value-judgements and the economist can comment only on their implications, problems and inconsistencies and whether state action is likely to be a better technique for achieving the goals than any other techniques, and, if so, which techniques. Anybody who added to, or subtracted from, this list would not be engaged in a logical exercise but in airing their opinions. Just why these are commonly believed to be valid areas of government intervention and some of the problems associated with the relevant techniques will be dealt with later.

A second point is that this list would have been widely regarded as outrageous only a generation ago. Earlier government reports gave quite different purposes, thus demonstrating that the whole style of state policy in the economy is a reflection of the public opinion of its time as much as of the current state of economic analysis. Accretions to, and dismissals from, the area of economic life regarded by the government as its responsibility can be briefly traced.

Most of this sort of change springs from contemporary experience. The *Cuncliffe Committee on Currency and Foreign Exchanges after the War* (1918)[4] reported that a chief aim of government economic policy was to return to, and maintain Britain on, the Gold Standard.

Within a generation this has become a curiosity in the museum of dead ideas. The Macmillan Committee[5] still gave a high priority to the question of exchange rates but did add both stability of the price level and the maintenance of high and stable employment. The White Paper on *Employment Policy* of 1944 was much more explicit: 'The government accepts as one of their primary aims and responsibilities the maintenance of a high and stable level of employment.'[6]

The White Paper on the *Economic Implications of Full Employment* in 1956 added an obligation to promote economic growth.[7] The other aims seem to have slipped into policy unheralded by official statements, apart from the general tone of the National Plan. Their existence is evidenced by budget statements and policy measures; their wide acceptability is shown by the lack of public comment.

Thirdly, the goals of government policy are inconsistent in that achieving one of them can hazard a second. A well-known example is the need to restrict spending to safeguard the Balance of Payments which conflicts with the twin needs to encourage spending, both to maintain employment and to promote economic growth. This polarises the government's priorities, produces inconsistent measures and the familiar stop-go routine. The very familiarity of this routine emphasises that it is largely the product of the inconsistency of government goals combined with the bluntness of present techniques. And it has very little to do with which political party is in power.[8]

It is not worth solemnly listing all these goals in some form of matrix and then pointing out which one is inconsistent with which. We need only say that goals are inconsistent if two conditions are satisfied. Firstly, they must *actually* be inconsistent in given circumstances and they also must not be positively associated in the *minds* of the public—however this might be estimated or discovered. Thus economic growth and Balance of Payments surplus have been actually inconsistent for the United Kingdom in recent years. This last phrase emphasises that often it is the given circumstances that make two goals inconsistent and only seldom is it an immutable law. The exchange rate largely made these goals mutually exclusive in Britain by producing 'import-led booms' while Western Germany found no such inconsistency, largely experiencing 'export-led booms'. But all this comes to nothing, there is no inconsistency, if the two goals are positively associated in the mind of the public. If, for example, the public does not mind about a payments deficit to get economic growth, or an increased National Debt to get full employment then the two go together, there is zero opportunity-cost and no choice need be made.

The two goals, Balance of Payments surplus and economic

growth, must thus be alternatives generating a choice frontier like *FF* before any choice need be made. Of course, there is no choice problem if the two goals are wholly independent (a possible example is redistribution of income and stable exchange rates) or are related like *NN* in Fig. 1 where more of *Y* means more of *X* (full employment and economic growth are possible examples). It is a matter of positive economics to establish which government policies are unrelated and which are functionally related either like *NN* or *F′F″* The following chapters should help clarify which goals are in fact inconsistent.

Once this matter of positive economics has been resolved—and it may by no means be easy—a normative problem then arises. Society

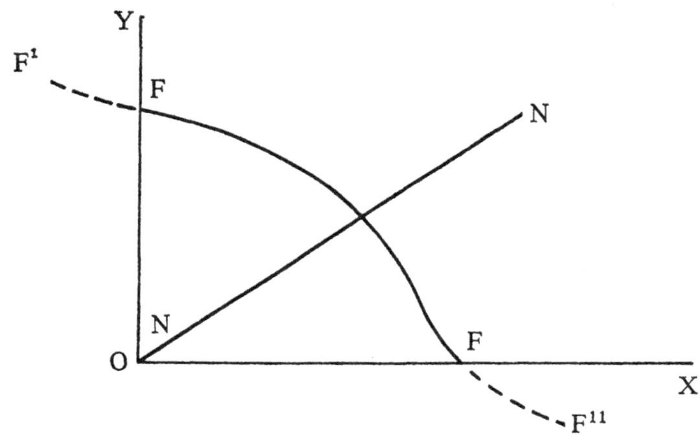

Figure 1

must choose whether it cares sufficiently about both goals to want the community on the *FF* segment, and so positive values to both goals, or on *F′F* which might mean Balance of Payments deficit (negative value on *X* axis) with economic growth or on *FF* with a large payments surplus but a fall in G.D.P. (negative value on *Y* axis). Such a decision is a value-judgement; the economist can only hope that it is a well-informed one.

Economic analysis should, therefore, force us to recognise that choices are forced on us by our value-judgements and to ask ourselves the exact slope of these choice frontiers, so that we can decide just how much economic growth we are willing to forego for a given increase in the Balance of Payments, and so on. Policy aims are inconsistent only if, first, the public regards two aims as worth while and, second, if they are in fact inconsistent.

It is convenient to look a little further behind these reasons and ask why the government cares about the exchange rate at all and to provide a more general catalogue of the purposes of state economic policy. Many laymen do not bother to ask these questions, taking the disadvantages of sterling devaluation, for instance, as self-evident. Enquiring into the apparently obvious can bring the ignominy of trivial answers but it can also avoid fallacies of fact or policy. After all, the importance of the Gold Standard was as clear to the Cunliffe Committee as it once was that the world was flat.

It should be emphasised that this chapter is concerned with the goals of economic policy; this necessitates some comment on government economic policy, but this should *not* be mistaken for a general account of government policy. Some parts of a general analysis are selected, but solely for their relevance to the *purposes* of the government, many more factors would deserve mention in a comprehensive account. A full consideration of government policy would include, for instance, some mention of the price of gold, but an account of the goals of economic policy need not do so, since the government broadly regards the price of gold as a datum, as a constraint, rather than as an end in itself.

Full employment is now within the government's responsibilities for two reasons, one social, the other economic. Firstly, unemployment is degrading and demoralising for the person concerned. Secondly, if labour is unemployed, then a productive opportunity is lost and gone forever. The opportunity cost to society of unemployment is the goods and services which were not produced.

The government is interested in *economic growth* because this tends to be equated with a higher standard of living for every member of the community. In fact this need not be so, for economic growth can have the opportunity cost of unemployment for some members of that community. A further disadvantage is that it has proved rather difficult to promote economic growth without also allowing some measure of inflation. There is also a non-economic motive for the government's interest in economic growth; it has become commonplace for the growth rate to be a matter of international political prestige quite as much as the actual income level.

Economic growth can have very real costs especially in the form of externalities. Unfortunately, the disutility thus caused is unquantifiable and, until recently, it went unnoticed as well as unmeasured. This is largely explained by 'growth mania', that is the prestige attached to a country's growth rate already noted.[9] (Whatever value-judgement is taken towards 'growth mania' it could be argued that economic growth can be self-justifying, that a *rate* of growth itself generates welfare independently of the extra goods and services produced.)

The government is interested in the *redistribution of income* for a political reason; it tends to accord with contemporary ideas of 'fairness'. Most people find it anomalous that income levels are largely determined by the market for a particular kind of labour rather than by any ideas they may have of the merit or importance of this particular kind of work. The income levels of nurses and 'pop' stars present, for most people, an uncomfortable disparity.

An economic reason for redistributing income is that this may lead to a general rise in economic welfare; although this is rather plausible it is in fact quite impossible to demonstrate because it remains unscientific to make inter-personal comparisons of utility in which the benefit to the gainer of the income distribution is compared with the loss to the other member of the community. The most common method for redistributing income is through taxation and subsidies; in fact experience with tax policies to raise the average standard of living has shown that they have not been a very effective technique[10] and this has led to further interest in the growth rate in order to achieve a general rise in the standard of living. Both the growth rate and the redistribution of income can be seen as goals of economic policy which are, in fact, aspects of a more general goal, that is the raising of the general standard of living; neither are the foregone conclusions that they might appear to be. However, the redistribution can be helpful to this goal in that it can influence the expenditure level which is very relevant to economic growth.

Aid to under-developed countries has a threefold basis. Some hold there is a moral obligation which they cannot rightly ignore. Development policies also have a political motivation in that if Western countries do not aid the poor ones, then Communist countries might well do so. Aid programmes also, however, have a self-centred economic motive; if poor countries become richer as a result of the aid then they also become much better markets than otherwise. This leads to higher exports and incomes in the aid-giving country through the foreign-trade multiplier.[11] The nineteenth-century investment by Western Europe in Australia, Canada and the United States may have had this effect.

Inflation has become as chronic and as world-wide as unemployment once was and has now become the preoccupation of the governments of most developed countries. It is normally accorded five economic difficulties. The rise in prices means that a given sum of money will purchase less goods and services after a period of time than it originally did and so the inflationary process erodes the real purchasing power of savings. A further consequence of inflation is that the prices of some goods will rise faster than the general rate of increase; in recent years antiques, property, jewellery and some share prices have been in this category. The consequence is that those who have their wealth in the form of money lose purchasing power, while those who have their wealth in the form of these particular assets gain purchasing power when they convert the assets back into money. Effectively this is an arbitrary redistribution of purchasing power. Both these processes are widely condemned, but, in fact, to deplore inflation because it erodes savings, or produces a redistribution of purchasing power within the community, is a value-judgement. Inflation does redistribute purchasing power between savers and borrowers and also between money-owners and some asset-owners, but this merely makes the inflationary process a fit subject for economic analysis. There is nothing in economics to say that savers are more worthy than borrowers or those who hold their wealth as money more deserving of respect than those who own assets that increase in value.

A point commonly made is that inflation is particularly severe on the middle classes. This seems doubtful: all classes will suffer from the erosion of money savings though they certainly will not suffer equally, but the middle and upper classes seem much better able to defend themselves against this process by converting their money saving into those forms of asset which benefit most from inflation. The opinion that the middle classes suffer most from inflation must be regarded as unproven.

In fact quite the reverse presumptions arise; that is that the middle classes are more able to exploit the inflationary process than others both absolutely and proportionately. They can do better absolutely because they hold more of the assets it is advantageous to hold and they can divert a higher proportion of their income to these assets whereas the very poorest members of the community cannot exploit this process at all because the relevant assets are indivisible and so cannot be bought in very small quantities. For identical reasons, not only are the middle classes better able to exploit inflation but also are better placed to defend themselves against it.

Thirdly, it is sometimes believed that inflation discourages savings. Thus, not only does it erode existing savings, but it might also diminish the rate of new savings. There is little evidence for this relationship. Economists tend to emphasise the level of income as the most important determinant of savings rather than changes in the price level. In fact, between 1938 and 1964, a period of inflation and rising National Income, savings rose as a proportion of the National Income from 5·4% to 8·6%.[12]

Fourthly, inflation lowers the real income of those whose money income is fixed, such as pensioners. This is undoubtedly so; the question to be asked is normative: how significant is this disadvantage and can it be ameliorated by redistributing some of any economic growth which accompanies the inflation?

Fifthly, inflation makes exporting more difficult if other countries are experiencing a stable price level or a slower rate of inflation. This difficulty only assumes positive significance if exchange rates are stable, and normative significance if the Balance of Payments is anyway a goal of government policy. Inflation can sometimes bring an advantage in that so far it has proved difficult to sustain economic growth while keeping prices stable.[13] Although most of the disadvantages of inflation will not withstand economic analysis because they are not economic in nature at all, the fact remains that these value-judgements are widely held and that in choosing this goal the government is probably reflecting general public opinion.

The government is also interested, almost obsessed, in gaining a *Balance of Payments surplus*, that is that the value of all exported goods and services in a year should exceed the value of those imported.[14] The government takes this attitude because this accounting relationship has now become a matter of prestige. There are few people who take the reverse attitude, which would be to feel that if exports are less than imports then it is the foreign country which has come off worse in that it has foregone goods to a greater value than it has gained.

There are economic reasons, as well as political reasons, for favouring a Balance of Payments surplus. If in one year a country earns more abroad than it spends, then it can use the surplus to give aid to other countries or to buy investments abroad which in future years may yield a higher National Income than otherwise. This is comparable to the potential personal advantages of spending less than is earned. A further attraction of a payments surplus is that it can be used to increase the gold and currency reserves which the government holds to defend the exchange rate. This point has particular importance for Britain in that sterling is a reserve currency.[15] It is these reserves which have been the source of most of Britain's international difficulties since the 1939–45 war, rather than her ability to export. They have nowhere near kept pace with the rise in National Income and in the value of exports and imports and so they are unable to perform their functions properly. These reserves are roughly comparable to that proportion of an individual's savings which are intended not for the purchase of future goods but to guard against random fluctuations in future incomes caused by such unpredictable factors as ill-health. In the case of the U.K.'s savings in the form of gold and currency reserves,[16] the random fluctuations spring from volatile elements in the payments position of non-sterling countries, the movement of capital sums in response to international difference in interest rates and to rumours of devaluations. A country such as Britain, in which foreign trade plays a large part in the National Income and whose currency is also a reserve currency, is particularly vulnerable to fluctuations of this sort and must give a higher priority than other countries to the maintenance of reserves solely to meet these difficulties, rather than for other purposes such as investment abroad.

A Balance of Payments surplus is thus deemed desirable partly for political reasons and partly for economic reasons. The economic reasons are as follows: firstly, so that the government may accumulate currency reserves which it may use as a working balance of savings with which to meet future difficulties with the Balance of Payments, secondly, to accumulate savings which will be invested abroad, thirdly, to accumulate reserves to the level appropriate if sterling is to be used as a reserve currency.

These three reasons would not be supported by all economists. The following comments are not offered as '*obiter dicta*', or even as a polemic, but merely to illustrate that it is possible to hold a different set of attitudes to the government, so that, though its priorities may be 'right', they are not foregone conclusions but simply value-judgements. It is possible to think of a system which would not involve foregoing resources in the present in order to accumulate reserves to cope with future trading difficulties; temporary trade imbalances between countries could be met by a system of international credit rather than from past currency savings. This would involve committing future savings to repay current debt. The principle of committing future resources to cover present known debt is quite different from committing present resources to cover unknown future debt. These remarks are intended merely to show that the idea of maintaining currency reserves to meet future difficulties is not an inescapable obligation. Firstly, an implication is sometimes seen that it is the only method, secondly, there is an assumption that it is the best method. The first assumption is wrong and the second is a value-judgement.

Nor is it by any means apparent that investment abroad contributes more to the Balance of Payments than does investment at home. There is no convenient general law which can be applied to all circumstances in all countries which enables any accurate prediction to be made of the Balance of Payments benefit to be gained from foreign investment; this whole problem is very complex indeed, with a great number of interdependent factors governing any benefit to be gained from foreign investment.[17]

Nor is it clear that a country gains, in economic terms at least, by having its currency used as a reserve currency in international trade. There are economic benefits in the form of greater invisible exports due to the extra financial business which is likely to result from the role of sterling and to this must be added the various political benefits. These benefits are, however, gained at the cost of the extra vulnerability placed on the reserves and the consequent priority that this tends to give to the community's need for a Balance of Payments surplus. This means that resources are used in accumulating Balance of Payments surpluses which could have been used elsewhere. They might, for instance, have been devoted to economic growth.

It should thus be clear that a Balance of Payments surplus is a government goal which only appears to have an economic basis; it really has a largely political basis in that it depends upon accepting the present system of world trade and the present role of sterling. Neither are beyond improvement. It is also intimately connected with the question of devaluation in that Britain tries to accumulate reserves in order to forestall the rumours of devaluation or devaluation itself.[18] Economists can only point to the costs of accepting the present international trade system. In another, quite feasible, world there might well be less priority given to the Balance of Payments as a goal of government policy.

The last goal of government policy is the maintenance of a *stable exchange rate*. It is particularly difficult to unravel the political motives from the economic motives in the government's hostility to devaluation. A devaluation is simply a price change; a pound sterling previously bought, say, \$2·80 and, after the devaluation, buys \$2·40. The government takes a very different attitude to this price change compared with the way it would regard a fall in the price of tomatoes. Why is this so?

It is particularly paradoxical that the government should be hostile to devaluation as this is a technique for righting the Balance of Payments. The effectiveness of devaluation in this respect depends upon the elasticity of demand for exports and imports.[19] 'Experience has revealed no other instrument as powerful as devaluation that can be used to restore competitive power; in conditions in which the failure of exports to make headway is plainly restricting the level of domestic activity, and other countries are not experiencing similar difficulties, it offers a way of escape that cannot be excluded.'[20] However, the government's attitude is not to regard devaluation as a technique for restoring equilibrium in the Balance of Payments but to regard avoiding devaluation as a goal of government policy.

This is because as a member of I.M.F. it takes a particular attitude to fluctuations in exchange rates. These are deplored because stable exchange rates stimulate trade and greater trade is thought to be beneficial. If an exporter did not know how many pounds sterling he would get for the foreign currency he had earned he would be much less likely to export and a persuasive case can be made that at least in the long run, in most circumstances, an increase in trade is worth while.[21]

World trading countries cannot seriously expect stability in exchange-rate prices any more than in tomato prices, as like any other prices they are under the influence of a market and the factors operative in that market are not constant.

The signatories of I.M.F. recognise three kinds of fluctuations. Firstly, there are day-to-day fluctuations and these are allowed in the official foreign exchange markets on the condition that the fluctuation will be within 1% of the official exchange rate. Secondly, there will be fluctuations which are due to a serious change in the market position but are not expected to be permanent; I.M.F. tries to suppress these fluctuations. It does so to accommodate the prestige requirements of the countries concerned.

By suppressing this kind of fluctuation the trading countries also gain economic benefits. By promoting certainty and confidence in exchange rates they reduce the premium necessary before a manufacturer will engage in exporting and thus they expand the volume of international trade. If the deficit country denies itself exchange-rate changes and has insufficient currency reserves, then the remaining possibility is that they have recourse to credit from I.M.F. and elsewhere.

International trading countries much prefer this system to the system of fluctuating exchange rates. This is not because changes in exchange rates cannot put right the Balance of Payments, it is because they do so at a heavy cost. If one pound sterling exchanges into less foreign currency than hitherto then an article manufactured at a cost of one pound now costs less in foreign currency, becomes more attractive to foreign consumers and so exports rise. The reverse process happens to imports; they fall because each pound sterling now buys less foreign currency so that an article produced abroad at a given cost in foreign currency now costs more in sterling.

Thus, if the required technical conditions are satisfied, it becomes possible 'to export the deficit' and correct one's own deficit at the cost of damaging the export trade of another country. This is a game that two can play. Countries deny themselves the weapon of exchange-rate variations so that other countries do not in their turn use that weapon against them. It is a kind of economic disarmament because countries do not trust one another to use this particular technique selflessly. Their suspicions are based on the harsh experiences of the 1930's in this respect. The detailed discussion which preceded the November 1967 sterling devaluation indicates how seriously countries now regard their interdependence in this matter.

The present system thus acknowledges the reality of the market by allowing day-to-day fluctuations, and, in the case of more serious fluctuations, such as the sterling crisis of 1956, providing credit while the country concerned rights its Balance of Payments equilibrium by internal methods.[22]

It is also recognised that a third kind of exchange-rate fluctuation exists; there may be a very serious market change of a chronic nature leading to a payments deficit from which a country cannot escape by taking internal measures and using its access to international credit. This situation is known as one of 'fundamental dis-equilibrium'.[23] Only in these circumstances is a country permitted to devalue under I.M.F. rules.

Exchange-rate stability becomes a goal of government policy for two reasons which are general to most countries. Firstly, devaluation is damaging to political prestige because of the mystical overtones which accompany this particular price change; secondly, it is an effective technique which countries deny themselves because they do not wish other countries to use it.

There are two other reasons for opposing devaluation which are particular to the United Kingdom. Although there have been successful post-war devaluations by France and Canada, which have not lost long-run prestige and which have gained a stronger trading position and a faster growth rate at least partly in consequence, it is more difficult for Britain to take this course for practical reasons. As a great deal of the world's trade is carried out in sterling, the effect of a sterling devaluation on other countries is more serious than is devaluation by the average country. Britain thus faces a greater likelihood of a damaging response from other countries. Secondly, the fact that sterling is a reserve currency also leads other countries to keep their trading reserves in the form of sterling. This means that if sterling is devalued then so are their savings, in that, originally, they could be exchanged for a given amount of their own currency, and thus goods, but now they can be exchanged for less currency, and so less goods. This would mean that Britain would have made an inadequate banker and the government is hostile to devaluation for that reason. It could be regarded as a breach of faith, it would probably lead to less international banking business in the future and this could damage future invisible export earnings. These possibilities have not really been successfully measured.

Thus, devaluation is a technique only available, in restricted circumstances, to most countries, for a mixture of economic and political reasons, and in very restricted circumstances to Great Britain because of political value-judgements and possible economic advantages of reserve currency status.

Some may regard reserve currency status as politically worth while and others may regard it as economically worth while; the latter viewpoint is unsubstantiated. Even those who would like to abolish the present role of sterling have to accept its present implications for devaluation and the Balance of Payments until a system can be devised to replace the present arrangements. This is very difficult without the agreement of other countries. A number of alternatives have been suggested, such as the creation of extra international credit; Special Drawing Rights were introduced in January, 1970. It is particularly difficult to opt out of this goal of government policy.

It should be said that value-judgements, or priorities, are changing in this matter and it seems that by international agreement, sterling will be withdrawn from its reserve role by a gradual process subject to negotiations in the 1970's. The exact institutional arrangements are not yet clear and will make little difference to the general point that this development will lessen the force of the preceding comments and give the United Kingdom more room to manœuvre both in its attitude to devaluation and to payment surpluses. It need not then give the maintenance of the exchange rates, or the earning of a surplus, quite such a high priority.

The above should not be mistaken for an analysis of government economic policy; it is merely an introductory account of the reasons for choosing particular economic goals. It is convenient not only to have a catalogue of the goals of government policy but also of the reasons for government intervention in the economy.

A long list can be assembled of particular reasons for government intervention. Many of them are informed by a general attitude that freedom brings obligations as well as rights. This is because our own actions impinge on the lives of others and we cannot pretend otherwise nor escape the interdependence of our society.

> 'No man is an island entire of itself, every man is a piece of the continent, a part of the maine; . . . if a clod bee washed away by the sea, Europe is the lesse . . . as well as if a manner of thy friends or of thine owne were; any man's death diminisheth me, because I am involved in mankinde.'[24]

This belief is widely shared and manifests itself in many aspects of life. Our collective responsibility to one another is recognised in that we all agree to drive on the same side of the road, and at restricted speeds on particular roads, and we all accept the spirit of the Town and Country Planning Act, 1947, in restricting a property owner's freedom to do what he likes with his property, as this impinges on other people's amenities.

A particular example at the moment is the attitude of some people to Incomes Policy:

> 'The best prospects do not lie along the road of legal compulsion. They do lie in the recognition that any group of people who are arguing about their incomes, whether it is workers about their wages or landlords about their rents, must accept and recognise that the bargaining strength of the two parties is not the only factor that can be allowed to decide these issues in the future. The public is in these negotiations as a third party, as an interested party.'[25]

This is a specific example of this general belief. The technical problems are choosing those areas of life where the impingement of a person's actions on another is sufficiently serious to merit government intervention and then to choose the best method of serving the public interest. The choice of the aspects of life in which the government is to intervene is always a political one; the choice of the best technique of intervention is partly political and partly economic.

One well-established justification of the government changing the use of productive factors by taking a person's wealth and then spending it for him in a way different from his intentions is that it is the only practical way to provide for internal and external law and order, for example, to provide police services, the judiciary and armed services.

An identical justification is a recognition that there are collective goods which it is physically possible to provide privately—like some transport, health, education and recreation amenities, but the problem is that when these goods and services are provided privately they are seldom produced at a price which the majority can afford and the government comes to feel they should be available for everybody to enhance the life of the individual and also to promote the welfare of the state.[26]

Thirdly, there is a portmanteau of assorted, strictly pragmatic goals which in the opinion of the community are important and cannot be provided in quite the way desired by a freely operating market. An example is those industries where the public demand is for some particular level of production, that seems to want the National Coal Board, for instance, to offer a level of employment inconsistent with profit making. It also denies profits to British Railways when it demands both cheap fares on resource-expensive commuter services and little demanded services in rural areas. The Forestry Commission brings planting up to a level quite impossible for profit-seeking companies because this level of forestry is deemed to be in the public interest. The state can afford to lock up assets in trees for a time quite unsuitable for a company. Other examples are that the state needs closer control over some industries than it can achieve through the general mechanism of the Companies Acts and so, for instance, atomic energy is in public hands. Sometimes national prestige is held to require a non-commercial policy and so air corporations have to buy British aircraft as it is held that it is their duty to pay attention to matters other than their balance sheet. The provision of recreation amenities is not always profitable to a profit-seeking company and so the government intervenes in the use of resources through the Town and Country Planning Acts and gives financial grants to the arts, theatre and sport. In a sense all this is summarised by the conventional definition of a public corporation which distinguishes it from a limited liability company and from a government ministry as 'a private body with public responsibilities'. This contrasts with a limited liability firm which has responsibilities only to its private owners, within the limits of the law, while a ministry is a public body and has responsibilities to the public through an elected Parliament. Further examples of practical goals are that nationalisation is one way of getting economies of scale. This was a major reason for the formation of the Electricity Board in 1926.[27] Part of the pressure for the nationalisation of the coal industry was to improve labour relations;[28] while some industries were nationalised so they could serve as a link in the general control of the economy by varying their price and investment policies. All these are practical examples of this general theoretical attitude.

In sum, the government intervenes in the economy for some severely practical reasons and in response to the widely held opinion that this is a suitable technique for providing an enhanced society and raising material living standards. Having decided to intervene for political and economic reasons, it then chooses particular goals out of the wide range of possible goals. These choices, too, are made for political reasons, for there is no economic reason for believing that nationalisation, of whatever form of intervention is used, is either the only, or the best, method for achieving the goals. It should by now be clear that the economists' role is an advisory one; the choice of government economic goals, and the choice of methods for realising those goals, is essentially political.

A note on the Balance of Payments

This chapter has been concerned with the goals of government policy and it is normally safe to assume that the meaning of the various terms is self-evident. In fact, the Balance of Payments is not what it might appear to be. Once a payments equilibrium has become a goal of economic policy, for whatever reasons, it becomes necessary to know the significance of a surplus or deficit; this seems simple enough, but in fact the significance can be elusive, for it varies with the accounting procedure used. Thus countries with equal deficits might need different economic policies if the deficits are the results of different accounting methods.

Accountancy has two aspects: conventional accountancy records the money flows into and out of the firm and provides valuable information for some purposes such as the detection of fraud; management accountancy deals with the same material but manipulates it so that it becomes relevant for other purposes such as the identification of the opportunity costs of a project as well as its money costs.

A similar duality is found in Balance of Payments accountancy. The accounts are kept on double-entry book-keeping principles and so every transaction appears twice, thus ensuring that the accounts do balance. They are not, however, normally published in double-entry form. In principle every transaction is entered twice, in practice there is inadequate information and so the accounts are completed with an entry for 'Errors and omissions'. But although the Balance of Payments must balance, deficits and surpluses are a common feature of the world. This is because the imbalance refers not to the total accounts but only to selected items within them. Despite its name the Balance of Payments is not a balance sheet and it is not a statement of assets; it is a revenue account showing the flows of exports and imports. In no circumstances whatsoever is it a measure of a nation's wealth.

There is no objective way of defining which items should, and should not, be included for these purposes. The definition of a surplus or deficit is normative in that it reflects the purpose for which the information is required. Usually, it is so defined that the resultant figures provide a sensible basis for policy decisions on the righting of any disequilibrium.

International financial transactions can be presented in a number of ways but, *for our purpose*, the most helpful division is to place some items 'above the line' and some 'below the line'. Any imbalance can only occur above the line, the below the line movements are those which finance the above the line inequality into a total balance. The placing of items above and below the line is a critical matter because economic policy will be based upon the surplus or deficit and so it becomes important that the size of the imbalance reflects genuine problems and is not obscured by transitory difficulties.

It is customary to place below the line, movements of official gold and currency reserves, the use of I.M.F. credit, movements of gold and foreign currency in private hands and 'swap' arrangements between central banks. Reserve currency countries also include changes in foreign holdings of the currency. All other money flows are normally recorded above the line; the chief kind are those corresponding to the movement of goods and services.

An example of the importance of placing an item according to whether its significance is such that economic policy should be based upon it is afforded by the case of international aid. Post-war U.S. aid to Western Europe was regarded as an appropriate case for the recipient countries to adjust their Balance of Payments and ultimately to do without the aid. On the other hand, aid to under-developed countries is regarded as a continuous process and they are not expected to adjust their Balance of Payments.

For many purposes, it is necessary to construct a 'basic' balance which reveals the underlying strength or weakness of the payments position and this excludes elements from the size of the disequilibrium which distort the underlying impression and so would form a misleading basis for policy decisions. Thus the inclusion of volatile speculative short-run capital movements in the case of the British Balance of Payments is helpful for short-run policy but would be misleading for long-run policy.

Notes

1 That is, a matter of opinion which cannot be proved or disproved by an appeal to facts. Positive economics contains no value-judgements within the analysis, normative economics does include value-judgements.
2 *Report of a Committee on the Working of the Monetary System*, Cmd. 827 (1959).
3 The Chancellor of the Exchequer in the House of Commons, Hansard, Col. 985 (9.9.57).
4 *First Interim Report*, Cmd. 9182, para. 10 (1918).
5 *Report of the Committee on Finance and Industry*, Cmd. 3897, paras. 275, 280, 282 (1931).
6 Cmd. 6527, para 1 (1944).
7 Cmd. 9725, para. 25 (1956).
8 See Chapter 5.
9 Mishan, E. J., *The Costs of Economic Growth*, Staples (1966) and Penguin (1969). This discussion will be elaborated in Chapter 4, p. 70–1.
10 See Chapter 6.
11 This concept attempts to dynamise the theory of the Balance of Payments mechanism. Among other things, it emphasises that a rise in the National Income of a foreign country, in this case generated by international investment, can increase the income of other countries through international trade, including the income of the country responsible for the original investment. See Robinson, R., 'A Graphical Analysis of the Foreign Trade Multiplier', *Economic Journal*, 62, pp. 546–64 (1952).
12 See 'Centrespread', *Barclays Bank Review* (1966). Further details given in Chapter 6.
13 See Chapter 5.
14 See page 34–6.
15 A country's currency is a reserve currency if it is used not only for trade involving that country but also for trade between two other countries. More important is that a reserve currency is also used by other countries as the form in which they hold some of their reserves. Sterling and dollars are the chief reserve currencies; gold also fulfils these functions.

16 Some commentators use the term 'savings' in rather an indiscriminate way. *Government savings* are only part of the *community's savings* from the National Income and these are different from the 'savings' for the purpose of international trade held as *gold and currency reserves*. Talk of Britain being 'poor' or of national 'bankruptcy' refers to the small size of savings in the last sense. The description, common in journalism, of the U.S. and U.K. in this way must seem a perverse misuse of words in Africa and Asia.

17 Reddaway, W. R., *Effects of United Kingdom Direct Investment Overseas*, Cambridge University Press, Department of Applied Economics, Occasional Paper No. 12 (1967). *Final Report*, Occasional Paper No. 15 (1968).

18 The pressure to accumulate reserves varies inversely with their existing size.

19 A detailed analysis of the circumstances in which devaluation improves the Balance of Payments is ignored as the present concern is with the government's aim of exchange-rate stability. Details of post-war devaluations are given in Chapter 6.

20 See *Radcliffe Report*, para. 716, p. 258.

21 For an account of the theory of international trade, see Samuelson, P. A., *Economics* (Seventh Edition), McGraw-Hill (1967).

22 See Chapter 5.

23 This vital term is not explicitly defined, in any operational sense, by I.M.F.

24 Donne, John *Devotions*, XXII.

25 Chancellor of the Exchequer, 5.10.66, in a speech reported in *The Times*, 6.10.66. Reproduced by permission of *The Times*.

26 Government expenditure on education is often motivated for these reasons, e.g. the pressure for the 1871 Education Act in Britain.

27 See Shanks, M. (Ed.), *Lessons of Public Enterprise*, p. 34, Jonathan Cape (1963). This argument is hardly convincing as economies of scale are available in large firms whether nationalised or privately owned. In some circumstances, nationalisation may seem the most reliable route to large production units. However, the I.R.C. is a way of achieving these results without nationalisation.

28 This argument, too, hardly seems sufficient in itself as ownership is only one of the factors relevant to labour relations.

Bibliography

The following books contain some analysis of the goals of the government within their treatment of economic policy:

DOW, J. C. R., *The Management of the British Economy 1954–60*, Cambridge University Press, 1964

HARROD, Sir Roy, *The British Economy*, McGraw-Hill, 1963

LIPTON, M., *Assessing Economic Performance*, Staples, 1968

MCMAHON, C., *Sterling in the Sixties*, Oxford University Press, 1964

Report of the Committee on the Working of the Monetary System *(Radcliffe Report)*, Cmd. 827, 1959

A detailed analysis of one of the government's goals can be found in:

MCCRONE, G., *The Economics of Subsidizing Agriculture*, Allen and Unwin, 1962

Chapter 3

CONVENTIONAL THEORY OF RESOURCE ALLOCATION

As has been emphasised, the economist cannot give final decisions regarding matters of economic policy. There is no scientific analysis available to determine whether nationalisation is 'right' and, if it is, which industries should be nationalised, nor whether budgetary policy is intrinsically preferable to rationing. The economist cannot solve this kind of problem at all although he is often treated by the layman as though he can. Another widespread assumption is that a free market mechanism is preferable to any form of government control on *economic* grounds; this latter assumption is read into economics by non-economists.

The role of the economist in any discussion of government economic policy is quite modest. It is to analyse the economic content of any points made, to point out the economic implications of a given policy, emphasising any contradictions with other policies, and to quantify these implications where possible. Whether all the advantages, economic and otherwise, outweigh the disadvantages of, say, Britain entering the European Common Market is an inherently political problem. The economist is to the politician as the doctor is to the patient. A doctor could tell obese patients that on a fruit diet they are likely to be spotty but slim while on a normal regime they are likely to have a clearer skin but to be fatter. Choosing between complexion and obesity is the patient's business. Similarly, an economist could say that a given policy might promote economic growth but hazard the Balance of Payments while another policy might do the reverse. Choosing between economic growth and the Balance of Payments is a political business, though, of course, the economist can help to make it a more conscious choice.[1]

The economist has nothing to say in his professional capacity on choosing which industries should be allocated to the group in which goods and services are provided by the state rather than by private enterprise. The list usually includes military service, refuse disposal and roads, but there is nothing logically necessary about these arrangements. There have been, and are, mercenary soldiers and private toll roads while some municipalities have sub-contracted refuse disposal. There is, therefore, no question of any economic 'law' which fits particular industries into one category or another.

These kind of industries are largely provided by the state as a matter of convenience. A similar attitude must be taken to a second group of industries in which the government intervenes. These are those activities which although conveniently provided by a freely operating market then produce results which the community finds unacceptable. The working conditions of women and children in the early nineteenth century is a well-known example. Similarly, private scientific research is commonly judged to be inadequate in scale so the government finances research and development at the public expense. Questions such as what are proper working conditions, or the proper size of industries in the national interest, are again value-judgements. The economist can contribute his special knowledge to the discussion but it does not entitle him to any prerogative. Political scientists, sociologists and theologians can claim likewise special knowledge but not complete knowledge.

The economist does begin to come into his own when attention passes to the obverse of the coin, which is the unspoken assumption that there is an economic law that the government should only intervene in the economy when a special case exists because a freely operating market has *economic* advantages.

This presumption, that government action in the economy is suspect, is based on two value-judgements, the second of which is often presented as a proven economic principle.

Hostility to the intervention of the government in the economy is based firstly on the avowedly political principle that such intervention must diminish private liberty. How much individual freedom should be given up for the benefit of the community is a wholly political problem and it will now be largely ignored; not because it is unimportant, but because we are concerned not with 'proving' that government intervention is 'right' or 'wrong' but with analysing its economic impact and the economic content of the case for and against it.

The second premise behind the antagonism to the government operating in the economy is the widely held belief that a free market is preferable because it will lead to the production of the goods and services which the community requires. This is wholly fallacious for the price mechanism does not, and cannot, lead to the best use of resources. It must be emphasised that this does *not* mean that government intervention is 'right', for it can also be shown that a planned economy cannot, with present knowledge, guarantee an optimal pattern of production. In other words, the economist can say quite a lot about these two kinds of economy but he cannot scientifically demonstrate that one will lead to the best use of resources and the other not. The decision is again essentially political in nature. However, because many textbooks give the impression that the price mechanism, or at least a special case of it called 'perfect competition', does lead to the best use of resources and because something similar is often assumed in political discussion it is worth elaborating why the price mechanism cannot, at present, do so.

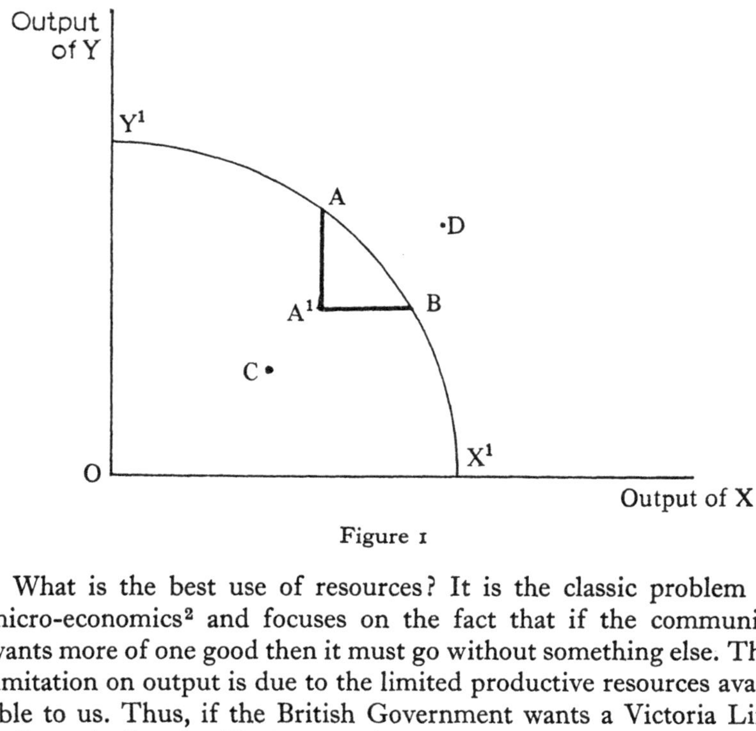

Figure 1

What is the best use of resources? It is the classic problem of micro-economics[2] and focuses on the fact that if the community wants more of one good then it must go without something else. This limitation on output is due to the limited productive resources available to us. Thus, if the British Government wants a Victoria Line built on the London Underground system it cannot, at the same time, build a Channel Tunnel. There are not enough Irishmen to go round.

Fig. 1 expresses the problem. Amounts of two goods, Y and X, are shown on the axes. If all the community's resources are devoted to the production of X, then the production level is X_1 and there is a zero production of Y. The community could alternatively have Y_1 of Y and no X at all or any one of the various combinations of X and Y

shown on the line $X_1 Y_1$. The general shape of this line clearly implies that more of one good necessitates less of another.[3] An example is the amount of Y shown as AA', which must be foregone to gain $A'B$ of the X good. The amount of Y that must be foregone in this way is the *opportunity cost* of X. This opportunity cost varies at different positions according to the quantities already owned of the two goods. Changes in it are shown by the slope of the line, Y_1X_1, which joins all possible combinations of the two goods and is called a 'technology frontier'.

A combination of goods such as A or B is called an *efficient* production pattern contrasting with an *inefficient* combination such as C where more of one good can be produced without foregoing any of the other. A combination such as D could only be reached by the *growth* of the whole economy over time.

Out of all the possible efficient combinations on the technology frontier, such as A or B, the price mechanism is sometimes held to produce that *particular* combination which the community actually prefers and thus lead to the best use of resources. Laymen's political discussions sometimes also claim that a freely operating price system would lead to production on the technology frontier, that is to full employment, and that it would also promote economic growth. The second and third claims can be analysed by the techniques of macro-economics and growth theory.[4] Attention will here be focused on the micro-economic problem of whether the price mechanism can be expected to lead to the use of resources most preferred by the customer.

How was a freely operating market economy expected to guarantee the best possible combination of goods and services? The most popular layman's attitude is simply a matter of faith and has a respectable precedent:

> '. . . every individual . . . neither intends to promote the public interest, nor knows how much he is promoting it . . . by directing [his] industry in such a manner as its produce may be of the greatest value, he intends only his own gain, and he is in this, as in many other cases, led by an invisible hand to promote an end which has no part of his intention. . . . By pursuing his own interest he frequently promotes that of the society more effectually than when he really intends to promote it.'[5]

Modern economic theory has less need of a blind trust in an 'invisible hand' and the Theory of the Firm has appeared to lead to the same conclusions. The following is a brief summary of its results, rather than an elaborate account and proof, which concentrates on those aspects relevant to the best use of resources.

Briefly, price theory holds that changes in product prices provoke those changes in the use of resources that are required by the community.

Demand Theory explains the level of the prices of given goods and services and of changes in the prices. The price is explained by resorting to demand and supply curves like those in Fig. 2. The demand curves, such as Da_1 and Da_2 in the diagram, are held to slope downwards to the right, thus implying that more is bought at lower prices.[6] The price is shown on the vertical axis and amounts bought and sold on the horizontal axis. On the other hand, supply curves, like Sa_1 are held to slope upwards to the right showing the different amounts that would be supplied at different prices with the implication that more will be supplied the higher the price.[7] The demand curve represents the summation of the demands of all the customers attracted into the market at the different prices and the supply curves the total amount supplied by all the firms attracted into the market at different prices. The market price is where the two curves intersect such as Pa_1 where Da_1 crosses Sa_1. This is because only at that price are the buyers and sellers agreed about the amounts to be exchanged and so only that price actually exists. Other possible prices such as Pa_3 do not actually exist as the buyers and sellers cannot agree the quantities exchanged at that price.

Once a market price has been established in this way, it can only fluctuate due to a change in the position of either the supply curve or the demand curve; that is that *at all prices* either the buyers or the sellers are now interested in different amounts. This might take the form of a movement of the demand curve like that from Da_1 to Da_2 in Fig. 2 leading to a new price, Pa_2. It is held that demand curves can move in either direction like this due to changes in incomes, tastes, the prices of other goods and the size of the market. If for any of these reasons the community wants more of the goods then the new price Pa_2 does indeed lead to a higher output at A_2.

Meanwhile, it is supposed that the community requires less of some other goods, B, the market for which is shown in Fig. 3. In this case, the demand curve moves from Db_1 to Db_2 and, at the lower price Pb_2 thus caused, production contracts to B_2 instead of B_1.[8]

The movement of supply curves, such as Sb_1 to Sb_2, will be dealt with later.

Thus prices in the product market change to induce the new pattern of production now required by the community. The product prices

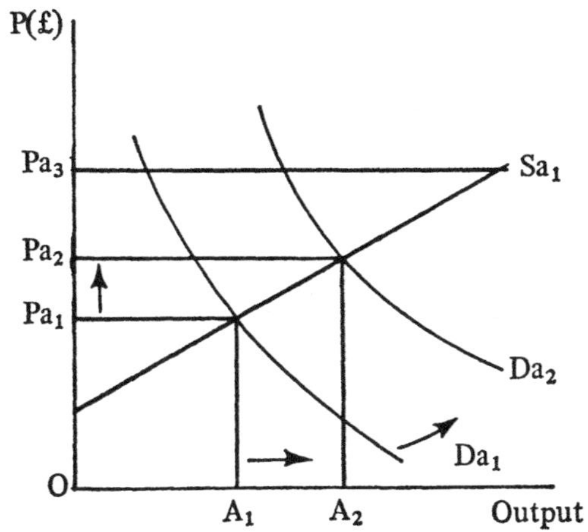

Figure 2

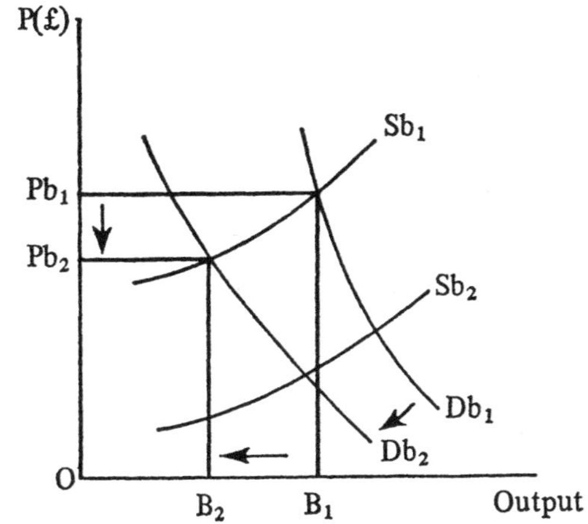

Figure 3

are regarded as signals of the community's preferences and the Theory of the Firm shows how the firms play their part in responding to the signals.

The firm's responses are largely explained by use of the concepts of average and marginal revenue and marginal cost. Now the price of a unit multiplied by the number of units sold must be the total revenue of the firm, and the total revenue of the firm divided by the number of units sold must be the average revenue. *Thus 'average revenue' simply means price.* Marginal revenue is the difference made to total revenue by the last unit sold. Clearly, if the price does not need to be lowered to sell the extra unit, then marginal revenue equals average revenue like ARa_1 and MRa_1 in Fig. 4. The firm does not need to lower its price to sell the extra unit if the firm itself is quite insignificant when judged against all the suppliers of the good. This kind of market situation is technically called '*perfect competition*'.[9] If, however, the firm is an important producer of its product then the extra output will be significant in the total market output and so the firm will need to lower its price as it expands its output and the relevant *AR* curve will be like *ARa* in Fig. 8 (p. 54). This market situation is known as '*imperfect competition*'. An important distinguishing characteristic of imperfect competition is that, if the price has to be lowered to attract extra custom, then the change in total revenue (that is marginal revenue) is always lower than the price (that is average revenue). For instance, if four units are sold at 7s. each then the total revenue is 28s., but if the price has to be lowered to 6s. each to sell five units the total revenue becomes 30s. giving, of course, an average revenue of 6s. but a marginal revenue of only 2s. *So in perfect competition average and marginal revenue are equal and in imperfect competition average revenue exceeds marginal revenue.* Marginal cost is a symmetrical idea and is the difference made to total cost by the last unit produced.

With these definitions and these relationships economists are able to explain how the firms respond to the changed prices in the product market to give the combination of goods and services that the community requires.

An important premise is that the firm attempts to maximise its profits. It achieves this by adjusting output until marginal revenue equals marginal cost. Profits may be substantial at other outputs but will nevertheless be non-maximum, because if marginal revenue exceeds marginal costs, an increase in output will add more to revenue than to costs and so add to the earlier level of profits which could not therefore have been maximum profits. Similarly, if marginal costs exceed marginal revenue then a contraction of output must

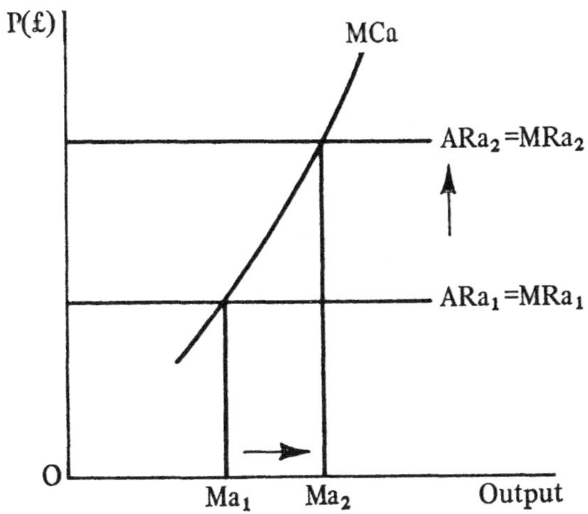

Figure 4

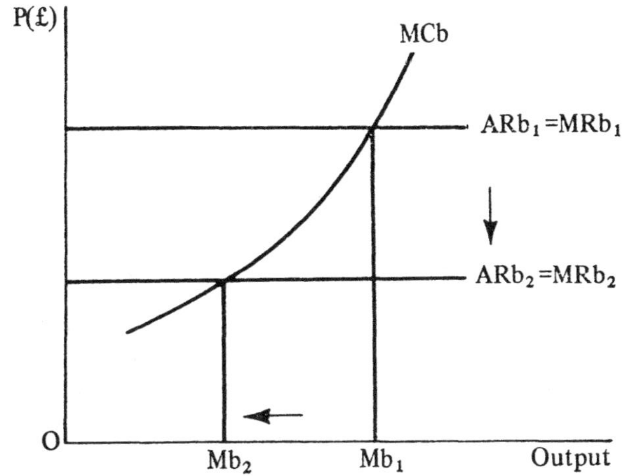

Figure 5

decrease total costs more than it decreases total revenue and thus widen the interval between them and so increase profits. It thus follows that, whenever marginal costs and revenue are unequal, profits can be increased by changing the level of output in one direction or another; only when marginal revenue and costs are equal does this opportunity not exist and that must therefore be the profit maximisation output.

With a given price, such as ARa_1 in Fig. 4, firm A would produce OMa_1 units thus maximising profits because at that point marginal revenue, MRa_1, equals marginal costs, MCa, while for similar reasons firm B producing a different product has an output of OMb_1. If the community's demand for A's product now increases, the price will rise to ARa_2 and output expands to the new profit maximising output of OMA_2. Meanwhile, the community's demand for B's product (Fig. 5) diminishes and so the price falls to ARb_2 and the output of OMb_2 in Fig. 5. In this way, the product prices act as signals to the firms, which then respond to give the community the various levels of output that it requires.

The remaining problem is how the firms will recruit the productive factors needed for the new levels of output. The Theory of Distribution analyses in a consistent manner the employment by the firms of the factors of production which are categorised for convenience into land, labour and capital. The key to the explanation is the concept of marginal revenue productivity. This is the difference to total revenue attributable to the last unit of the factor employed. This sum of money clearly depends on the actual production and the price of the product. Normally, *MRP* would be expected to slope downwards to the right as in Fig. 6, showing that if extra men, equipment or land are used they will add less to total revenue than did their predecessors because the product price may have to be lowered to sell the extra units and also because the extra factors might have a smaller impact on output than did those already employed.[10] As marginal revenue productivity is the difference made to total revenue by that last unit employed it is also what that factor is worth to the firm and it must therefore be the firm's demand curve for the factor. The firm's policy will be to recruit factors until its demand for them at any factor price equals the supply of factors at that same price, and to pay the corresponding income such as OY_1 to OE_1 factors because $MRPa_1$ equals *Sa* in Fig. 6. There are, of course, many other problems in Distribution Theory, like monopolistic exploitation, but they are irrelevant to our present interests.

If firm A is in an expanding industry in Fig. 6, the change in the product price provokes the firm into increasing output to a new output and it also alters marginal revenue productivity from $MRPa_1$ to $MRPa_2$ and thus leads to the recruitment of more land, labour and capital at the level OE_2 at the new income OY_2. Meanwhile, firm B in Fig. 7 in the contracting industry has seen its product price fall and its marginal revenue productivity shift from $MRPb_1$ to $MRPb_2$ and consequently factor incomes have fallen from OY_1 to OY_2 and employment from OE_1 to OE_2. In this way factors of production are released from the contracting industry to the expanding industry and the firms are thus able to move to the levels of production now required of them.

All this seems to be an attractive theory which gives an equilibrium not only in the product and factor markets but also in the output of the firm. The price mechanism seems to lead to that point on the technology frontier most preferred by the community. It would thus follow that the price system itself, quite autonomously, gives an optimal solution to the problem of the use of resources and that any interference from the government could only be damaging. This kind of theory, with varying degrees of rigour, has become a large part of the received doctrine of economics,[11] especially in elementary and intermediate textbooks, thus giving some students the idea that economic analysis could prove that state action in the economy was deplorable. A similar idea, favourable to competition and hostile to government interference in the economy, especially nationalisation, has become the philosopher's stone to the laymen.

There are two questions to be asked about the price mechanism, and the attitude to the government in the economy, that spring from placing faith in a market economy. Firstly, does the price system in fact allocate resources in something like this manner and, secondly, does it distribute the factors of production between the competing industries in the best way?

The unreality of economic theory has decoyed many readers and students into a mistaken disdain for micro-economics. It is not a criticism of a *theory* to say that it is not a factual description. It is, after all, *not supposed* to be descriptive; it is in the very nature of a theory that it abstracts from the real world to focus on critical relationships between only those factors which are significant. The question to be asked of a theory is not whether it corresponds with the real world but whether its abstractions from reality damage its explanatory powers.

The first disparity between the theory and the real world is that the actual price mechanism cannot make minor adjustments to the

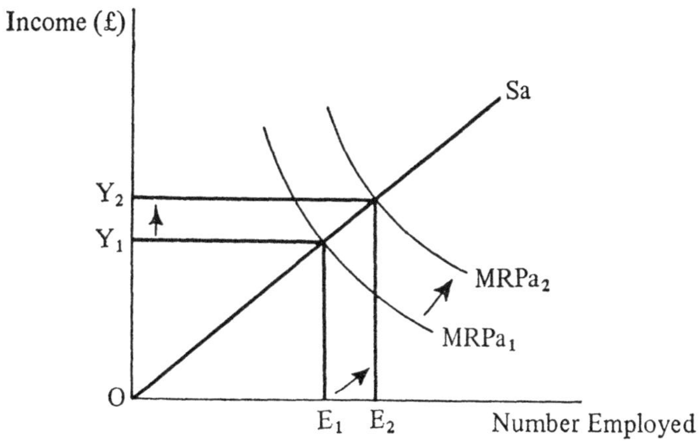

Figure 6

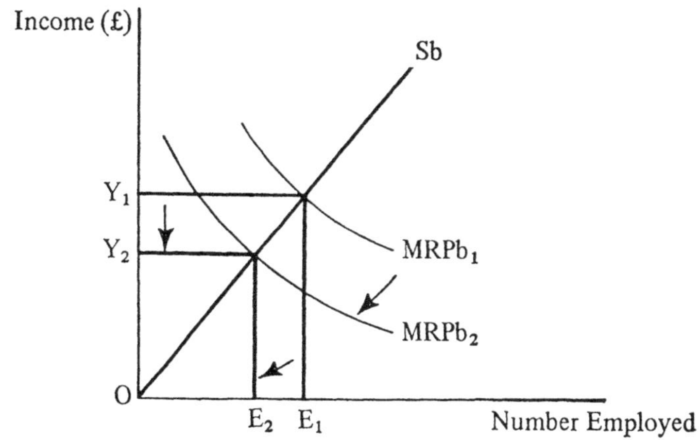

Figure 7

use of resources in the way predicted by the theory. In the first place, due to the casual nature of some human preferences, a consumer who finds a given brand of chocolate unavailable tends to take another brand and neither manufacturer finds that the demand for his product has faltered because the customer cannot be bothered to alter it even when he does have some preference for one of the brands. In the second place, many industries are incapable of making a minute adjustment to a changed demand because of the indivisible nature of their input. An electric-power company or an Electricity Board cannot, for instance, buy a tenth of a turbine because a new housing estate has been built in the town. The scope for buying smaller turbines is also restricted. Thus the price mechanism is not a fine enough instrument for minute adjustments to resource-use and the most that we can expect from it is a rather clumsy response to society's needs.

A second factual weakness is that firms cannot really be expected to react to the signals from the product market in the manner presumed in the Theory of the Firm all of the time. A firm can have many other goals beside that of profit maximisation. A company may be interested in a quiet life as long as a certain level of profits are maintained or it may seek to maximise sales, total revenue, its own rate of growth or even 'tax losses'. A convincing list of alternative goals can be easily assembled. Those entrepreneurs who do attempt to maximise profits may still not act in the manner characterised in the Theory of the Firm simply because they do not have the managerial skill to identify the optimum output.

Thirdly, even when firms do respond to price changes in the way described, it can take a very long time indeed to change the output of an industry simply because of the protracted time necessary for building a factory, sinking a coal-mine or bringing in an oil-well. Thus the most that can be hoped for is that production levels correspond to the preferences at sometime in the past.

The theory concentrates on new prices and output due to shifts in the demand schedule as in Fig. 2. A higher price could also be associated with *lower* outputs due to shifts in the supply curve like that of Sb_2 to Sb_1 in Fig. 3 producing Ob_2 output at PB_1 as the supply curve moves along Db_1. An entire supply curve might move in this fashion for a number of exogenous reasons such as changes in factor incomes or in production conditions. Given the new supply conditions, the new price and output may well be that which the community now prefers out of those available to it but it may not at all welcome the change to the new range of choices and to describe this new position as 'optimum' is ingenuous.

The theory of the price mechanism proceeds all the time on the idea that the expanding industry will recruit land, labour and capital from the contracting industry but this assumes that the released resources are, in fact, employable in the burgeoning industry. This presumes a coincidence that may well be unwarranted; not to mention the immobility of resources even if, conveniently, they are employable in both industries.

Yet another difficulty is that the government now plays a large part in the economy and often specifically does not do what private companies would do in the same circumstances. A nationalised transport concern, for instance, may operate at a level that guarantees a socially adequate service while running at a book-keeping loss—though, as we shall see, a commercial or financial loss need not be an economic loss.

As normally presented, the theory of the price mechanism assumes that the economy is on the technology frontier and so more of one article must mean less of another. This assumes both full employment and no economic growth. In fact, more *can* be had of one without giving up another, if there is economic growth, or, if the extra goods are produced by resources previously unemployed, rather than by transferring employed resources. In other words, it is an implicit assumption of this approach that the economy is already on the technology frontier.

So any picture of freely operating markets giving the consumer what he wants is only a rough-and-ready approximation of part of the economy, functioning unrealistically smoothly, part of the time.

The second problem is how far those prices which do influence the allocation of resources do so in a manner which corresponds to the use of resources that the community would prefer. That is, will they produce the optimum output on the technology frontier? There is a case for a rather sceptical attitude.

There are reasons for believing that the demand which helps to govern product prices is a poor guide to the demands of a society for some goods rather than others. Firstly, individuals are sometimes irrational consumers in that they exercise demand for what they do not really want. Sometimes it is because they are the victims of a marketing technique rather than the masters of their own spending. Or it may be because their expenditure is partly determined not by what they want but by what they want their neighbours to see them buy. This is technically known as the demonstration effect.

Another way in which the demand for goods and services may be a poor guide to the preferences of a society is that the demand which is actually exercised in the market is the demand which is actually backed by money and that is not the same as the community's needs because of the non-optimum distribution of income. The optimum distribution would maximise the community's welfare in that, after redistribution, no member of the community could gain in welfare except at the expense of another member. The existence of a non-optimum distribution can lead to an ineffective market demand for, say, hospitals. The price mechanism may allocate the available resources to office-building while the community might prefer otherwise.

The concept of supernormal profits is also useful in analysis of the price mechanism. They are defined as a level of profits above that required to keep the firm in the industry. Their existence in the *A* industry means that sums of money have been paid to that industry which need not have been paid for the level of output. Therefore, that money could have been spent in the *B* industry without foregoing any production from the *A* industry. Thus the community could have had a more advantageous production pattern but was thwarted by the existence of supernormal profits. These are most likely to occur where firms can stop other firms entering their industry to compete away these attractive profit levels. Monopolistic firms, in the common-sense use of the word, are most likely to be able to do this by use of such techniques as patents, restrictive practices and control of the supply of raw materials.

There are two important criticisms of the price system which focus on the fact that market prices are likely to be a poor guide to the opportunity costs of various products. This means that the consumer has an inaccurate idea of the slope of the technology frontier, and so, although he must choose between competing goods, he does not know what the real choice is. He is only aware of the money prices and is forced to make his choice in these terms which need bear no relation to the real choice. The consumer becomes a colour-blind man choosing a décor!

Firstly, the price mechanism distorts consumer's choices in the kind of market known as imperfect competition. In this case, price has to be lowered to attract extra custom and so average revenue (*ARa*) slopes downwards in Fig. 8 and for the reasons already given[12] marginal revenue (*MRa*) is lower. This means that, as price is greater than marginal revenue and the firm equates marginal revenue to marginal cost, price must be greater than marginal cost in all those markets in which the firm is a significant part of total supply. Economists have fussed a great deal about the relationship of price and marginal cost. Why does it matter that price is greater than marginal cost?

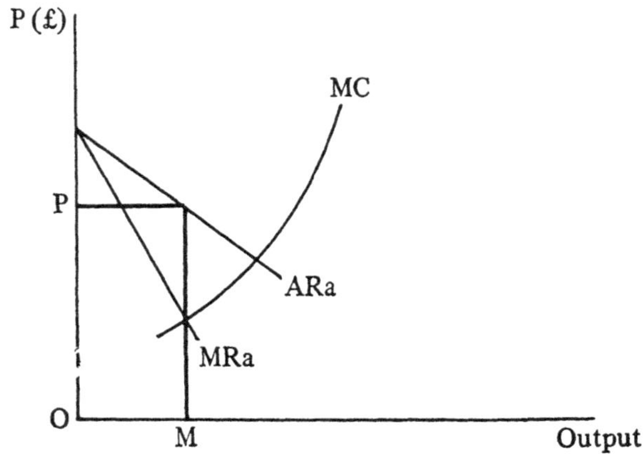

Figure 8

The 'price to marginal cost ratio' is of critical importance because of the impact it makes on the continual choices the consumer has to make between alternatives whether they be between guns or butter, holidays or furniture, Mozart or Bach records, a Channel Tunnel or a Victoria Line, *A* or *B*. The consumer can only make the choice correctly if he knows how many units of *A* he can get if he gives up one unit of *B*. The only information the consumer has is the money prices of *A* and *B* which tell him the quantity he can actually *buy* of *B* if he foregoes a unit of *A*, and not the quantity of *B* which could be *made* by the transferred resources from the *A* industry. This might be quite different. *Money prices* can, therefore, be quite misleading criteria when choosing between alternatives. If, for instance, the price is greater than the marginal cost it means that the resources used up in the production of that last unit have been overestimated to the consumer because the money price exceeds the opportunity costs (marginal costs) and so he thinks that *in real terms* the good is more expensive that it is. He therefore mistakenly restricts his purchases because he has been faced with a bogus measure of the choices open to him. In such circumstances only the innocent would hope that price mechanism will yield prices that will manœuvre the economy to the optimal position on the technology frontier.

The manner in which money costs can lead to a misapprehension of real costs can be shown by the following example. The U.S. space programme is sometimes attacked on the grounds that it costs, say, $\$X$m. and wheat costs, say, \$2 per bushel so that if the space programme were abandoned the money could be spent on $\frac{X}{2}$ million bushels of wheat and so, by a simple switching of its expenditure, the U.S. Government could produce millions of bushels of wheat and ease world starvation. It is emotionally appealing to suggest we cancel a trip to the moon to save people's lives. It is, however, arrant nonsense to postulate such a choice, for if the real resources, the scientists, laboratories, computers and launching pads, were put to growing wheat the result would be laughable. The main effect of spending $\$X$ million on wheat would not be on output at all; it would be on the price of wheat. Our first point then is that money prices can be a misleading guide in thinking about the costs of the alternatives open to us.

Secondly, doubt is cast on the price system as a successful method of running the economy autonomously by the question of externalities. These are money costs or money revenues which originate in one firm but show in the accounts of another. They are important because again the consumer can be misled about the real choices before him and, consequently, industries may expand to the wrong size and the economy be on the non-optimum position on the technology frontier.

An example chosen for its simplicity rather than its urgency is the effect of farmers' fertilisers on commercial fishing in an inland lake or sea.[13] River drainage into the lake will ensure a nutritional gain for the fishlife which will eventually benefit the catches of the fishermen. This externality is a cost to the farmers and a benefit to the fishermen. Our present concern is not with the random nature of all this or the policy of taxing the fishermen and subsidising the farmers but with the effect on the use of resources. The farmer will consider only the cost and benefit to himself in *money* terms, which are quite different to the costs and benefits to society in *real* terms. He will thus underestimate the quantity of fertiliser he should buy. From the point of view of society he should expand his activities while the benefits are greater than the costs incurred to produce them. From his point of view the farmer will expand while *his* money benefits are greater than *his* money costs. The externality does not interest him because to him it means a greater money cost than benefit. The economy does not achieve the optimal position on the technology frontier; industries with external benefits are always underexpanded, those with external costs are overexpanded.

An important point is that conventional book-keeping pays attention only to private costs and benefits, that is to money flows into and out of the firm. This is quite inadequate as a test to determine the allocation of resources between industries. The size of different industries should take account not only of the real resources used and produced by a firm and appearing in its accounts, but also the total resource-use and production for which the firm is responsible.[14] An accountant is concerned, quite properly, solely with the money costs for which his firm is responsible and the money benefits which they gain whereas the economist is concerned not solely with money flows but also with the total of real resources actually used up and the total real benefits actually produced.

Other examples of externalities are found in smoke and river pollution, increased road-transport costs due to slower throughput imposed on one firm if another factory is built next to it and the effect on the road system of opening or closing a railway line. In those and many other ways commercial costs and benefits are merely a subset of all costs and benefits and so private and social interests can sharply diverge.

Two further points are that when a price system 'transfers labour' from one industry to another, it in fact produces at least temporary unemployment, and, indeed, permanent unemployment for those workers whose skills are too specific to be employed in other industries or who are too old, or too immobile geographically. This offends the value-judgements of many people, as does the tendency of the price mechanism to produce widely different incomes between persons because income depends on demand and supply, that is on accident rather than on effort or intrinsic skill or 'value'.

We may then conclude that prices in the product market are inadequate signals of the community's requirements; that when they are good signals it is unlikely that all the firms will try to answer them; that those firms that do try may be incompetent at their task or that they may need a long time; that even when they can respond the prices of their products may be a sham measure of the resources used up.

An important point about this critique of the price system is that it is not original and is not presented as such. It is commonplace enough economics.[15] What is extraordinary is that it gets a poor place in orthodox textbooks, or no place at all, so that it is not surprising that hostility to state action in the economy and a belief that there can be an economic *justification* of free enterprise has become part of the conventional wisdom of too many people, thus confirming Keynes's suspicion of the potency of ideas:

'I am sure that the power of vested interest is vastly exaggerated compared with the gradual encroachment of ideas. . . . There are not many who are influenced by new theories after they are twenty-five or thirty years of age, so that the ideas which civil servants and politicians and even agitators apply to current events are not likely to be the newest. But soon or late, it is ideas, not vested interest, which are dangerous for good or evil.'[16]

The next stage is to state the condition which *would* result in the optimum use of resources. They can be expressed in a number of ways. We could expect optimality if the money price was an accurate guide to the resources foregone in production, that is if price equalled marginal cost. Strictly, this is only a necessary condition and not a sufficient condition, e.g. a firm might have its price equal to marginal cost at a profit minimising output, i.e. a firm must maximise its profits as follows: with R as profits, P as price, Q as number of units produced, so that PQ is total revenue, and C as costs, then the firm tries to maximise $R = P.Q - C$. Now R is maximised when its derivative vanishes, that is when:

$$\frac{dR}{dQ} = \frac{d(PQ)}{dQ} - \frac{dC}{dQ} = 0, \quad \text{or} \quad \frac{d(PQ)}{dQ} = \frac{dC}{dQ}$$

The first order condition is simply that marginal revenue, $\frac{d(PQ)}{dQ}$ equals marginal cost, $\frac{dC}{dQ}$ but the second order condition is that $\frac{d^2R}{dQ^2}$ should be negative, that is that the firm was already making profits when marginal revenue became equal to marginal costs.

Now price equals marginal cost in perfect competition which is the market situation in which the firm does not need to lower its price to sell more units and the firms have equal costs at any given level of production.[17] A nationalised industry could also adopt a policy of setting the price of its output equal to its marginal costs. Strictly, the economy would only be in an optimal condition if $P = MC$ in every industry. There is no way of distinguishing the situation in which the economy has only one imperfectly competitive market from that in which it has many.[18] So the irony arises that some politicians feel that they have a justification for a free-market economy in scientific economics while other politicians think that government intervention in the economy can be shown to be advantageous because a nationalised industry can make its price equal to marginal cost.

The diagram below presents the optimal position in another way.

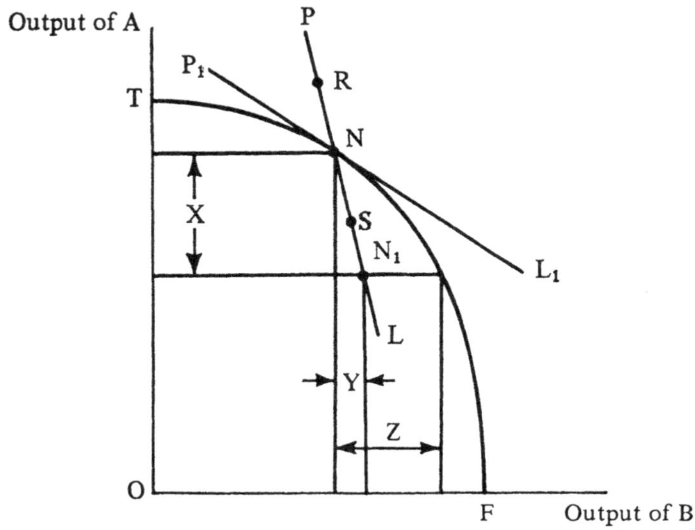

Figure 9

Fig. 9 shows the technology frontier as *TF* giving the various combinations of *A* and *B* which the economy is actually physically capable of producing and so it shows the real amount of *A* which could be produced if a unit of *B* were foregone. The choice ratio between these two goods is different at different points on the frontier as production conditions differ at varying outputs. A tangent to any point on the frontier, such as P_1L_1, to *N*, will show the real ratio at which choices between the two goods could be made. However, the prices in the market at which the consumer actually has to make his choice may be quite different. A price line, such as *PL*, shows all the combinations of *A* and *B* which can be bought at current incomes and current prices. It is quite sensible for the price line to suggest that combinations can be bought which the economy cannot produce, as at *R*, or vice versa, as at *S*; this is merely the realistic implication of imports and exports. Now, if the price line should not be a tangent but should cross the frontier as does *PL* at *N*, then the prices are such that the consumer has to choose between combinations of *A* and *B* such as *N* and N_1. This informs the consumer that prices are such that if he foregoes *X* of article *A* he can have *Y* units of article *B* but this is misleading data, as the technology frontier shows quite clearly that the economy is physically capable of foregoing *X* of *A* and producing an extra *Z* units of *B*.

Only if the price line was a tangent to the technology frontier can the two lines have the same slope and thus show a similar rate of substitution between the two goods. And only then would the prices be an accurate guide for the community in choosing between different goods. The price line, P_1L_1, is such a tangent to the frontier at N and in such conditions price would equal marginal cost,[19] and the prices would be an accurate measure of opportunity costs.

There is a debating device called the '*ignoratio elenchi*'. This is an argument that appears to refute somebody else's point of view by disproving something he did not actually say. In the present context, for instance, a critique of the price system is not subverted by detailing the shortcomings of a controlled economy. It should then perhaps be re-emphasised that economics cannot prove that the government should intervene in the economy; just as price competition is unlikely to result in optimal production, neither is a state-controlled economy. The latter is likely to have difficulties with externalities, with getting information about consumer preferences and costs and with meeting the second order conditions.[20]

Economists have a role to play in government policy but it is in analysing the economic content of rival policies and in predicting their consequences. It is not in arbitrating between the claims. Unfortunately for their morale, economists are not the priests of politicians but their acolytes.

Government intervention in the economy is unlikely to yield Utopia, but then relatively few people in the Western world ever really thought that it would. A much greater number do think that state action in the economy distorts an economically optimum situation produced by free market prices.

State action will not produce optimality, its function is much more modest. The role of the government in the economy is in fact to promote particular goals chosen by the community and this choice is entirely value-loaded. They might be full employment, price stability, maintenance of the Gold Standard or the control of monopoly. In the latter case, for example, there is no point in a monopoly policy that reproduces the perfect competition equilibrium by making price equal to marginal cost since that merely meets the necessary condition, and even if sufficient conditions were met in a particular industry, the Theory of the Second Best shows that in the context of the entire economy this need not be an advantage.

This is because, although it is possible to define the optimal allocation of resources—and to note that one of its characteristics is the price-marginal cost equality—it is difficult to *rank* alternative positions as second best, third best and so on. In *principle* they can be ranked but it is only possible with detailed knowledge of the production and utility functions so that in *practice* they cannot normally be ranked. For welfare purposes, they are all second best in that they cannot be scientifically distinguished but the community *has* to choose between these alternatives and so it can only do so by means other than welfare economics.

This can be illustrated diagrammatically. Fig. 10 shows a techno-

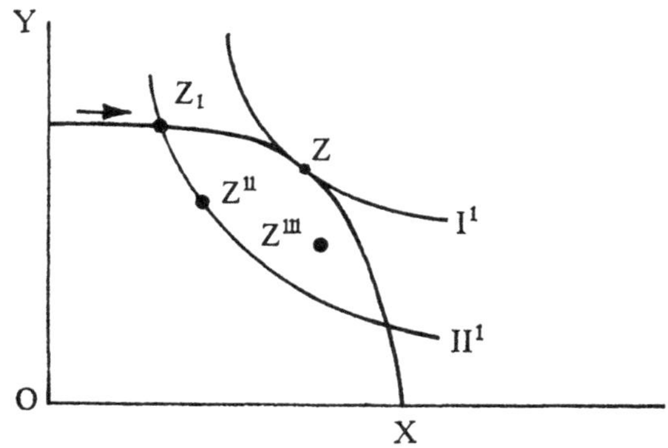

Figure 10

logy frontier offering various output combinations of goods *Y* and *X*. *I'* and *I''* are community indifference curves (see any of the welfare textbooks in the bibliography) joining output combinations which each yield the same welfare to the community. The point *Z* is the optimal resource-use yielding the highest welfare available. It is called the Constrained Bliss Point. Once this position is not available because one of the optimality conditions is broken—that is a constraint exists—the community moves to, say, Z_1, it *need* not mean lower welfare to break other conditions and move perhaps to *Z''* and it may even lead to higher welfare at *Z'''*.

Thus, once the economy is in a sub-optimal position—and we may safely assume it is—it need not be disadvantageous for a particular firm to have price unequal to marginal cost. Our difficulty is thus twofold: first, there is the absence of any general rule that removing a constraint will necessarily improve the community's welfare and, second, although in principle appropriate criteria are available, in practice they seldom are because we know little about real opportunity costs—because money prices show us budget line ratios and not true opportunity costs—and even less about welfare functions—that is the indifference curves—as was seen in Chapter 1.[21] The diagram *expresses* the problem exactly but cannot solve it, for we can hardly ever put exact values on real world positions and thus know which policy gives Z, Z' and so on.

Government policy can usually be aimed only at pragmatic goals such as the control of restrictive practices and not at producing the optimum position on the technology frontier. In this perspective, government action becomes a technique for achieving some given purpose to be compared with other techniques and other goals; it is not a betrayal of a scientific economic principle handed down by Adam Smith.

Notes

1 The choice is not in fact a straightforward matter, in which choosing one goal excludes the other, due to the reciprocal relationship, between economic growth and the Balance of Payments. See Chapter 6.

2 Briefly, the study of a single price rather than the general level of prices, the employment offered by one firm rather than the general level of employment, etc., etc.

3 Its general shape, downwards to the right, is agreed but there is no need for it to be smooth or linear as we would expect production to expand at varying rates as resources are recruited to an industry.

4 The problems of unemployment, that is of avoiding production positions such as *C*, are dealt with in Chapter 5. The problems of economic growth, that is of moving the technology frontier so that it passes through *D*, are considered in Chapter 4.

5 Smith, Adam, *The Wealth of Nations* (1776).

6 Any general reader innocent of economics is advised to take this as received doctrine. If curious, he should consult any standard textbook on price theory of which a list is given at the end of Chapter 1.

7 As for note 6 above.

8 This kind of theory is 'comparative statics' and does not attempt to explain the path between the equilibria, e.g. whether it was one or a series of steps. This is the concern of 'dynamic economics'.

9 Technical details of the different kinds of markets can be found in any of the textbooks in Chapter 1, Bibliography.

10 This statement relies on the Law of Non-Proportional Returns. See any book in the Chapter 1 Bibliography.

11 It should be re-emphasised that this is only the briefest summary of those parts of price theory which relate to the use of resources. Details and proofs can be found in the references at the end of Chapter 1. Economists do have alternative, less well-known, theories of resource allocation, such as input-output analysis (see Chapter 7).

12 See page 46.

13 This deft example is owed to Dorfman, R., *The Price System*, pp. 139–40, Prentice-Hall (1964).

14 Economists have developed the technique of cost-benefit analysis for dealing with the problem. Details are given in Chapter 8.

15 Robinson, J., *Economic Philosophy*, pp. 70–1, Penguin (1964).

16 Keynes, J. M., *General Theory of Employment, Interest and Money*, p. 343, Macmillan (1936). Reproduced by permission of the Trustees of the estate of the late Lord Keynes.

17 For details, see any of the textbooks in the bibliography.

18 Lipsey, R. G. and Lancaster, K., 'The Theory of the Second Best', *Review of Economic Studies*, Vol. XXIV (1), No. 63 (1957).

19 There are yet other ways of identifying the optimum conditions available in the references given in the section on welfare economics in the Bibliography at the end of this Chapter.

20 A planned economy meets an interesting difficulty if it regards land as 'free'. This means that its opportunity cost is ignored and a zero price is as misleading as a positive price in that it is unequal to marginal cost. For this reason land has been misallocated in the U.S.S.R. (See 'Caring for the Land' in *Morning Star*, 30 October 1968).

21 An example of these difficulties is given in Chapter 8 on nationalised industries.

Bibliography

The following books deal with Welfare Economics:

REDER, M. W., *Studies in the Theory of Welfare Economics*, Oxford University Press, 1947

GRAAF, J. de V., *Theoretical Welfare Economics*, Cambridge University Press, 1957

LITTLE, I. M. D., *A Critique of Welfare Economics* (Second Edition), Oxford University Press, 1957

QUIRK, J. and SAPOSNIK, R., *Introduction to General Equilibrium Theory and Welfare Economics*, McGraw-Hill, 1968

The following deal with more modern theories of resource allocation, such as input-output analysis:

BAUMOL, W. J., *Economic Theory and Operations Analysis* (Second Edition), Prentice-Hall, 1965

COHEN, K. J. and CYERT, R. M., *The Theory of the Firm*, Prentice-Hall, 1965

CYERT, R. M. and MARCH, J., *The Behavioural Theory of the Firm*, Prentice-Hall, 1963

Chapter 4

ECONOMIC GROWTH

The apparatus of government policy directed at consumption, investment and so on is only comprehended by those who know the significance of these variables and this needs an understanding of micro-economics, macro-economics and economic growth. This brief chapter is thus focused on the main determinants of economic growth so that, in later chapters, the purpose of government policy towards these variables can be properly appreciated.

Economic growth, as here considered, is the rate of growth over time of the National Income per head. It is commonly expressed as a percentage increase per annum. It is sometimes a mixed blessing; it can carry real costs, it may be distributed in a non-optimum manner and, certainly, a rise in National Income per head does not necessarily mean a proportionate increase in welfare per head and might even mean a fall.

There is a possible ambiguity in that increases in real output per head are sometimes effected by moving from an inefficient position on to the technology frontier itself, Z_2 to Z_1 in Fig. 1. This is a matter of full employment rather than economic growth which is concerned with moving the entire frontier, *TF* to T^1F^1, in Fig. 1. From the public's point of view they come to much the same thing, as real income unquestionably rises, and government policy is quite properly concerned with both. Analytically they are quite different; making better use of existing resources needs certain policies and is a once and for all improvement, economic growth can be a continuous process and needs, with exceptions, a quite different set of policies. We are here concerned with this latter problem of the growth rate and the policies relevant thereto. This is not to imply that these conceptually different policies may not affect one another to some extent: sometimes they may be mutually consistent as when an increase in investment leads to further employment and faster growth and sometimes they may be mutually inconsistent as when a growth policy may require a transfer of labour from one sector of the economy to another and so at least temporary unemployment.

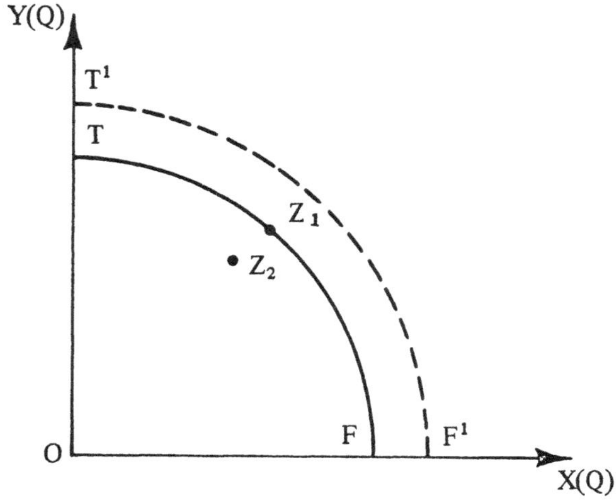

Figure 1

A clear distinction must be drawn between understanding any of the models of economic growth and an appreciation of economic growth in *practice*. This dichotomy is professionally embarrassing; economists have put a great deal of intellectual input into growth theory for a small output in terms of testable non-trivial propositions. As Hahn and Mathews comment:

> 'The authors of these [economic growth] models have naturally had in mind as a rule that they should contribute to an understanding of the way that economies actually grow over time; but this approach to growth theory is none the less different from that which would be used if the immediate purpose was to provide the best available explanation of the variety of historical growth experience.'[1]

Our interest is with the relationship of theory and public policy and so, though we cannot wholly escape growth models, our main theoretical interest is elsewhere.

It should be emphasised that there is no such thing as *the* theory of economic growth; there are many competing theories, because theories are assembled from assumptions and concepts and so can be constructed in a number of quite different ways. Our main concern is not with the weighty problems of assessing, comparing or testing these theories but with a more pragmatic approach to the variables relevant to the growth process.

Like other chapters, this chapter must not be mistaken for a survey of a whole body of theory, it uses parts of the economist's theoretical apparatus to comment on the sources of, and form of, government economic policy. One of the problems of teaching economics is that micro- and macro-economics can be taught from a spectrum of elementary, intermediate and advanced theory but growth economics is quite different in that it is available for the most part only in an elementary or in a rather advanced form.

Three separate factors, or sets of factors, are relevant to growth, though they are also interdependent. Firstly, growth is affected by the quantity and quality of land, the number and skill of the labour force, the stock and mechanical efficiency of capital assets such as computers, lorries and factory equipment.

A second factor—into which the first can in fact be subsumed—is the ratio in which the production inputs are enjoyed by a country. This is a more helpful formulation of the first point as it says that we are not concerned with increasing simply the absolute volume of a factor. This is because we would run into the diminishing returns case and eventually the case of negative returns. Our concern is instead with factor ratios. The most common form of this concern with factor ratios is found in the problem of overpopulation. This notion regards the optimum labour population as that which, combined with existing land and capital resources, maximises output per head. Now this idea is disadvantageous in that it poses the problem in a prejudicial manner; it is sensible to regard India as overpopulated with regard to labour but it is just as sensible to regard it as underpopulated with regard to capital. In fact it is overpopulated not in absolute terms at all, but only with regard to capital and land, and similarly it is capital and land poor only when viewed in the perspective of its population.

Presumably we habitually focus on labour overpopulation instead of more generally on the input ratios because the labour population size can be more easily altered than that of land—though hardly that of capital. A further reason for this traditional approach is probably the Malthusian concern with population. The important thing is not to attribute causal significance to one factor because it has too great or small a magnitude but to regard the land, labour, capital *ratio* as non-optimal It is not then, for example, simply the quality and quantity of labour in the U.S. compared with the U.K. that generates a higher *per capita* output but also the other inputs with which the labour has to be combined.

It is a common misapprehension that all overpopulated countries are under-developed but this is not so; the U.K. is overpopulated in some senses. Overpopulation carried implications about the growth *rate* rather than merely current living standards.

Now these considerations—the quality and quantity of factors and their input ratios—are commonplace in comparative statics in explanations of unequal National Incomes at a given time. They are also vital to the growth process by which a country moves from one equilibrium to another. The absolute investment level, for instance, is relevant to the capital-output ratio found in most growth models.

The third factor relevant to growth is how much current production society is willing and able to forego in order to gain greater production in the future. This is sometimes thought of as money savings and the interest earned thereon but these are merely the financial manifestations of one aspect. In real terms it is the production foregone while the labour force is more elaborately educated by day release schemes, and so on. It is, of course, hoped that the real extra production so generated in the future exceeds production foregone in the present—even when expressed accurately in present values.[2] In real terms it is also the production foregone while land is irrigated, drained, laid fallow to gain greater future crops and when consumption goods are foregone by allocating resources to capital production for greater future consumption output. Economic growth has thus clear opportunity costs even if their size is unclear due to the measurement of the price mechanism. The size of the opportunity cost may also be unclear where there is widespread *unemployment*. The community, knowingly or otherwise, still has to make such choices which are critical to the growth path.

Just as we have seen that resource allocation is sub-optimal in a free market and will see that a free market is unlikely to produce full employment or maximise G.N.P. so it should be clear that the variables relevant to economic growth are unlikely to autonomously reach the values appropriate to any given growth rate chosen by the community. Thus, once the government makes the initial normative judgement of promoting economic growth, state intervention in the economy naturally follows.

Government policy towards economic growth may now be classified into this threefold division: operating on the quantity and quality of the factors of production, their relationship to one another and the volume of production foregone.

Almost any policy, for example the U.K. joining the E.E.C., might have some effect on growth. However, there is no need for a boring list of all such policies, for it will be sufficient to give an example of each major kind, more or less specifically directed at growth. As far as the *quantity* of *labour* is concerned the Australian Government encourages immigration and the Mexican Government promotes birth control. Most advanced countries operate more on the *quality* of labour—in effect, of course, this can be identical to an increase in the absolute quantity of labour as far as output is concerned but, significantly, not as far as output per head is concerned. An increase in labour quality raises income per head, an increase in quantity need not. For this and other reasons most governments encourage education; the U.K. Government increases its expenditure—absolutely and relatively—on the traditional forms of education and in recent years has manœuvred industry through Industrial Training Board grants and levies into financing more vocational education.

The government can do next to nothing about the total *quantity* of *land* but they can influence the supply of certain kinds of land. The Town and Country Planning authorities can vary the proportions of residential, recreational and industrial land and subsidies are available for marginal farmland. This latter technique also affects the quality of land.

Not only is the government concerned with the factor ratios and so changes the factor quantities, but also it is interested in where these quantities are available, that is with a geographical equilibrium. It is pointless to have the appropriate volumes of land, labour and capital available but in quite different places. It fosters the occupational and geographical mobility of labour by legislation like the Housing (England and Wales) Act 1961, which gives local authorities the power to allocate council houses to skilled workers needed from elsewhere. Capital mobility is encouraged by regionally differentiated grants through the location of industry.[3]

The government, in principle, encourages us to forego today to enjoy more tomorrow, but in practice the U.K. Government has been imprecise in its ideas of how much must, or should, be foregone to gain a given increment of future production. The problem can be expressed in the following diagrammatic fashion. The community has to choose a combination of present and future production on the choice frontier *CF* in Fig. 2 which shows that it can only have more present consumption by foregoing future consumption and vice versa. Thus to get the highest possible growth rate *C* it must give up all present consumption. Of the combinations of present and future consumption open to it the community obviously chooses that tangent to the highest community indifference curve represented as U, U_1, U_2 etc. In other words, faced with a resources constraint on its mix of present and future consumption, society maximises its welfare

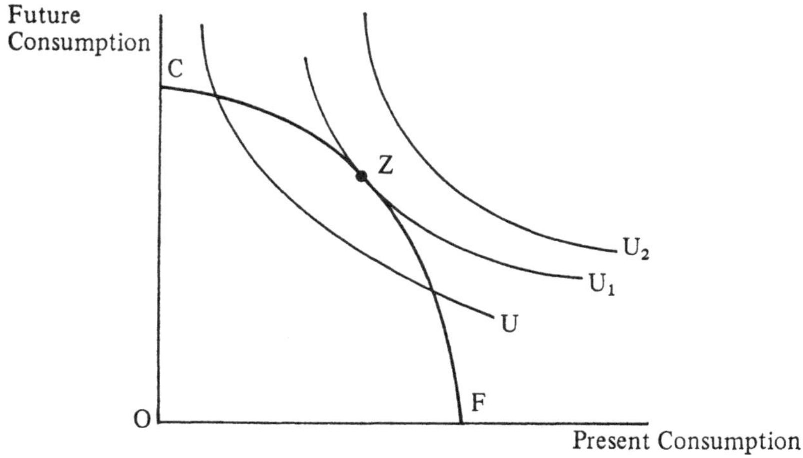

Figure 2

at *Z* where the marginal rate of transformation between growth and current consumption equals their social marginal rate of substitution.[4]

Unfortunately, the actual physical trade-off rates on choice frontiers like *CF* are seldom known, for we know little about the opportunity cost of economic growth. Nor, for the reasons given in Chapter 1, is much known about the community's preferences between present and future consumption. This casts an unflattering light on the British National Plan,[5] for this document announced a target growth rate of 4% and then discussed the ways and means. It contributed nothing to our knowledge of the trade-off rates and the public was presented with no evidence that it was, or should be, their choice. The public was told something of what had to be done, for instance about exports, but this is not the same as being told the cost in terms of foregone opportunities. An apparently bold plan of action is no substitute for knowing what you are doing. To choose scientifically a growth rate you must know the opportunity cost of growth, which is the consumption foregone, including the consumption generated by alternative growth rates, and you must know the preferences between present and future consumption. The National Plan presented no rationale of why the target growth rate was the appropriate one, nor did it identify the costs of growth. All this is scarcely democratic planning.

It is worth re-emphasising that economic growth has costs and so is not necessarily a good end in itself.[6] The costs take three main forms. Firstly, the re-allocation of resources necessitated by the growth process means lower incomes and unemployment for labour in the industries contracted by the growth. Secondly, there are externalities in the form of deleterious effects imposed by some on others. If, for instance, more people have radios then more people's peace can be damaged by irresponsible noise-levels and if more people can afford supersonic air travel then more people have to listen to it. Thirdly, there are costs in the form of present production foregone. This latter point can be conveniently expressed by means of Fig. 3. The economy is already on some growth path such as *gg*. The growth rate is assumed constant $\frac{\triangle Y}{\triangle T}$. The government decides at some moment, T_1, to promote the growth *rate* g_1g_1 which offers $\frac{\triangle Y'}{\triangle T}$. As this means more present consumption must be foregone, the living standard in terms of consumption declines absolutely by Y_3. The economy, in its new faster growth rate $G'G'$, does not even reach the old absolute consumption level Y until T_2 and it does not even catch up the income levels it could have had on the old growth rate

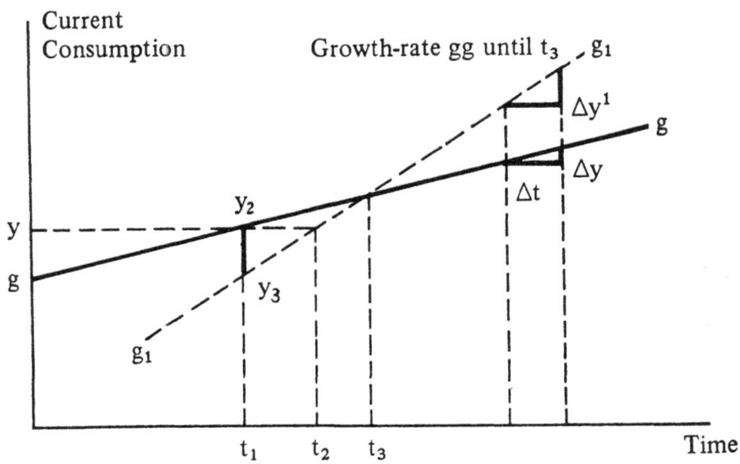

Figure 3

gg until T_3. Once past T_3 it greatly benefits since for a given period of time $\triangle T$ it now gains $\triangle Y'$ instead of $\triangle Y$, but society has the difficulty of assessing short-run lower incomes against long-run higher incomes. It can only reliably do this if the social rate of time discount is known.[7]

We have so far talked in general principles of the need for, and likely form of, government policy directed towards economic growth. Our concern is with economics and policy so it is now worth looking at precise and tentatively tested economic hypotheses to see their implications for economic growth.[8]

There is a well-established relationship between National Income growth rates and productivity increases in the manufacturing sector of the economy. More precisely, the fastest growth rates are related to the greatest excess of productivity in the manufacturing sector over the rest of the economy. In so far as some countries have experienced faster growth than their manufacturing productivity would predict, the explanation seems to lie in how much a country invests in relation to its growth rate. So a country that finds productivity in manufacturing difficult to increase can partially escape the constraint by investing a higher proportion of its income than previously. A third relationship is the evidence that every 1% increment to the growth rate needs a 0·5% increase in productivity and 0·5% increase in employment man hours.[9]

The search for an appropriate policy might go as follows. Are there likely to be endogenous increases in productivity and investment and, if not, how might the government generate them? How might the government increase available manpower in the manufacturing sector to further increase the growth rate?

These are questions of positive economics. Productivity depends partly on scale economies resulting from output changes within the firm. In the United Kingdom, the government can, and does, stimulate these developments through the Ministry of Technology and the I.R.C. However, there are other sources of productivity. Goods and services are exchanged against other goods and services so that economic growth also depends on demand elasticities for some goods and supply constraints for others, and vice versa. Now it seems difficult for the government to much affect demand elasticities so attention switches to supply constraints. The government can encourage technological change—though it is an open question of positive economics how it might most easily do this.[10]

A critical question is the significance of the supply constraints for policy, especially since manpower apparently needs to be disproportionately increased in manufacturing industry. Since a shorter working week is part of a rising standard of living for most people, longer hours are not an available solution. The pattern is obviously to transfer farm labour to the manufacturing sector of the economy but, by its nature, this process must have an end. This has broadly happened in the U.K. which has the lowest percentage farm-labour force in the world. It is in this light that manpower policies like S.E.T. and Payroll Tax must be seen. Such tax devices are worth consideration; it is, so far, not clear whether they can in fact produce the manpower-investment patterns apparently needed in different sectors of the economy and it is not known what would be the optimum rates at which to levy them. Other writers, besides Professor Kaldor, place emphasis on the small pool of agricultural and self-employed labour in the U.K. and on economies of scale.[11]

There are, of course, other hypotheses available—mostly at a journalistic level—to 'explain' the slow U.K. growth rate. They included poor management, trade-union restrictive practices, the education system, the social milieu, the attitude to technology and innovation, the government of the day. Such hypotheses tend to reflect their author's prejudices. They have the conceptual difficulty that they are often framed in a uni-causal fashion and the practical difficulty that they are unquantifiable.

The Harrod-Domar model[12] is the best known growth theory, if we can pass our attention to formal growth models rather than particular hypotheses. This model contained two remarkable properties; it concluded that there was nothing to make an economy autonomously operate at full employment with the maximum attainable growth and, once off this steady state growth path, it would experience either continuous inflation or continuous unemployment. Enough will be said about growth models and public policy if we concentrate on the first 'knife-edge' problem that the economy cannot easily have full employment levels consistent with maximum growth.

The Harrod-Domar pattern can be expressed in a number of ways. Using linear difference equations, the following can be constructed.

$$S_t = \alpha Y_t \text{ (propensity to save)} \qquad 4(1)$$
$$I_t = \beta(Y_t - Y_{t-1}) \text{ (a form of accelerator)} \qquad 4(2)$$
$$S_t = I_t \text{ (equilibrium)} \qquad 4(3)$$
$$\alpha Y_t = \beta(Y_t - Y_{t-1}) \qquad 4(4)$$
$$\alpha Y_t = \beta Y_t - \beta Y_{t-1} \qquad 4(5)$$
$$\beta Y_{t-1} = \beta Y_t - \alpha Y_t \qquad 4(6)$$
$$\beta Y_{t-1} = (\beta - \alpha) Y_t \qquad 4(7)$$
$$Y_t = \frac{\beta}{\beta - \alpha} Y_{t-1} \qquad 4(8)$$

This is to say that income in a given period is related to that of the former period by the factor of the ratio of the accelerator[13] to the accelerator minus the saving propensity.

A rather more significant form of the Harrod-Domar problem is as follows. Firstly, it is assumed that there is one item in the economy that can either be used as capital or can be consumed. Apart from this capital input, the only other input is labour. There are constant returns to scale and zero technical progress. It is further assumed that the saving propensity is constant, that the input coefficients are fixed and that the labour force grows at a constant rate n fixed by non-economic (demographic) forces.

Clearly, the income growth rate cannot be any faster than that of the two inputs of labour and capital. The first difficulty is that these two input growth rates are separately determined since the capital growth rate is endogenous (related to S) and the labour growth rate (n) exogenous. A second problem arises in that if capital growth is slower than n then the income growth rate, g, is slower than *n which must imply increasing unemployment.* If $g=n$ then this becomes the steady state (full employment) growth path for the economy; it is called the natural growth rate and is the highest growth rate permanently attainable. Unfortunately, there is no reason why g should equal n.

Consideration now turns to the other input, capital. The capital market is in equilibrium when $S=I$. If the capital stock is K, and planned investment is I, then the capital growth rate is $\frac{I}{K}$ and so $S=\frac{I}{K}$ in equilibrium. Now income cannot grow faster than capital and this growth rate is the *warranted* growth rate. Using subscripts and writing V for the capital-output rate, we get

$$g_n=g_w=\frac{I}{K}, \qquad 4(9)$$

but $\frac{I}{K}$ can be re-written $\frac{I}{Y}\cdot\frac{Y}{K}$ but $\frac{I}{Y}=S$ and $\frac{Y}{I}=\frac{I}{V}$ so 4(9) can be re-written

$$g_n=g_w=\frac{I}{Y}\cdot\frac{Y}{K}=\frac{s}{v} \qquad 4(10)$$

This well-known result, that the condition for the warranted growth rate (capital determined) to equal the natural growth rate (labour determined) is for them both to equal $\frac{s}{v}$. But the difficulty is the n, s, and v are determined quite independently so that $g_n=g_w$ is a special case only. There is thus nothing in the model to yield full employment and also the highest possible growth rate.

It is important to see the origins of this pessimistic view. We are forced to it by the Harrod-Domar assumptions which demand that $S=I$, while S is endogenously determined, and then requires the labour stock to grow at the same rate. Furthermore—and this is critical—there is no escape in the form of substituting labour for capital or vice versa, if we should have 'too much' of one or the other (due to $\frac{I}{K}=N$) because we have fixed co-efficients. Nor are economies of scale available.

It will be apparent that steady state growth becomes possible with full employment if we relax one, or some, of our assumptions about savings, labour demand, labour supply and technology. The Harrod-Domar model is important because it draws attention to the importance of these sorts of assumptions. We will follow through just one of them. If we abandon fixed co-efficients in favour of a range of alternative production techniques, each with its own capital-labour ratio, then V becomes adjustable to make $\frac{S}{v}=n$ and so produce full employment and the fastest possible growth. This is the germ of the 'neo-classical' approach to growth problems. A general conclusion is 'when production takes place under neo-classical conditions of variable proportions and constant returns to scale . . . there may not be any knife-edge. The system can adjust to any given rate of growth of the labour force, and eventually approach a state of steady proportional growth'.[14]

Our concern is with economic theory and government policy; as Sir Roy Allen says, 'The models . . . despite their formidable appearance at times, are many stages removed from policy applications.'[15] Not quite all is lost. The Harrod-Domar model does specify some important variables and helps the policy-maker to ask the right questions; the less formal economic theory also provides a useful filing system whereby ideas and policies can be classified. Some of these ideas are now in the form of testable hypotheses and carry some encouraging implications for government policy.

Notes

1 Hahn, F. H. and Matthews, R. C. O., 'The Theory of Economic Growth: A Survey', *Economic Journal*, Vol. LXXIV, p. 779 (1964).
2 See Chapter 7 for some consideration of the present-value technique.
3 See Chapter 11.
4 For the purposes of exposition we are equating greater future consumption with the concept of the growth rate. This need not be quite the same thing.
5 *The National Plan*, Cmd. 2764 (September 1965).
6 Mishan, E. J., *The Costs of Economic Growth*, Staples (1966), and Penguin (1969).
7 See Chapter 8.
8 See Kaldor, N., *Causes of the Slow Rate of Economic Growth of the United Kingdom*, Cambridge University Press (1966).
9 Kaldor, *loc. cit.*
10 See Chapter 9.
11 Denison, E. F., *Why Growth-Rates Differ*, Allen and Unwin (1968).
12 Harrod, R. F., 'An Essay in Dynamic Theory', *Economic Journal*, Vol. XLIX (1939), and Domar, E. D., 'Capital Expansion, Rate of Growth and Employment', *Econometrica*, Vol. 14 (1946).
13 Savings propensities and accelerators are developed in Chapter 5.
14 Solow, R. M., 'A Contribution to the Theory of Economic Growth', p. 53, *Quarterly Journal of Economics* (1956).
15 Allen, Sir Roy, *Macro-Economic Theory*, p. xii, Macmillan (1966).

Bibliography

ALLEN, Sir Roy, *Macro-Economic Theory*, Macmillan, 1966

The National Plan, Cmd. 2764, H.M.S.O., 1965

DENISON, E. F. assisted by J. P. POULLIER, *Why Growth Rates Differ*, Allen and Unwin, 1968

DENISON, E. F., *Growth and Efficiency*, Part III in Caves, R. E. and Associates, Allen and Unwin, 1968

ELTIS, W. A., *Economic Growth*, Hutchinson University Library, 1966

KALDOR, N., *Causes of the Slow Rate of Growth of the United Kingdom*, Cambridge University Press, 1966 and Penguin, 1969

MISHAN, E. J., *The Costs of Economic Growth*, Staples, 1966

Chapter 5

THE DETERMINATION OF NATIONAL OUTPUT: THE THEORY

The purpose of this chapter is to show that—given the assumption that the government wishes to maximise employment subject to constraints of both a high growth rate and price stability—it necessarily follows that the government will intervene in the economy. It has been shown that these policy goals are value-judgements; the economists' job is to show which policies are consistent with these goals. Technically, as opposed to politically, all that we can ask is consistency between ends and means.

Government intervention is consistent with the goals; it can be shown that the levels of employment and output and the rate of change of prices which will occur *autonomously* are seldom those which the government would choose.

Now if we can find the factors governing the level of income we have also found at least the main factors affecting the level of output and employment. This is because, for the moment, we will assume that prices are constant so that a rise in income must mean a greater production. This can only be brought about by an increase in resource employment.[1] Production *can* be increased in the long run without extra employment due to economic growth but in the short run extra output entails some extra employment. It is a characteristic of Keynesian economics that it is concerned with immediate practical policies; it has a great deal to say about the short run but much less about the long run.

What are the determinants of income? It is a straightforward proposition that if people are to receive incomes then other people must spend. The basic notion is thus the simple identity:

$$Y \text{ (income)} \equiv E \text{ (expenditure)}^1 \qquad 5(1)$$

which is customarily taught by means of flow diagrams. Now as long as expenditure is maintained at some given magnitude then income will also be so maintained. And it is an equilibrium income: to say that income is in equilibrium is to say nothing about its level. But if, out of income, some proportion is saved[2] instead of spent, then expenditure falls and so must future income. Similarly, if more is spent than is earned—that is if investment[3] occurs—then income will rise. Because savings and investment need not be equal, income can in fact change in one direction or another. Savings and investment need not be equal because they are determined by quite separate factors with different groups of people —though some people could be both savers and investors. It is immediately clear that $Y=E$ is equilibrium but it need not be a stable equilibrium. Our explanation may now be generalised. Saving (S) are a form of 'withdrawal' and investment (I) a form of 'injection'. There is another pair of withdrawals (W) and injections (J): imports (M) generate incomes in other countries and, along with government taxation (T), represent the two other withdrawals from the circular flow. The other injections are, of course, the corresponding items; exports (X) are expenditure in another country that generate income in the home country and government expenditure (G), too, creates extra income. The factors governing these items are largely independent of one another so that it is only a charming coincidence if $S=E$, $X=M$ and $T=G$. Nor is there anything in the model to make the withdrawals sum to the same value as the injections.

The economic consequences can be easily summarised:

1 If $J > W$, then National Income rises.
2 If $J < W$, National Income falls.
3 If $J = W$, National Income is stable.

So far we have an explanation of why National Income is likely to fluctuate upwards or downwards. The resultant changes in income lead to changes in I, S, T, and M which take values that set up a process whereby Y and E approach one another in value. It is a characteristic of the Keynesian model that Y must equal E by definition in equilibrium, and, if $W \neq J$, then the National Income changes until W becomes equal to J and thus $Y=E$.[4] We thus have an explanation, first, of why we might expect the economy to be in disequilibrium, but also we have an implication that the very disequilibrium will produce changes in the income level that move the economy towards equilibrium. This carries an implication that the economy is in autonomous operation and will reach equilibrium without government intervention. This is true. However, the Keynesian model also shows that *equilibrium* employment and output is not the same as *full* employment and output.

We first asked ourselves what determined income and the answer was the level of expenditure. Our question must now become what determines expenditure and the most convenient method of answering this is to fragment equation 5(1) into the form:

$$Y \equiv E = C + I + G \qquad 5(2)$$

and then discuss the determinants of consumption, investment and government expenditure.

The latter can be dealt with easily. *Government expenditure* is determined by a prior decision to balance or unbalance the government's budget. Once this decision is made, other decisions can follow which implement the basic policy; the government will spend enough to get the balance, surplus or deficit that it is prepared to countenance. Thus government expenditure is governed by exogenous non-economic factors, mainly a particular government's concept of the role of the budget and its (partly) independent policy decisions about the required level of spending on roads, education, defence and so on.

Most governments are now quite happy with an unbalanced budget. They decide what proportion of resources it is appropriate for them to take over and then allocate these resources between competing claims.[5]

Consumption expenditure is related to income in a form called a consumption function thus:

$$C = f(Y, m.p.c) \qquad 5(3)$$

which rather asserts the obvious in saying that consumption depends on the level of income and the proportion spent of the marginal increment to income $(m.p.c./\frac{dc}{dy})$; this notion is the marginal propensity to consume. Fig. 1 shows the position graphically. Consumption savings and income are shown on the axes and the 45° line represents equality of consumption and income (scales on axes the same). Thus at income level Y_1 the entire income is spent on consumption, C_1. At higher incomes like Y_{11} only a proportion of income, C_{11}, is spent, the remainder being saved, S_{11}. Obviously, unless there is a countervailing injection then this withdrawal will dis-equilibriate the economy.

If we can discover what factors govern the shape and position of the consumption function, then we have variables to which government policy might be addressed in order to yield required levels of consumption and savings.

The shape of the consumption function simply implies that, at lower incomes, people spend their income on immediate consumption and that, at higher incomes, money is available for saving. This seems unexceptional: the explanation is that at higher incomes most needs are already met and, secondly, that people can take time to adjust their real living standards to higher money incomes. We would not expect every individual to have the same consumption function but we would expect the *m.p.c* of even the most profligate to eventually become less than unity. We would expect the national *m.p.c.* to display these properties and we would expect the *m.p.c.* to sometimes alter its position, perhaps from $m.p.c._2$ to $m.p.c._1$. This would alter, at a given income level, the magnitudes of consumption and saving.

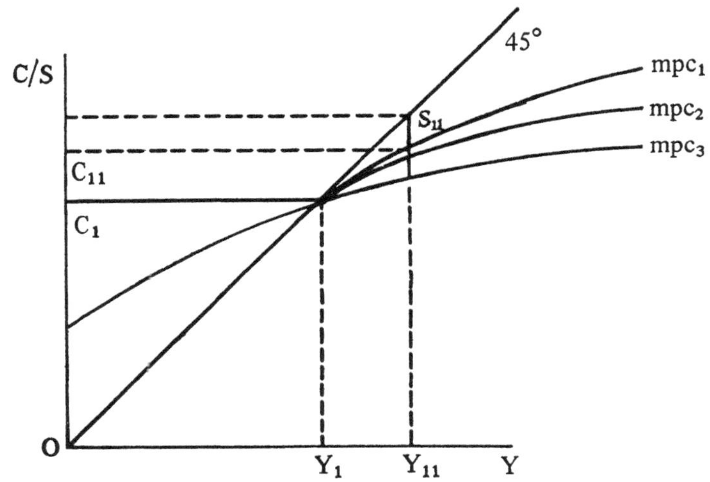

Figure 1

Such movements could be responses to changes in prices, taxes and tastes. The government can easily alter prices and taxes but tastes have proved to be more intractable. Savings campaigns, for instance, attempt to alter choices between spending and saving and are not notably successful. Rather than its total, the government can sometimes affect the form of a given magnitude of savings.

The factors governing the *shape* of the consumption function (changes in consumption at different incomes) and its position (changes in consumption at a given income) carry implications for government policy explored later. To take a simple example, for the moment, the redistribution of income from the rich, who save, to the poor, who do not, cannot be considered simply as social policy for it is not economically neutral; it can be expected to raise aggregate spending and this carries implications, as we have seen, for income, output and employment levels and, as we shall see, for the price level. There is no economic reason why, at a given moment, the consumption function should not intercept the Y axis at a positive value like *m.p.c.*$_3$ in Fig. 1.

The determinants of *investment* spending are less self-evident; they can be summarised as:

$$I=f(m.e.c.,i) \tag{5(4)}$$

This means that investment depends on the current interest rate and the marginal efficiency of capital; that is, that the investor will only purchase a physical capital asset if the percentage return on it exceeds or equals what he could earn by lending at the current interest

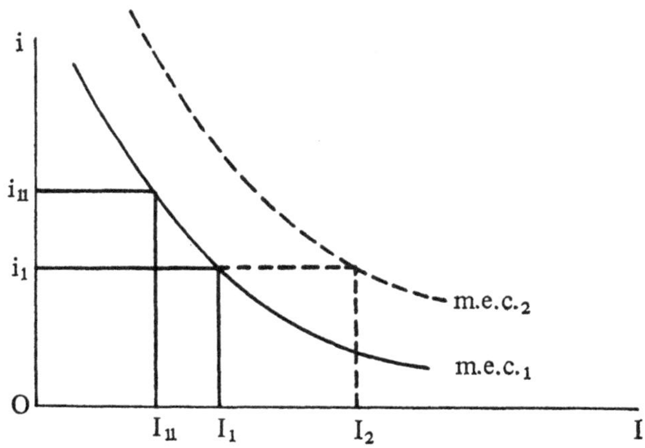

Figure 2

rate. This is simply to say that the gain from the capital asset must exceed the opportunity cost of ownership, the interest foregone. It is convenient to express this notion graphically in Fig. 2 and then state these concepts, and their developments, more explicitly.

An *m.e.c.* schedule is assumed to be negatively sloped, thus implying that the first unit of a given type of investment asset, say a machine tool, yields a higher return than a later unit.[6] There will be exceptions but it is plausible that this has a general applicability; what is less clear is the elasticity of this negative slope (our diagram carries no implications in this respect as no scale is shown). Given that an *m.e.c* schedule has these general properties, the diagram simply asserts (it does not prove), that, given an interest rate, say i_1, itself determined by exogenous factors, equilibrium I will be at the level I_1. Should these exogenous factors raise interest rates to i_{11}, then I falls to I_{ii}. Similarly if the factors governing *m.e.c.* shift it from $m.e.c._1$ to $m.e.c._2$ then I will increase from I_1 to I_2 at the given interest level i_i.

What factors govern changes in interest rates and in the level of *m.e.c.*? The answers to these questions will suggest approaches to policy problems regarding investment both as an injection and as a part of aggregate expenditure.

The *m.e.c.* is the rate of discount that makes the *prospective yield* of capital equal to the *purchase price*. This is a manipulation of the familiar notion of an interest rate: in general, if the interest rate is denoted by r (say 7%) and the sum lent by P_0 (say £100) and the sum received at the end of the year by P_1 (£107) then

$$P_1 = P_0\,(1+r) \qquad 5(5)$$

$$107 = 100\,(1+7\%)$$

If P_1 is now re-lent for a year then

$$P_2 = P_1\,(1+r) \qquad 5(6)$$

but equation 5 means equation 6 can be re-written as

$$P_2 = P_0\,(1+r)\,(1+r) \qquad 5(7)$$

after a third year $P_3 = P_2\,(1+r)$ 5(8)
which, due to expression 7, can be re-written as

$$P_3 = P_0\,(1+r)\,(1+r)\,(1+r) \qquad 5(9)$$

which is better written as $P_3 = P_0\,(1+r)^3$ 5(10)
or more generally

$$P_n = P_0\,(1+r)^n \qquad 5(11)$$

This tells us the value, after n years, of an asset originally valued at P_0 returning a yield of $r\%$ per annum. Our immediate concern is with the present value of an asset which is expected to yield $r\%$ per annum for n years.

Clearly $$P_0 = \frac{P_n}{(1+r)n} \qquad 5(12)$$

Now this P_0 is the present value,[7] of the prospective yield of the asset and the rate $r\%$ per annum is the marginal efficiency of capital.

As we have seen, if this *m.e.c.* exceeds the current interest rate, then it is better to buy the asset which promises these returns rather than lend at the current interest rate.

What factors can we expect to govern *m.e.c.*? If the government can alter the purchase price of the asset (technically, its supply price), it will still generate the same income flow, but this must now represent a higher percentage return, as it was earned from a smaller sum from the entrepreneur's viewpoint. Thus, investment subsidies are a first candidate as a policy technique; a difficulty is that we are talking not of known future yields but expected yields.[8] Expectations have proved generally unresponsive to government propaganda.

If the *m.e.c.* proves intractable, or at least insufficiently responsive, the government might look to the factors governing interest rates as a means of influencing the investment decision.[9] The interest rate is the charge made (normally on an annual percentage basis) for the use of money. This price, like any other, depends on demand and supply, in this case for money.

A number of factors govern the demand for money—which is conventionally defined as anything generally acceptable in settlement of a debt and this means, in practice, currency and bank deposits, including 'near-money' such as deposits in merchant banks and building societies. People want currency and bank deposits, as opposed to other forms of wealth, because money can be turned quickly into other forms of wealth: that is it is liquid. Now *liquidity preference* has its genesis in three motives for holding money. People have a transactions motive for day-to-day purchases which might well depend on the price level and the level of money income, there is a precautionary motive which manifests itself in a sum of money held to meet emergencies and which probably depends on temperament and money income and there is a speculative motive in the form of money held ready to take advantage of 'investment' opportunities as they arise. This presumably depends again on money income, temperament, expectations and the current interest rate—since money held in this way involves an opportunity cost in the form of interest foregone.

The *supply* of money varies between economies. It will normally depend on the government, firstly, as it controls the currency supply and, secondly, in so far as the government can control the creation of bank deposits (and other forms of credit) by the banks. As we shall see, its ability is, in this respect, somewhat circumscribed.

We have examined so far the determinants of government, consumption and investment spending as a necessary preliminary to considering government policy. A further form of expenditure within a country is the *exports* resulting from the spending of other countries. Their level depends on domestic and foreign price levels and the international exchange rate plus any government regulations like tariffs, quotas or exchange controls.

A summary so far would re-write equation 2 as

$$Y \equiv E = C + I + G + X - M \qquad 5(13)$$

These are our variables and we have discussed the chief factors relevant to them. Consumption spending depends on Y and *m.p.c.*, I spending on *m.e.c.* (and so a supply price and prospective yield) and on i (and so on liquidity preference and the money supply). G is likely to be determined exogenously and $X—M$ by price levels and exchange rates which are, at the moment, goals rather than means of government policy. However, there are techniques for exercising some influence on the level and pattern of $X—M$.

Now that we have seen the determinants of spending it is appropriate to return to the equilibrium level of income. Fig. 3 represents expenditure on the Y axis and income on the X axis and the 45° line represents equality between the two. If Y were always and autonomously equal to E then the community's expenditure function would be the 45° line and there would always be the appropriate level of spending needed to maintain any given income level. However, as we have seen, there is nothing to make $W = J$ so that if at some income level Y_0, $J > W$, then spending exceeds income and income must rise from Y_0 and continue to rise while the excess expenditure exists;

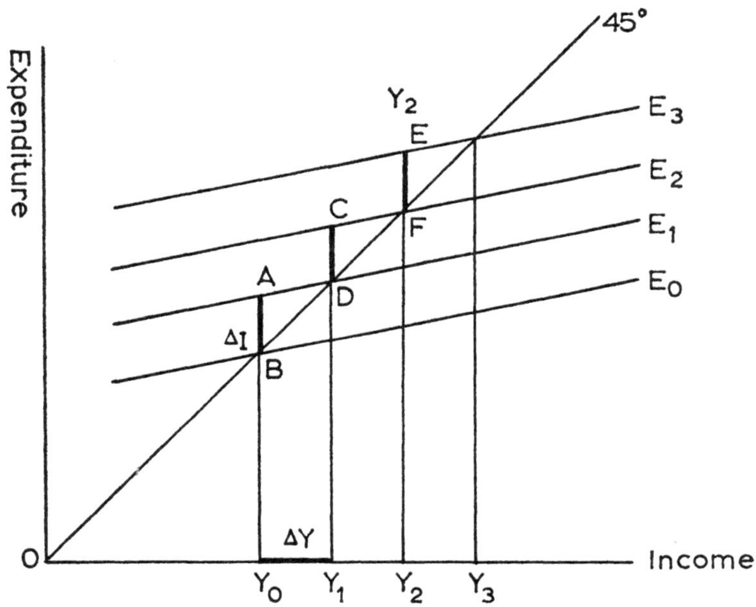

Figure 3

that is until income reaches Y_1. These expenditure functions relating E to Y at different levels of Y, are *aggregate demand* functions representing the level of spending, for a given community at a particular time, expected at each level of income. How much is spent will depend on C, I, G and S and these, as we have seen, are governed by a number of exogenous factors. The aggregate demand functions are the summations of C, I, G and X functions which are not separately shown. *When aggregate demand exceeds the 45° line* such as AB at Y_0 then *income rises till* $Y=E$. Of course, at the same time employment and output are also increased.

The critical point is that though for this aggregate demand function, equilibrium income is at Y_1, there is nothing in the system to say that this represents the income level corresponding to full employment: equilibrium employment and full employment are not the same thing.

If the full employment income happens to be at Y_2, then the government must shift the aggregate demand function to E_2 by manipulating the relevant variables. Because the new aggregate demand E_2 exceeds aggregate supply at the income level Y_1 by CD, income shifts as aggregate demand shifts. This simple notion is the basis of government macro-economic policy. This is not to say that the execution of such policy is easy; the variables may not respond adequately to the government's measures.

We may now relax our assumption that prices are constant. When income moved $Y_0-Y_1-Y_2$ it was an improvement in *real income*. Now there is a limit to this process, though *not* to the possibility of excess aggregate demand. It is not true that real income can always be increased by increasing spending. If this were so, economic growth would be a simple matter. The process stops, say at Y_2, when real income cannot be increased in the short run because there is no spare capacity available to generate the extra real production. This is the *full employment constraint*. (We are normally thinking of labour in 'full employment', but, conceptually, it could be land or capital.)

Now if there is excess aggregate demand at full employment such as EF at Y_2 then there is undoubtedly a rise in expenditure and so income still rises. The point is that it is *money income* that is rising and not real income. If the real production of goods is approximately constant, while expenditure rises, then prices rise; an excess of aggregate demand at full employment, like EF at Y_2 when E_3 is operative, is called an *inflationary gap*.

It is not implied that there is a sharp break before which there are only *real sector* changes in income, output and employment and after which all changes are *money sector changes*. It is a question of degree; at some incomes changes in expenditure fall on unemployed resources and lead mainly to real changes, at other incomes they fall on employed resources and so lead to money changes and at some incomes they cause both real and money effects.[10]

Our model now tells us that an economy left alone by the government will produce an equilibrium; but the equilibrium employment need not be full employment, equilibrium output and income need not be the maximum output or income and the price level autonomously produced need not be stable. The Keynesian model also helps to formulate our thinking about policy measures. It should be said that the full employment constraint limits output and income changes, but its strictures can be lessened, in the short and long runs, by changing the labour input for a unit of output, that is by increasing productivity. It is a rigid constraint only if input ratios are fixed.

A formal model of income determination in a closed economy

Equilibrium $Y=C+I+G$ 5(14)

[Consumption function $c=a+b$ 5(15)

where a is intercept on Y axis, b is *slope* of consumption-function, *m.p.c.*]

So from 14 and 15

$Y=a+bY+I+G$ 5(16)

There is only one unknown, since a, I and G are all given. C is stated in terms of Y, so solving by subtracting bY from both sides.

$Y-bY=a+I+G$ 5(17)

and so

$Y(1-bY)=a+I+G$ 5(18)

Divide both sides by $1-bY$

$$Y=\frac{a+I+G}{1-bY} \quad 5(19)$$

This says that National Income depends on the shape of consumption-income relation [given by a and b] and the level of I and G.

So far we have used comparative static analysis and seen that if $W=J$ then the National Income moves from one equilibrium to another. The concepts of the multiplier and accelerator, which are common to static and dynamic analyses, show that these income changes need not be part of a step by step process. In fact, the process of change itself can stimulate yet further changes.

The *multiplier* comes in many guises. The investment multiplier explores the paradox that the change in income resulting from a change in investment can exceed the change in investment in size. At first look, this is impossible since $E \equiv Y$; however, a verbal explanation says that the income receivers themselves spend at least a part of that income in their turn and so $\triangle Y > \triangle I$. This is because I is a once-and-for-all change and Y is the sum of a series of 'rounds' of income.

The point can also be made diagrammatically in Fig. 3. This shows an equilibrium position at Y_0 with an expenditure function E_0. Now if this function E_0 is displaced by an investment injection $\triangle I$ the increase in income is Y_0 to Y_1 shown as $\triangle Y$ which from inspection exceeds $\triangle I$. Clearly the extent of the excess of $\triangle Y$ over $\triangle I$ depends on how much of a given 'round' of income is passed on, that is on *m.p.c.* or *m.p.s.* The interval between Y_0 and Y_1, $\triangle Y$, is not a single change but the sum of a series of 'rounds' of income change. There is a clear relationship between the magnitude of the multiplier (K) and *m.p.s.*

A formal derivation of the multiplier (K)

$$\triangle I.K = \triangle Y \qquad 5(20)$$

$$K = \frac{\triangle Y}{\triangle I} \qquad 5(21)$$

Equilibrium before injection $\quad I_{t1} = S_{t1} \quad$ 5(22)

Equilibrium after injection $\quad I_{t2} = S_{t2} \quad$ 5(23)

from (22) and (23) $\quad \triangle I = \triangle S \quad$ 5(24)

but $\triangle S$ depends on *m.p.s.* $\quad \triangle S = sY \quad$ 5(25)

from (24) and (25) $\quad \triangle I = sY \quad$ 5(26)

and so $\quad Y = \frac{\triangle I}{s} \quad$ 5(27)

from (20) and (27) $\quad \triangle I.K = \frac{\triangle r}{s} \quad$ 5(28)

so $\quad K = \frac{1}{s} \quad$ 5(29)

or $\quad K = \frac{1}{1-c} \quad$ 5(30)

where $s = $ *m.p.s.* and $c = $ *m.p.c.*

Thus the multiplier varies with the reciprocal of *m.p.s.*, the less is saved from a given injection, the greater the final effect on income. We have considered an investment multiplier, which is one form of injection, but similar (not identical)[11] relationships are available for all injections which relate the final effect on income to the size of the withdrawals. So, in general

$$\triangle Y=\frac{\triangle J}{1-b} \qquad 5(31)$$

where $1-b$ is any withdrawal, b the expenditure level and J is any injection.

All this does not say that the economy cannot reach an equilibrium; it does say that if withdrawals are low it can be a long and erratic business since what starts by manifesting itself as a single change can become a series of changes, real or monetary, or both.

The *accelerator* is the relationship between a rate of change in consumption and the increase in capital goods necessary to produce the extra consumption goods. It might seem plausible that if we need 10% more production then we need 10% more production capacity; the world is not so simple.

In fact the investment goods industries experience much wider fluctuations of demand (and so employment, income and output) than do consumption goods industries.

There are three reasons at work. First, investment goods commonly have a greater value than one year's output. So a permanent increase in consumption of £1 million p.a. may need an increase in investment of £3 million for just one year.

Second, an *increase* in the stock of investment goods seem to depend on how fast incomes are rising rather than their actual level.

$$\text{Thus } \triangle I=f\left(\frac{dY}{dt}\right) \qquad 5(32)$$

This assumes that entrepreneurs expect incomes to continue. Third, some investment is a *replacement* of a part of the stock of capital; that is, it is a 'hiccup' of previous investment, but even such echoes are not regular, as capital is replaced partly because it is physically worn out and, partly, because it becomes obsolete as a result of technical change, itself a fluctuating matter. The 'hiccups' are also irregular because they follow increases in extra capital assets, themselves irregular, due to their dependence on the rate of change of income as expressed in equation 32.

In the accelerator and the multiplier we have the seeds of dynamic change and possible instability. Fortunately, we need not build up a formal model of the trade cycle nor referee between rival trade-cycle models. Such models do not yet influence policy: we are concerned with the *fact* of policy which follows from the community's value-judgements about economic goals and the inability of the economy to independently produce them. The *form* of policy depends on the variables we have discussed rather than any of the available trade-cycle models.

EQUILIBRIUM IN THE PRODUCT AND MONEY MARKETS Attention must now pass from a consideration of a largely Keynesian model to the monetary aspects of these problems which have led to a refinement of macro-economics and are also helpful for policy analysis. This branch of theory is still in some state of flux; we will concentrate on the I.S.L.M. model which attempts to resolve the problem of 'money-neutrality'; that is, does money simply perform the 'functions' shown in introductory textbooks, or does it play a part in the determination of the *relative* prices of goods and the level of output? We are thus concerned with the link between the monetary sector and the determination of income and employment.[12]

Of the three motives for holding money, rather than other forms of wealth, the classical (pre-Keynesian) economists acknowledged the precautionary and transaction motives. Under this system the demand for money is largely a function of income levels and in particular it does not respond to the level of interest: conceptually to plot the demand for money at different interest levels would be a pointless exercise as there is no functional relationship. Keynes's monetary innovation was the speculative motive (money kept ready for speculative opportunities) and it *does* respond to interest levels. However, it is not negatively sloped for its whole length: there would be some quite high interest rate at which a further increase would not lead to a redistribution of assets from money to bonds—and so less money demanded at the new higher rate. There would be no response because, at this high interest rate, the loss (interest foregone) from holding speculative funds would be so great that there would be no such funds, and also because bond prices are so low there is little capital risk and so only the classical motives for holding money would be operational. Thus the money demand would be interest-inelastic above this rate. Below this level, the demand for money would vary inversely with the interest level until, at some low interest level, the demand for money becomes infinitely elastic with respect to interest because the interest loss is now so low and the capital risk so great on bond prices[13] that investors would just as well hold idle balances as earning assets. The demand for money would take on the character shown in Fig. 4 where the demand function aggregates all three motives for holding money.

Given such a demand for money, the level of interest will correspond to the intersection of the supply function of money—this is largely government determined and largely independent of the interest level. If the supply is S_1then i interest is at i_1, if S_2 at i_2 and so on.

A change in the money supply affects interest rates directly and indirectly. Directly, because interest is partly determined by the supply of money and, indirectly, because an interest change affects investment, and so spending, and so income, and so the transactions and precautionary demands for money and so interest rates again. There can be a similar chain reaction in the real goods market: an invention may alter *m.e.c.* and so increase the investment demand function at all interest rates, and so increase income and so alter the classical demands for money. Now if the necessary funds are to be released from speculative hoards then interest rates must rise and so investment must fall, incomes thus fall and there is another round of reactions.[14] It will help to have a model that will yield an equilibrium solution.

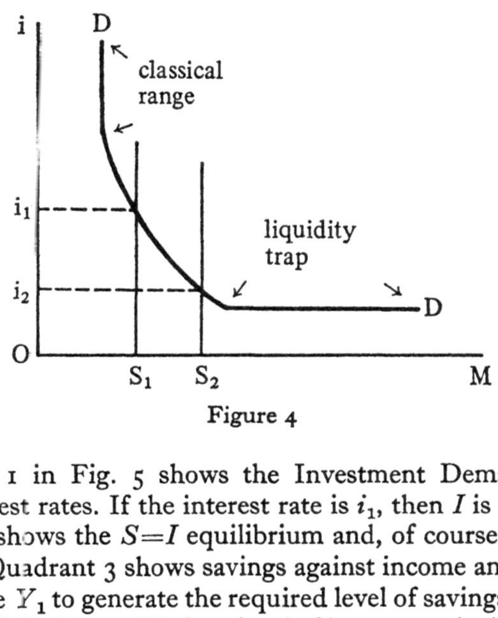

Figure 4

Quadrant 1 in Fig. 5 shows the Investment Demand function against interest rates. If the interest rate is i_1, then I is I_1 and so on. Quadrant 2 shows the $S=I$ equilibrium and, of course, the relevant level is S_1. Quadrant 3 shows savings against income and the income level must be Y_1 to generate the required level of savings. Quadrant 4 shows that Y_1 is the equilibrium level of income at the interest rate i_1 in that it calls forth the required savings that are needed for the investment level consistent with that interest rate. If the income were other than Y_1, then S_1 and this income level would be in disequilibrium in that it would produce a different volume of savings than the level of investment generated by the interest rate. Quadrant 4 shows the income level appropriate for every interest rate, Y_2 for i_2,

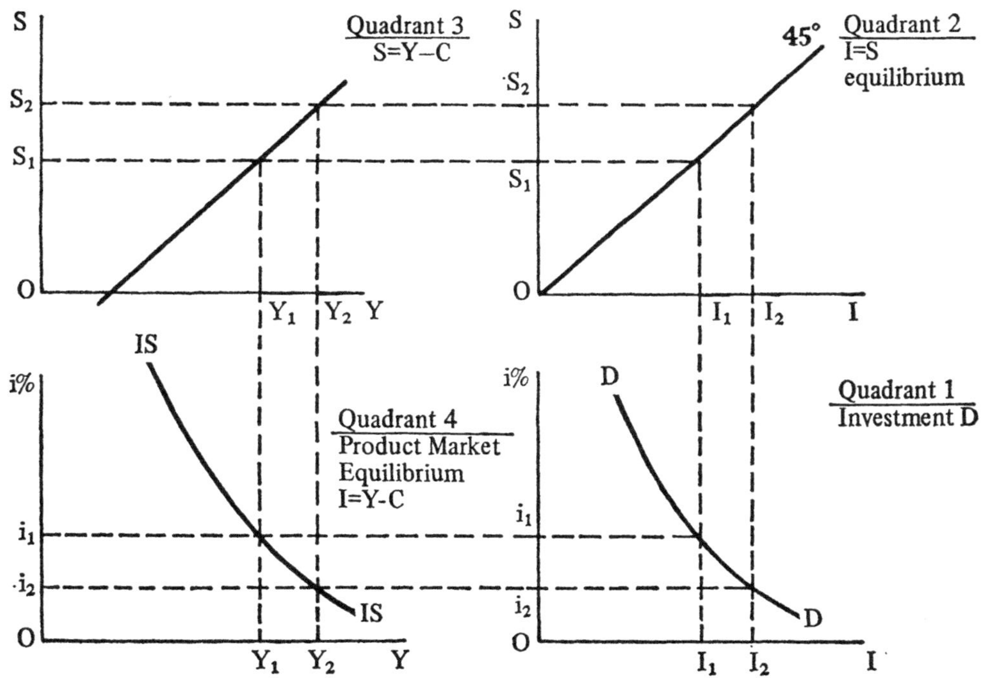

S
Quadrant 3
S=Y–C
S2
S1
O
Y1
Y2
Y
S
45°
Quadrant 2
I=S
equilibrium
S2
S1
O
I1
I2
I
IS
i%
Quadrant 4
Product Market
Equilibrium
I=Y-C
i1
i2
IS
O
Y1
Y2
Y
i%
D
Quadrant 1
Investment D
i1
i2
D
O
I1
I2
I

Figure 5

and so forth. These equilibrium income levels form the I—S function. There being no government or international trade in this model, the equilibrium conditions are simply $I=S$. But the investment demand schedule is $I=f(i)$ 5(33) and the savings function is $S=Y-C(Y)$ 5(34) so the I—S function shown in Quadrant 4 is where

$$I(i)=Y-C(Y) \qquad 5(35)$$

This means that for any interest rate there is *some* income where $I=S$ and so there will be equilibrium in the product market.

What of the money market? If the supply of money is m_s (normally constant) then

$$m_s=ky+L(i) \qquad 5(36)$$

since the demand for money is ky (the transactions and precautionary motives for money, proportional to income) and $L(i)$ (the speculative motive, a function of the interest rate). Equation 35 gives equilibrium in the product market, the I—S function, and 36 in the money market the L—M function. But both are the functions of two variables—interest rate and income. It should therefore be possible to solve the two simultaneous equations to yield interest and income levels that give equilibrium in the product market ($I=S$) and in the money market ($D_m=S_m$). It will be advantageous to continue graphically.

In Fig. 6, Quadrant 2 shows a given supply of money (presumably determined largely by the government) and it can be divided between the speculative balances (m_2) and the classical balances (m_1) in the range of ways shown, MS. If $m_2 1$ is held speculatively, then clearly $m_1 1$ is held for transactions and precautionary motives.

The volumes held for these purposes vary with income as shown in Quadrant 3 and only at $Y_1 1$ will $m_1 1$ be held for these motives. Quadrant 4 shows that $Y_1 1$ is the income level consistent with i^1 in just enough money is held under m_1 motives to leave the appropriate amounts in speculative balances to give the required investment demand. This is monetary equilibrium. For each interest rate an appropriate income level can be found and this is the L—M curve. Similarly, in the real goods market, for each interest rate there was also an income level such that $S=I$. The I—S curve shows a range of incomes consistent with interest rates and so does the L—M curve so we now have (graphical) values for our two equations. They are *both* satisfied in Fig. 7 which shows the 'Hicksian Cross'; there is only *one* interest rate (i) for one income level (y) that yields equilibrium in both the real and monetary sectors. This gives a general equilibrium and thus no tendency for the magnitudes of any of the variables to alter.

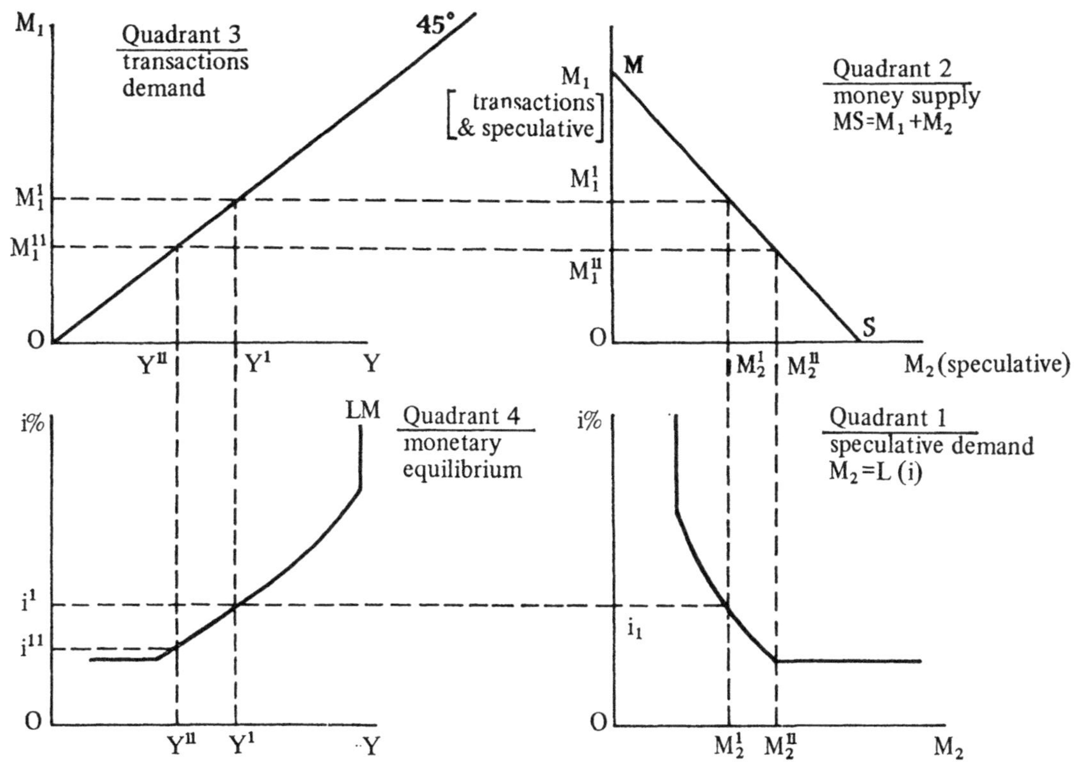

Quadrant 3
transactions demand
45°
M_1
M_1^1
M_1^{11}
O
Y^{11}
Y^1
Y
Quadrant 2
money supply
$MS=M_1+M_2$
M
S
M_1 [transactions & speculative]
M_1^{11}
M_2^1
M_2^{11}
M_2 (speculative)
LM
Quadrant 4
monetary equilibrium
i%
i^1
i^{11}
Quadrant 1
speculative demand
$M_2=L$ (i)
i_1
M_2

Figure 6

So far attention has been given to a model with an equilibrium condition of $S=I$. It is now convenient to generalise to a model where $W=J$, in Quadrant 2 of the real sector model. So Quadrant 1 now shows an injection function $I(i)+G+X$ 5(35) and Quadrant 3 now shows all leakages at different incomes so instead of equation 34 the following: $S+T+M=I+G+X$ 5(37)

We may now adapt all this into Fig. 8 to investigate the problems of money neutrality.

Quadrant 1 shows the level of J at different interest rates. (It is assumed that only I actually responds to i and that the other components of J, (X and G), are independent of i.) Quadrant 2 shows $W=J$ and Quadrant 3 shows the different level of W at different incomes. (It is assumed that only S directly responds to Y.) Now only income level Y can produce the appropriate withdrawals so Quadrant 4 shows Y as a point on IS and real (and monetary) equilibrium. What are the consequences of a shift in J? This could be due to new levels of G or X or I.[15] If J moves to J^1, at the given i, then we must

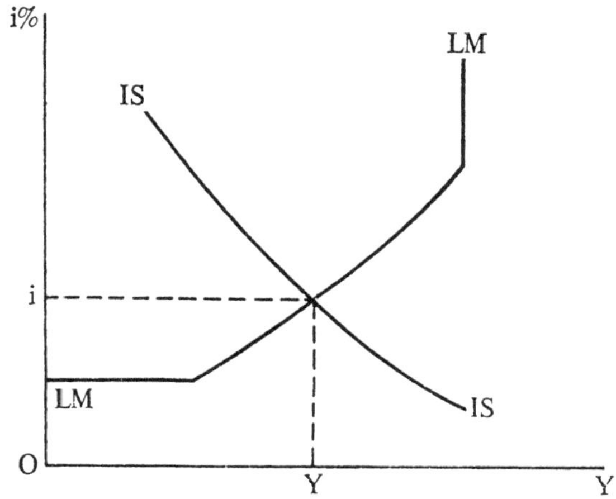

Figure 7

move to W^1 (to provide at each income level the necessary withdrawals to equal the new injections for each income level). This new W function gives equilibrium in Quadrant 4 at Y^1 *and has created a new interest level* i^1 which exceeds i. It is this which explains the anomalous results of the models.

1 The increase in the IS function ($\triangle IS$) exceeds the increase in the J function ($\triangle J$). However, this was to be expected due to the workings of the multiplier.

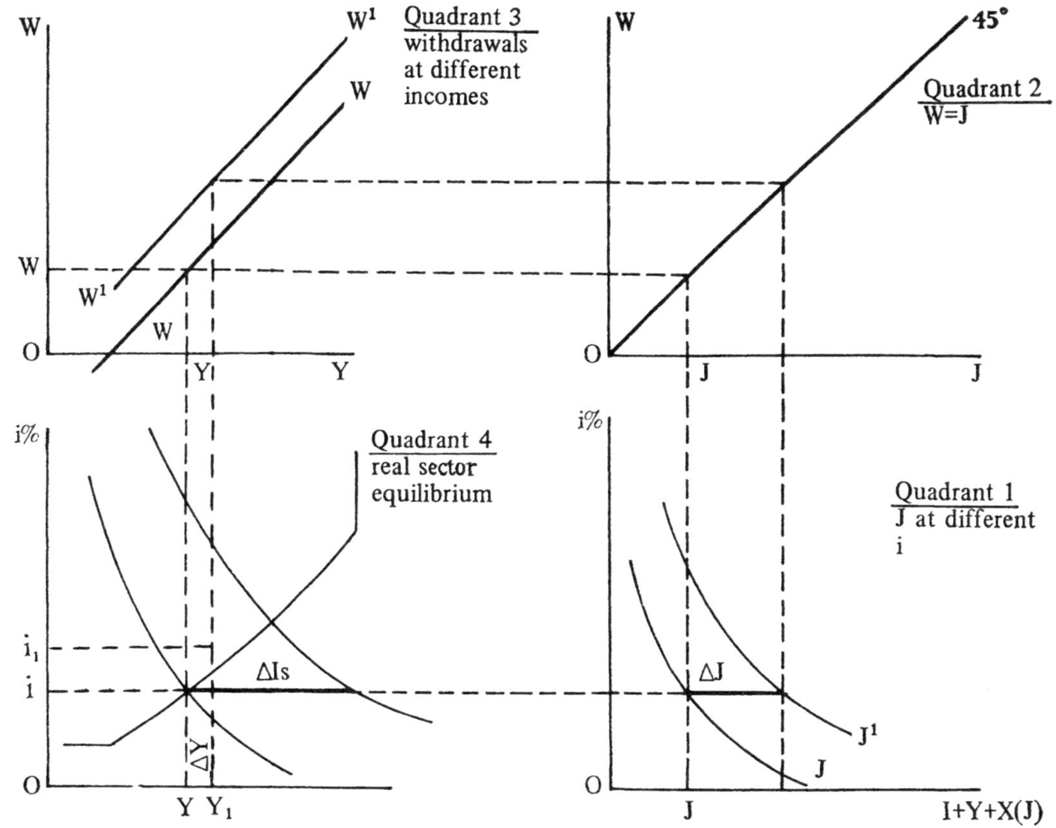
W
W¹
Quadrant 3
withdrawals
at different
incomes
W
W
W¹
W
O
Y
Y
W
45°
Quadrant 2
W=J
O
J
J
i%
Quadrant 4
real sector
equilibrium
i₁
i
ΔIs
ΔY
O
Y Y₁
i%
Quadrant 1
J at different
i
ΔJ
J¹
J
O
J
I+Y+X(J)

Figure 8

2 The increase in the IS function ($\triangle IS$) exceeds the increase in income ($\triangle Y$). That is, the full multiplier failed to operate.

It is the increase in the interest rate that explains this. If the money supply is fixed, the increase in W can only come from speculative or transaction balances; but the latter are a function of Y, which is rising, so the funds *have* to come from speculative balances which is what necessitates the higher interest rate. But, in its turn, the higher interest rate means less I and so less Y. The stimulus given by J is thus diminished by a decline in investment spending. Three conclusions follow. First, our earlier multipliers were crude because they assumed money neutrality, that a change in J would not affect i and so investment; second, that money is clearly not neutral; third, an increase in J could have no effect at all on income if monetary repercussions lead to a fall in investment that exactly equalled the injection.

The I.S.L.M. model thus shows that our simple multipliers only hold good if the changed expenditure can be financed without interest rate changes. It can tell us much about policy but, first, we must investigate the sources of changes in $I—S$ and $L—M$ functions and have a more technical definition of fiscal and monetary policies than hitherto.

The $I—S$ schedule may shift in one or other direction due to changes in G or T (exogenous), S (a function of Y, tastes, total taxation and tax rates, prices), I (a function of i, itself a function of money supply and LP), and *m.e.c.* (a function of innovation, and profit expectations).

The $L—M$ function responds to changes in the money supply (m, and m_2 of Quadrant 2), expectations and, possibly, payments practices.

A 'pure' fiscal policy changes the magnitude of Y without affecting the money supply. A 'pure' monetary policy affects the money supply without *directly* affecting the income stream. There can be few examples of a pure fiscal policy; taxation must lead to the running down of balances and so in effect on the money supply.

We return in Fig. 9 to the Hicksian Cross to help formulate an approach to fiscal and monetary policy.

Fig. 9 (i) shows a given $L—M$ schedule and starts with $I—S$ and equilibrium with i and Y. If, due to fiscal policy, this moves to $I—S_1$, then, in this intermediate range, there is an effect on the interest level and the level of income, similarly with $I—S_2$. However a shift to $I—S_3$ in the classical range produces an effect solely on i and none whatso-

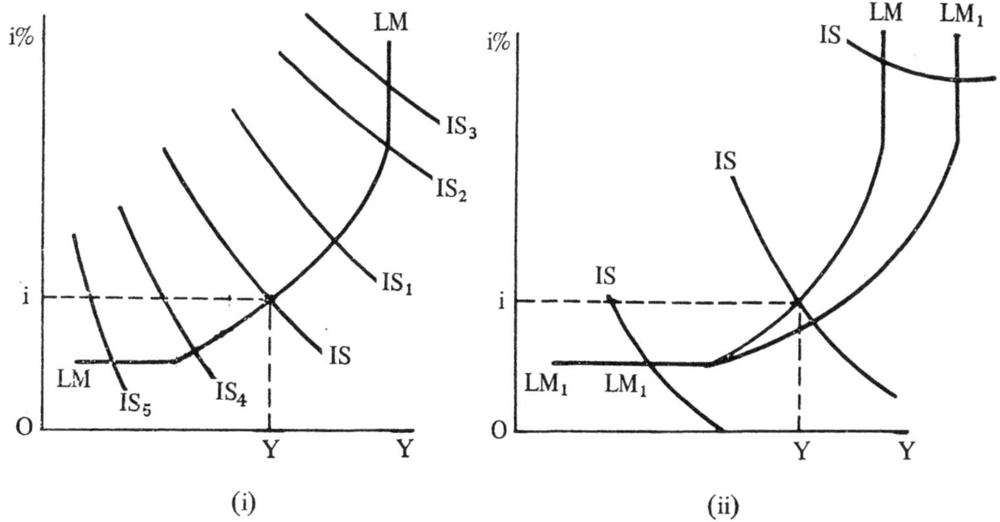
i%
LM
IS3
IS2
IS1
i
IS
LM
IS5
IS4
O
Y
Y
(i)
i%
IS
LM
LM1
IS
IS
i
LM1
LM1
O
Y
Y
(ii)

Figure 9

ever on Y. The liquidity trap zone gives the opposite effects: a shift from $I—S_4$ to $I—S_5$ affects income wholly and the interest rate not at all. Thus whether or not fiscal policy is appropriate depends on the range of the $L—M$ curve on which the $I—S$ curve is operating.

Fig. 9 (ii) has three given $I—S$ curves and it is the $L—M$ curve that is moved. If the $L—M$ function is moved by monetary policy from $L—M$ to $L—M_1$, the effects are easily classified. In the Keynesian trap (with a strong speculative motive operating), the effect is entirely on income. In the intermediate range, the effect is partly on interest rates and partly on income; this is also true in the classical range (with a zero speculative motive), save that the effect is now more fully on income and less on interest rates.

So again there are no general rules about the efficiency of monetary policy any more than there were for fiscal policy. The choice between fiscal and monetary policy can never be resolved by some economic criterion that will always hold good; each case must be judged on its own circumstances.

The I.S.L.M. model can say much more on macro-economic theory, but our concern is with policy so, for the moment, we need make only one more point. Earlier an increase in income was equated with a (non-proportionate) increase in output and employment provided there were unused resources available—otherwise it was equated with inflation. Now the version of the I.S.L.M. model presented was a two sector model but in fact there is a third sector—the labour market. It is perfectly feasible to have equilibrium in the real and monetary sectors without full employment.

So far we have presented inflation as being caused by an excess of spending at full employment. In fact, there are rival explanations of inflation[16] of which cost-push seems the most important.

Put simply, *cost-push theory* hypothesises that factor-price increases (particularly wages) lead to the more general price increases characteristic of inflation *independently of the level of demand. Demand-pull inflation* represents a reversed relationship, hypothesising that it is the level of demand that raises product prices and then factor prices.[17] Now, for policy purposes, it might matter a great deal which kind of inflation an economy was experiencing: fiscal policy restraining demand is rather irrelevant if the demand level is irrelevant to inflation. Incomes policy restraining wages can be irrelevant if costs are irrelevant.

Sectoral demand shift inflation occurs if some sectors of the economy experience rising prices and costs due to increased demand—and this is not matched by price and cost falls elsewhere—as prices tend to be rigid in a downwards direction. Thus the price rises in the prosperous sectors of the economy are not balanced by price falls elsewhere, leading to a stable price level; instead the prices in the other sectors are stable and it is the general price level that is unstable.

Where this process occurs, public policy would have to avoid acting on the major aggregates in the economy and concentrate on key elements within it. Thus there is no ready-made policy to deal with all inflations; each instance merits separate enquiry.

There is a similar story with regard to unemployment. So far the only source of unemployment recognised has been a deficiency in aggregate demand; but as well as this cyclical unemployment there is the possibility of structural, seasonal, frictional and voluntary unemployment and there may be a separate policy appropriate to each.

It is helpful now to pull together some of the threads of the argument to see *a priori*, as it were, the main candidates for consideration as techniques of government policy before looking at the facts and problems of policy in the next chapter.

Our goals were price stability, full employment, exchange-rate stabilisation, Balance of Payments surplus, economic growth, redistribution of income and aid to under-developed countries. Our main variables were G, T, C, I, S, X, and M.

The government has close control over its *expenditure* and it can expect increases in it to help to resolve some forms of unemployment and decreases to mitigate some forms of inflation. Components of its expenditure—as opposed to its total magnitude—can be controlled and can influence some forms of inflation, employment and payments problems; if deftly applied they can influence economic growth and both domestic and international income distribution.

The government is not only interested in the level of its own spending but also in the relationship between its income and expenditure, that is in the magnitude of the budget surplus or deficit. A budget surplus or deficit leads to a decrease or increase in the money supply. The change in the money supply need not be uniformly related to the size of the budget imbalance. The money supply is relevant to the interest rate and so to investment and thus to total spending and so to employment and price levels. It may be more directly related to the price level if this varies in some proportion to the volume of money.[18]

While it is clear that a budget deficit or surplus possesses positive effects, it must not be thought that a balanced budget is economically neutral. In some circumstances it can be economically positive with a balanced budget multiplier.

The generalised form of the multiplier was equation 31

$$\triangle Y = \frac{\triangle J}{1-b}$$

It is convenient to explain the balanced budget multiplier with a simple model showing the identical income change for changes in *C*, *I* and *G*. Thus

$$\triangle Y = \frac{\triangle I}{1-b} = \frac{\triangle C}{1-b} = \frac{\triangle G}{1-b} \qquad 5(38)$$

But for an increase in taxes, the multiplier is negative because the fall in income leads to a fall in consumption. The change in consumption leads to a fall in income of the magnitude of the consumption change times the multiplier $\frac{1}{1-b}$. So a tax increase of *T* does *not* lead to an identical fall in income (with $\triangle T = \triangle Y$) but to $\triangle T$ times *m.p.c.*

$$\text{So } \triangle C = -b\triangle T \qquad 5(39)$$

$$\text{but, from equation 37, } \triangle Y = \frac{-b\triangle T}{1-b} \qquad 5(40)$$

This shows the negative effect on income of a given increase in tax. If the government, balancing its budget, spends exactly that sum there is a positive effect on income through the government multiplier. But it does not cancel out. This is because the tax multiplier is $\frac{-b\triangle T}{1-b}$[19] and the government multiplier is $\frac{\triangle G}{1-b}$. So the effects of the tax and government multiplier, when $T = G$, and the budget is balanced, are unequal.

$$\frac{\triangle Y}{\triangle G} + \frac{\triangle Y}{\triangle T} = \frac{1}{1-b} + \frac{-b}{1-b} = \frac{1-b}{1-b} = 1$$

Clearly a balanced budget does not have fiscal neutrality and the level at which it is balanced is important. If it is balanced at £100 million then the income is £100 million greater than if it were balanced at zero government expenditure and zero taxes.

Government expenditure is important not only for the significance of its own size, the disposition of its components and its ratio to taxation, but also because part of it is commonly financed by borrowing and the form of government debt, structure has policy implications. Government bonds form the basis of the asset structure of the banks; the way in which these assets are managed—their total size and their form—can affect the banks and so the money supply and the cost of bank credit.

Taxation is a variable under fairly close control. Its size is important for the proportion of resources under government control and so for aggregate demand. Its form can affect the distribution of income; what proportion of U.K. taxes might have this effect, and their effectiveness, is considered in the following chapter.

Consumption (and its reciprocal, *savings*) is a vital determinant of total spending and so of a number of the government's goals. However, it is difficult to control and the government must do as best it can. Price control, taxes, subsidies and interest rates are possible policy techniques directed towards it.

Investment is also a variable more easily discussed than controlled. However, taxes and subsidies on capital goods, interest rates, and so money supply, are feasibly worth consideration.

Exports and *imports* are among the goals of government policy and one of the techniques relevant to the National Income determination. Their control too has proved elusive but tariffs, quotas and exchange rates are all possible techniques. For most people, however, these are politically dubious. The domestic price level is also relevant to exports and imports and in this case its stability is a government ambition which *is* consistent with maximising exports—itself a government goal. However, exports are an injection and so a potentially inflationary force. So achieving price stability can help to maximise exports but maximising exports de-stabilises prices. The policymaker's life is not a happy one.

It is not necessary to understand the form of the multiplier's conceptual gymnastics, and so on, to understand the fact of the problem and the need for government intervention. But it is necessary to understand the form of the multiplier to find the appropriate form of the policy. To this we now turn.

Notes

1 This is not to say that they have increased in the same proportion.

2 'Savings' in this sense must be purchasing power genuinely withdrawn. Money saved in a joint-stock bank account and then lent by the bank is not so withdrawn.

3 It does not matter, to our theory at this level, how the investment is financed, though it does matter to the individual.

4 The Keynesian model eliminates inequalities in W and J by changes in the National Income; pre-Keynesian models tended to rely on interest-rate changes to make $J=W$; in particular to make $S=I$.

5 As opposed to deciding the level of activity in the various government departments and then summing them up to find the proportion of national resources needed. Keynes, J. M., *How to pay for the War* and *National Income Statement* (1941).

6 Largely due to the wide occurrence of diminishing marginal physical returns and imperfect markets (see Chapter 3). The economy's *m.e.c.* is likely to be negatively sloped as it is the summation of the *m.e.c.*s of individual firms and because of the rising supply price of capital.

7 Chapter 7 shows why a time-stream of revenue needs to be adjusted to a present value for a sensible investment decision.

8 Expected incomes govern the investment decision: it does not matter to us whether expectations are fulfilled as our concern is with the fact of investment and its role in aggregate spending; it *does* matter to the entrepreneur as he is concerned with the profit of his investment.

9 We here discuss the conventional Keynesian interest theory: alternatives can be found in Shackle, G. L. S., *Recent Theories concerning the Nature and Rate of Interest*; *Surveys of Economic Theory*, Volume 1, Macmillan (1965).

10 'Mainly' because this model uses aggregated variables; for some purposes there is a need for the models to be *disaggregated*, usually on an industrial or regional basis. See Chapters 7 and 11.

11 See later and in Chapter 6.

12 I.S.L.M. models are derived from: Hicks, J. R., Mr. Keynes and the

'classics': A suggested interpretation, *Econometrica*, N.S., 5 (1937). Our model will generally ignore *G*, *T*, *X* and *M*.

13 Bond prices and interest rates move in opposite directions.

14 These two examples give the first indications that the changed income-level changes the demand for money and this changes interest rates and this changes investment and so income; money is not 'neutral'.

15 For details of the reasons why *G*, *X* or *I* might alter, see later, page 100–2.

16 e.g. imported, bank, gold, credit, administered price, sectoral shift and cost-push inflations.

17 Chapter 6 contains some discussion of the testing of these theories and their relevance to U.K. experience.

18 See note, p. 130–1.

19 It must not be thought that this is the only form of the balanced budget multiplier; forms can be derived involving transfers, etc.

Bibliography

Apart from the general textbooks noted in the Chapter 1 bibliography, the following give helpful accounts of macro-economics.

ACKLEY, G., *Macro-Economic Theory*, Macmillan, 1961

BROOMAN, F. S., *Macro-Economics*, Minerva Series No. 9, Allen and Unwin, 1965

DERNBERG, T. F. and MCDOUGALL, D. M., *Macro-Economics*, McGraw-Hill, 1964 (3rd edition).

SCHULTZE, C., *National Income Analysis*, Prentice-Hall, 1964

PART TWO

Chapter 6

THE DETERMINATION OF THE NATIONAL INCOME: THE PRACTICE

This chapter deals with the problems of maximands and constraints in economic policy and the relationship between theory and policy. It then concerns itself with the facts of consumption before looking at policy and the U.K. economic record.

CONSTRAINTS AND MAXIMANDS Attention has so far been called, explicitly and implicitly, to the inconsistent nature of both government goals and government policy techniques. It can be difficult to promote full employment and price stability; devaluation can generate exports but stable exchange rates are a goal of policy, and so on.

To the economist, the goals are maximands and the difficulties are constraints. A constraint narrows the range of options open to the policy-maker; in a problem that concerns two variables it can be represented as a choice frontier of which a technology frontier[1] is an example when the variables are outputs of two goals available in such a way that a choice must be made between particular combinations and so between alternative policies. Resort can be made to algebra in the case of an 'n-variable' problem, where n can be greater than 1. The maximands, too, can be simple but are more likely to be complex: simple goals are profit maximisation for a firm and economic growth for an economy. These are more than likely too simple, so that profit maximisation, subject to a given share of the market or of future profits, or economic growth, subject to a Balance of Payments equilibrium, are more realistic goals. On the other hand it might be appropriate to express the problem as the maximisation of the payments surplus subject to achieving a given level of growth. *We cannot really state our maximand until we have chosen our priorities.* There are similar problems in regard to the relationships between full employment, inflation, growth and payments problems . . . and so on.

There is a convenient mathematical technique—Lagrangean Multipliers—for solving multi-variable maximisation problems.[2]

Unfortunately, this technique is not really available for policy problems. We cannot specify either our maximands or our constraints carefully enough for this.

We have already seen[3] that it is not yet possible to specify a social welfare function and that interpersonal comparisons of utility are unscientific and will see that there is no reliable way of comparing society's preferences through time,[4] yet we constantly tax the rich and subsidise the poor, direct investment to a development region at the expense of other regions, arbitrate between monopolists and their customers and allocate resources to investment, and so increase future consumption and forego present consumption. We must, of necessity, do all these things and in an ill-informed way. Nor do we have reliable criteria with which to judge our clumsy attempts.

A further reason why we have difficulty in formulating policy goals is that we do not know enough about the policy options open to us—that is we do not know the constraints. This problem manifests itself in two different ways; first, because of externalities and of monopolies in the product and factor markets the money prices produced by the market mechanism are a poor measure of true opportunity costs and, second, because, for instance, we know very little about trade-off rates between regional growth and national growth. If we were sure how much national growth must be foregone in order to promote the growth rate in a particular region we would know the real cost of regional policy. Most national plans, regional plans, export plans and so forth tell us what policies are necessary and so what we have to do; this is not the same as telling us the costs.

Not only are we ignorant of the costs of our policies and unable to formulate knowledgeable goals but we do not express them all quantitatively and do not agree about the values when we do quantify even in this limited way. Aid to under-developed countries and income redistribution get no quantification at all. We clearly want no inflation but are unclear about how much inflation we will tolerate if it will gain another goal, say full employment. Full employment means 2% unemployed to some and 3% to others (a 50% difference) and there is disagreement about how wide industrial, or regional, deviations we will allow from this national average. The National Plan opted for 4% growth and the 1967 Green Paper for 2½%.[5] There are also disagreements about the range of official exchange-rate fluctuations we can allow and the size of payments surplus for which we might aim.

We thus have a situation in which we have to rely on value-judgements to rank our goals and to resort to guesswork in assessing the true costs. We do not avoid these difficulties by restricting the role of the government, for such a policy still produces a non-optimal situation, for we have seen that a free market cannot produce the optimal allocation of resources, full employment, economic growth and price stability autonomously and we will see later that it cannot produce an optimal location of economic activity. It is a matter of common observation that it does not produce a stable exchange rate, a redistributed income or a payments surplus autonomously. Government economic policy does not, therefore, take us from an optimal position to a non-optimal one; it takes us from one non-optimal situation to another one. We can rank these non-optimal positions only on political grounds but we can hope to choose policies consistent with such goals on scientific grounds. The Theory of the Second Best shows that we cannot, as yet, rank alternative positions by scientific criteria; whatever we discuss—the budget, tariffs, monopoly policy—there is always uncertainty and ambiguity. It is foolhardy to pretend otherwise, but this is frequently done.

THEORY AND POLICY Economics has two major roles to play in the analysis of policy. It contains a number of hypotheses, the predictive power of which can in principle be verified and, second, it is helpful in formulating an appropriate approach.

> 'Viewed as a language, theory has no substantive content; it is a set of tautologies. Its function is to serve as a filing system. And the criterion by which it is to be judged are those appropriate to a filing system. Are the categories clearly and precisely defined? Are they exhaustive? Viewed as a body of substantive hypotheses, theory is to be judged by its predictive power for the class of phenomena it is intended to "explain". Only factual evidence can show whether it is "right" or "wrong" or, better, tentatively "acceptable" as valid or "rejected".'[6]

The economist can offer his taxonomy and his hypotheses without partiality.

> 'Positive economics is in principle independent of any particular ethical position or normative judgement . . . its task is to provide a system of generalisations that can be used to make correct predictions about the consequences of any change in circumstances. Indeed not only is it abstracted from a political position, and is thus like the presumption that two and two are four, but it cannot of itself help us to form political attitudes.'[7, 8] 'Economics can never tell us what we ought to do, but only what will happen if we do certain things.'[8]

With these as our standards, we can now turn from theory alone to theory and facts. Do our theories about consumption and investment functions, multipliers and accelerators have any correspondence to the real world? Do they have predictive value? What difficulties arise in applying the various forms of economic policy which in theory seem worthy of consideration? Is our filing system a helpful one? It will come as no surprise that economics does yield a very helpful classificatory approach but that it is not beyond improvement nor that its hypotheses have some empirical content if stated carefully enough. Where economists are most in the dark is not in supposing what will happen but in supposing the magnitude of what will happen. They can make a good shot at the direction of the effects of a change in Bank Rate or a change in taxation, but only a passing shot at its size. The profession is, however, gaining competence in both these respects.

THE FACTS *A priori*, the *consumption function* leads us to believe that consumption spending—and so savings—responds to income, changes in taxation, prices and tastes. Do the facts correspond to all this?

It is by no means clear just how and what has been established by the various tests. When empirical investigations produce inconsistent data we are often driven to testing the tests rather than testing the hypotheses. The first difficulty which occurs in inductive reasoning of this sort is that of being sure that there is, in fact, a causal relationship between changes in the factor under consideration and in consumption spending. The long arm of coincidence always makes such enquiries hazardous. This is a form of the 'identification problem'.

However, it does seem that most of our difficulties can be resolved by distinguishing the short run—in which consumption spending does *not* seem closely related to income—and the long run—in which a closer connection *does* seem to exist. Let us look first at the form in which income is apparently relevant to consumption spending, and then at other factors which seem to affect consumption spending.

Our theoretical account so far relates consumption quite simply to income and it is expected to be positive, stable and less than unity. If this were the case, a redistribution of income from the rich to the poor would be expected to raise aggregate spending. Perhaps surprisingly, there is little evidence that this is so.[9]

There is evidence that, in the long run, the *m.p.c.* has a high fractional value, especially in Britain[10] but things are very different in the short run where *m.p.c.*s sometimes exceed unity. This can only mean dis-savings (perhaps drawing on former money saving), or the use of credit (drawing on future savings), or the sale of assets.

This has led to two rival hypotheses to the Keynesian hypothesis that related consumption to the level of *absolute income*.

THE RELATIVE INCOME HYPOTHESIS[11] relates consumption to the individual's income, relative to those incomes with which he makes comparisons, rather than his absolute income. The best-known case is that black Americans on a given income save more than white Americans on the same income because they compare themselves with other Negroes, rather than other people in general. There is evidence that the introduction of new products also stimulates consumption spending.[12]

THE PERMANENT INCOME HYPOTHESIS[13] reconciles the short-run and long-run anomalies by relating consumption spending to the income the individual expects to earn over a period of time, rather than to his current income. The size of a house mortgage frequently reflects not only a belief in a future stream of income, but in a trend of earning. Hire-purchase debt is another example of this. Young graduates, for instance, commonly spend more from a given income than non-graduates.[14]

There are factors, other than income, relevant to consumption spending; these include socio-economic characteristics,[15] age[16] and wealth.[17] All this amounts to saying that our previous uni-causal relationship between income and spending was too crude. The policy implications are that it may be more awkward than it would appear at first glance to control consumption spending; this is unfortunate as it is clearly an important variable in the determination of income, output and employment. What is the U.K. experience?

As might be expected, the relationship between consumption and income does not appear to have been a simple one. Generally, time lags have developed in the response of consumption to tax changes, expecially tax rises. It is clear that savings have increased, but mainly in particular occupations.

One variable to which durable consumption spending does respond is hire-purchase regulations. But this does not have to mean that total spending falls, for the expenditure may be switched elsewhere to non-durables or simply postponed for a while.[18] It is thus difficult to see what is the total effect on consumption, it is unlikely to be predictable and it is difficult to know what sections will be affected for it need not be the sections that are directly involved in the hire-purchase transaction. There is little doubt that the effect is considerable.

If it is difficult to tell the effect of government action on consumption spending then, by implication, little can be said about the effect on saving.

There is plenty of evidence that consumption does not respond to interest rates[19] and so we cannot expect personal savings to do so either. However, it is possible that interest-rate changes can affect the form of savings and lead to transfers from, say, the G.P.O. to, say, Trustee Savings Banks. When there is a net withdrawal of National Savings, as in the autumn of 1968, the impression gained by the public is that there has been a reduction in the nation's savings. *The proportional effect is probably small and need not, in fact, occur at all.*

It would appear that fiscal policy has a considerable effect on consumption spending but not always on the item taxed, or subsidised, and nearly always after a time lag. Consumption also responds to credit regulations, but again in a confused way. It is difficult to feel we know enough about the factors governing consumption to be confident that a particular policy is the one appropriate to produce a given level of consumption spending.

The investigation of the facts of the consumption function is a difficult enough exercise, but the *investment* function presents even more intractable problems. There are similar difficulties, of the identification problem, and of the short and long runs.

There are three separate problems: is investment governed by the factors suggested by economists and do the concepts of the accelerator and the multipliers manifest themselves in the real world? The theorem that investment depends upon the marginal efficiency of capital and the interest rate is hardly capable of investigation. This is because the *m.e.c.* is that rate of discount which equates the prospective yield with the supply price: but an individual's discount-rate is subjective and so is the prospective yield.[20] The most we could hope is that an investor equated what he thought was the *m.e.c* with what he thought was the interest rate! This phantom is not worth pursuing. We could, however, hope to investigate the relationship between fluctuations in the interest rate and investment.[21] While this could tell us whether investment is interest-elastic,[22] it could never confirm or deny the *empirical* content of the economists' investment function which, given that an investor's goal is to maximise his welfare in the form of a particular time-profile of an income stream, draws out the *logical* implications that investment is extended until the marginal efficiency of capital equals the interest rate. Logical implications are quite different from empirical content. Unfortunately, drawing out the necessary implications entailed in an assumption does not tell us whether the assumption is made in the real world nor whether those making the assumption know what is logically implied by it.

However, some comments are possible. Many statistical enquiries show only a weak relationship between investment and interest-rate changes. This is not altogether surprising, since the economic theorist did not offer a uni-causal relationship between these two variables, he offered a functional relationship between investment on the one hand, and both interest rates and the *m.e.c.* on the other. Once it is expressed in this way everything falls into place; investment can be constant, or even falling, while interest rates fall because of changes in these other factors.

One can summarise these other factors as the state of the business cycle and technological change. If there is unused investment capacity then a fall in interest rates will certainly not induce the construction of yet more unused capacity, and technological change can stimulate new investment even when interest rates are rising. The state of the business cycle is relevant to expectations and so to the prospective yield and thus investment.[23] However, it is difficult to formalise something so ephemeral as expectations so that often all this is expressed as

$$I = (i,\ Y) \qquad 6(1)$$

$$\text{or } I = (i,\ \triangle Y) \qquad 6(2)$$

where Y, or $\triangle Y$, assumed a relationship between income and expectations. Expression (2) takes us towards the accelerator hypothesis. This seems reasonable enough, provided it is remembered that expectations can occasionally respond to other factors. This attitude implies that there will be, at each interest rate, a set ofinvestment schedules for each level of income as in Fig. 1.

What is the U.K. experience with reference to investment?

There is little evidence that investment responds to interest rates or that house-mortgage rates are critical to house-building; although house-building is sensitive to the credit rationing systems used by many building societies. The factors governing investment in stocks are such that economists have not been able to formulate generally acceptable hypotheses. Thus, although stock holding is an important form of investment, no policy can be safely built on predictions about future stock holding. Much investment is at least partly insulated from fiscal or monetary policy. Thus, for instance, nationalised industries may be under quite different government pressures. Similar to the reaction of building societies, it is suggested by many studies that company investment responds to the availability of funds—especially internal finance, rather than interest rates.[24] It is not, therefore, surprising that the single most important government weapon appears to be the taxation of profits, especially the techniques of tax allowances.[25]

The *accelerator* has a strong basis in fact but it has proved difficult to formulate a version of the acceleration hypothesis that will withstand empirical investigation. Investment spending does fluctuate more than consumption spending, but can this be explained by the size of investment expenditure generated by a consumption change? Or by a relationship with the expected (or real) rate of change of

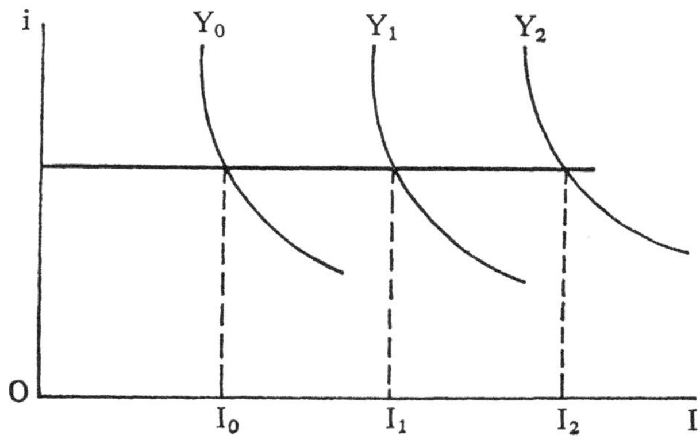

Figure 1

income and by replacement investment itself echoing the sequence of past additional investment concurrently with additional new investment? While not questioning the great plausibility of the economists' explanation, early attempts at verification were disheartening.

There is now some evidence that if the accelerator principle is carefully enough stated it can offer an explanation of at least some real world phenomena. It was originally felt by economists that there was little empirical evidence for the accelerator relationship,[26] but it is now clear that there is a strong accelerator in operation but that its identification is confused by the presence of complicated time-lags.[27] This means that while the government must allow for its effects, they cannot, in practice, use the concept in policy formulation as its predictive value is limited by the general ignorance of the exact form of the functional relationship.

Exactly the same comments are in order on the *multipliers*; first, the concept is formally correct in logic; second, it can be detected in a lagged form in the real world, and third, our knowledge is too imprecise to allow any detailed use of it.[28]

THE PRACTICE *Physical* policy is the use of direct legal sanctions and administrative apparatus to achieve particular resource-uses. Planning is a general case, licences and rationing are well-known examples. Two characteristics are immediately apparent: first, a rationing system, for instance, can allocate resources where they are most wanted rather than to those who can afford to pay for them. It thus has a potential 'fairness' against the 'unfairness' of the price system. Second, all governments resort to it in war time and in other crisis periods; this is a sure sign that it can be made to work, that it can achieve its ends.

If fairness and practicality were the only two characteristics of physical policy, the general hostility to it would be anomalous. Antagonism to physical policy is widespread; no political party ever won an election with a slogan that it would introduce rationing.

We will now discuss physical policy, taking rationing as our example. A common criticism of rationing schemes is that they interfere with the free play of market forces. This would be well founded if it could be shown that the market mechanism leads autonomously to the optimal use of resources. This is not the case; a non-optimal resource-use must occur in a world that contains monopolistic characteristics in the labour and factor markets and also externalities; nor is a free market likely to produce the growth rate, or output and employment levels, required by society. Those who are against physical policy because it interferes with the market are really against the purpose rather than the method; *of course*, it changes resource use, that is what it is trying to do.

The economist, as such, has nothing to offer concerning an explicit value-judgement in favour of personal freedom in all matters including the spending of money, but he can tell anybody who thinks that, as a matter of positive economics, a free market optimises the use of scarce resources that he is in error.

A quite different criticism of physical policy is that it has a high opportunity cost; that it requires an elaborate bureaucratic structure of offices, civil servants and paperwork. It is a matter of common observation that this is so; it is quite another matter—on which no cost benefit studies seem available—whether these resources could offer society a higher return in other uses or whether similar results could be obtained by fiscal policy, monetary policy or some other means at lower opportunity cost. Not only does it require a large civil service to be effective, it also needs a high quality one, as difficult decisions must be made between alternative priorities; it is easy to write that 'a rationing system can allocate resources where they are most needed' but it is much more difficult to *decide* where they are most needed. No scientific criteria are available to resolve whether scarce resources should be allocated to school or hospital building. Not only does physical policy need a large and well-qualified civil service, it also needs an uncorrupt one; something that is taken for granted in the Western countries but has, sometimes, proved elusive elsewhere.

Much of the hostility to physical policy draws on these last two difficulties; administrative imperfections can hardly be avoided. If a dairy farmer has specific rations of milk allocated for each customer, awkwardness must arise. The cows simply do not know the arrangements and so produce more or less milk than the ration allows. Human nature is such that from these, and other sources, black markets arise, but it is always the government which gets the blame.

It is difficult to avoid the conclusion that the antagonistic attitudes common to physical policy are politically motivated rather than soundly based in economic analysis. This is not to say that such an attitude is 'wrong', it is to say that it is a value-judgement.

What are the economic difficulties in using physical policy to manage an economy? They are very similar to the reasons why a market system also sub-optimises. Their problems are essentially problems of information of the kind touched on elsewhere. What economic goal does the community wish to maximise and how is it to be discovered? How are the 'shadow prices' which show the real opportunity costs of a particular product mix to be arrived at? Once rational prices are known, attention must then turn to the choice of rational investment criteria. A successful physical policy of rationing, or any other forms of planning, needs workable answers to all these questions.

In trying to reconcile the needs of the individual and of society, most rationing systems have three characteristics. We will illustrate them with reference to food rationing. First, some foods, judged to be of special importance, are put on a specific ration; the size of an individual's ration to depend on age and occupation—thus a child might get less meat than an adult and a steelworker more than a clerk. Second, some foods are put on a points system; an individual gets a given number of points, according, again, to age and occupation and is free to allocate them as he likes between, perhaps, tins of jam and tins of fruit, which will each call for a particular number of points from his total. This method follows the precepts of Welfare Economics in creating a system where the individual maximises welfare by himself allocating points, so that the ratio of points spent on alternative goods equals their marginal utility ratio. A second advantage of this system is its flexibility; the points needed to purchase a given good can be altered as supply conditions change. A third characteristic recognises that a person's need for food is not wholly dependent on age and occupation, and so those who desire more food can often find that, where possible, some of the bulk foods, like bread and potatoes, are off-ration.

These principles are most obvious when applied to food but are of some general applicability to any rationing problem. Transport, fuel or steel could be approached in a similar fashion with some forms on specific ration due to their importance, others available to a given limit in proportions decided by the purchaser and, perhaps, some forms available without restriction. The difficulties are what one would expect: how are priorities to be decided on a rational basis? The start is to choose a maximand and then find the constraints and the opportunity costs. A licensing system is a form of rationing in that it allocates a specific total to the individuals who hold the licence. Usually such a policy does not allow the consumer to allocate resources according to his own priorities, and so there is a chance of a lower welfare maximisation; thus, such a policy is less well founded in economic theory.

Another example of planning is the setting up of institutions concerned with planning, such as the National Economic Development Council and Regional Planning Boards. We will take as our example Economic Development Committees. Originally set up in 1964, as part of a panoply of bodies concerned with seeking and disseminating information regarding the National Plan[29] they were conceived as part of the necessary disaggregation involved in planning. They have grown to be widespread bodies still linked in a two-way exchange of information with their parent, the National Economic Development Council, whose major objective of increasing economic performance they share.

There are over twenty E.D.C.s covering over two-thirds of all workers in the private sector. Their membership comprises representatives of employers and the employed, together with representatives of a relevant government department, with a chairman from outside the industry.

They have, in general, been more concerned with changing the performance and structure of their industry than with the information aspects of their original role. Some of their work (e.g. standardisation) involves inter-firm comparisons which, if carried out by a Trade Association, would fall foul of the 1956 Restrictive Practices Act.[30]

Obviously, the exact work of the E.D.C.s varies from case to case. They have often shown interest in technical innovation (and so co-operate with the Ministry of Technology), in rationalisation, in management and manpower problems (and so co-operate with Industrial Training Boards and they also tend to have productivity sub-committees), in export promotion (there are levies for efforts by the whole industry and there is often an interest in the physical flow of goods), in import-savings studies (machine tool and chemical E.D.C.s) and in standardisation problems (electrical engineering E.D.C.).

To take the work of one Committee as an example, the Economic Development Committee for the Distributive Trades has sub-committees on training, stocks, statistics and wholesaling. It regards the main medium-run problem as one of manpower. If it can ensure that its manpower demands increase more slowly than sales, then this is a significant contribution to economic growth in the form of manpower released for elsewhere.[31] They have funds for the re-training of older staff and the training of management and school-leavers. They are interested in enhancing the quality of retirement, by offering a proper career structure and by adapting working conditions to attract part-time staff. They have made a case study of investment and productivity and published a booklet on optimal stock control, as stock-holding is resource-expensive, and is tending to increase with the extra variety of stock-lines and increasing sales of non-food items. Attention has been given to shop-hours, wholesaling and market research on the attractiveness of foreign imports—thus hoping to provide information relevant to the Balance of Payments.

The political scientist has most to offer in considering the effectiveness of such a body in achieving its ends. The economist is interested in the techniques that are used to identify goals and true costs.

In its present form in the U.K., *prices and incomes policy* is a combination of physical and exhortatory policy. Its forerunners include the Wage Freeze (1947–50), the Pay Pause (1961) and the Guiding Light (National Incomes Commission) (1963). Despite great publicity and popular attention, reflected in the fanciful titles, all were unsuccessful in controlling increases in incomes and prices, so that in 1964 a different approach was tried.*

* See *Special Note*, page 152.

'In the Joint Statement of Intent on Productivity, Prices and Incomes, representatives of the T.U.C. and Employers' organisations have accepted that major objectives of National Policy must be: To ensure that British Industry is dynamic and that its prices are competitive; to raise productivity and efficiency so that real national output can increase, and to keep increases in wages, salaries and other forms of incomes in line with this increase; to keep the general level of prices stable.'[32]

The 1964 Joint Statement of Intent had as its general objective, the pledging of the signatories:

1 to attack obstacles to inefficiency and to adopt more rigorous standards of performance at all levels.
2 to co-operate with the government in setting up machinery to
  (*i*) keep under review the general movement of prices and incomes and
  (*ii*) to examine particular cases to see whether they were in the national interest.

The institutional framework consisted of the National Economic Development Council (2.*i*. above) and the National Board for Prices and Income (2.*ii*. above). In practice the centrepiece of the policy has turned out to be the N.B.P.I. by virtue of the volume of its activities and the results of its reports. The N.E.D.C. contribution has been to act as a forum for discussion about the likely growth of the economy and thus the selection of the appropriate norm or ceiling.

Until 1966 the policy was one of exhortation, i.e. co-operation was voluntary and the recommendations of the N.B.P.I. could be ignored. In that year, however, a change of emphasis took place when the famous Part IV[33] gave the government statutory powers of enforcement. At the present time the policy remains both exhortatory and physical. We now turn to a consideration of the objectives of the policy. Since 1964 these have been three:

1 to control inflation
2 to promote growth
3 to encourage social fairness by relating earnings to work, and to help the poorest paid group of workers.

With regard to the first objective, we have already seen[34] that there are a number of forms of inflation, but of these, prices and incomes policy is relevant *only to the cost-push or sectoral demand shift type*. An accurate evaluation of the policy would require to know, firstly, the proportion of the total inflationary pressure from cost-push. This is a matter about which there has been no general agreement amongst economists. Certain models have achieved wide acceptance (e.g. that of Dicks-Mireaux, see note 35), but they related to the 1950's rather than the present situation. A model is necessary to enable the 'with policy' result to be compared with what would have happened without a policy. The N.B.P.I. is conducting research on this point.[35] What evidence there is seems to show that 1950's relationships no longer apply, that the policy was effective during the period of 'standstill' and 'severe restraint' and that 'the average annual increase in earnings in recent years may have been 1% less than it would otherwise have been'.[36] If it continues, this last result could be important since, e.g. if earnings had risen by 5½% but without a policy would have risen by 6½% the effect is 15%. Since productivity will have risen also,[37] the effect would be proportionately greater on the earnings/productivity difference.

The second objective is to use prices and incomes policy to promote growth. Apart from any indirect effects (e.g. on inflation and thus the Balance of Payments), it can hope to do this by improving efficiency. The fundamental problem here is that efficiency is a concept carried over from the physical sciences, involving an increased output from a given input, which presents great difficulties in economics. Firstly, inputs, such as hours of work and acres of land, cannot be summed; we cannot sum their money prices as these are greatly affected by market conditions. Outputs are similarly difficult to aggregate, particularly where different qualities of output are possible. As a result, attention turns to labour productivity: that is to output per worker instead of the ratio of output to all input.

This, however, is not the same thing at all. Output can increase while labour input is constant, for some reason attributable to labour itself; but it may also be attributable to changes in the other factors of production.[38] If extra units of, say, capital are used with the same unit of labour it would be a value-judgement to distribute all the rewards of any increased 'productivity' (of labour) in wages. At least, in such a case, some measure of change in 'capital productivity' could be made; it is much more difficult where, as a result of technical change, a new form of capital input causes a shift on to new cost functions. Now the theorist has no measure of the change in efficiency. Technical change in this sense need not be more advanced machinery, it may be new working methods—which are one of the objectives of productivity agreements. This does not, of course, mean that to relate a change in 'efficiency' to labour productivity is any more arbitrary than some of the wage changes generated in a free labour market, nor that it does not correspond to a widely held value-judgement.

The present machinery comprises an 'Early Warning' system, an official set of criteria to be applied to incomes, the N.B.P.I. to report on selected cases and powers of enforcement. We will examine each in turn, using them as specific examples of the economist's general approach to an incomes policy.

The Early Warning system[39] resulted from the realisation in 1966 that any commission would be swamped by the number of cases of price and income increases in a year. It was hoped that the T.U.C. and C.B.I. would co-operate by receiving all requests by their members and handing on selected cases to the N.B.I. This part of the policy has always been voluntary. In the event, only the T.U.C. co-operated, and has a Vetting Committee which sifts all claims and settlements for more than 100 workers. Selected cases are then referred to the N.B.P.I. Other forms of incomes are now examined; thus solicitors' and architects' remuneration have been referred to the N.B.P.I., the 1968 Act restricts increases in ordinary dividends to $3\frac{1}{2}\%$ p.a.[40] Price control is complicated because some prices fluctuate seasonally while others are directly related to import prices determined in world markets,[41] the former would involve reiterative requests for increases and decreases, the latter would be too sudden for the Early Warning system. As a result various government departments (e.g. the Board of Trade, the Ministry of Agriculture etc.) are responsible for receiving information and supervising:

1 goods and services subject to Early Warning arrangements;
2 goods of which the trend of manufacturing prices is kept under review; and
3 foodstuffs subject to constant watch.[42]

The rate of increase of other important prices, *viz.* local authority housing rents, and rates are also kept under review.

We next turn to the criteria to be applied to any proposed price or income increase. This consists, firstly, of an overall acceptable rate of increase p.a. based on official forecasts of the growth of National Income in real terms. Here jargon reigns supreme. The 'Guiding Light' was replaced by the 'norm'[43] which in 1968 was in turn replaced by a ceiling of $3\frac{1}{2}\%$ p.a. This was hoped to be more than mere playing with words; norms were held to have the unfortunate consequence of raising income expectations so that all felt entitled to the norm and claims then centred around abnormal increases.

Secondly, we have criteria laid down to apply to price or income increases.

> 'Wages and salaries are determined by many factors, including changes in the demand and supply of different kinds of labour. . . . They are also influenced by the policies which the government pursue. . . . The government have affirmed that their social objective is to ensure that the benefits of faster growth are distributed in a way that satisfied the claims of social need and justice . . . impractical and undesirable to inhibit the structural changes necessary in the interests of faster growth.'[44]

Now any incomes increase has to satisfy one of the following criteria:[45]

1 where the employees have made a direct contribution towards increased productivity. Some of this increase should also be passed on by lower prices.
2 where a pay rise can bring about a change in the distribution of manpower which is in the national interest.
3 where existing wages are too low to maintain a reasonable standard of living.
4 where pay of a group of workers has fallen out of line with the pay for similar work elsewhere and it is in the national interest to redress the change.

The basic assumption is that there should be no increase; the maximum agreed increase is 3½% p.a., but exceptional increases may be allowed where there is a marked contribution to increased output per man or a major revision of the pay structure.[46]

Any price increase must also satisfy one of four criteria:

1 If output per employee cannot be increased so as to allow incomes to rise at a rate consistent with the criteria and if no off-setting cost reductions can be made.
2 If there are unavoidable increases in non-labour costs which cannot be offset.
3 If there are unavoidable increases in capital costs per unit which cannot be offset.
4 If the firm cannot obtain the capital required to meet demand.

There are also criteria for price reductions. Since 1968 the government has had reserve powers to enforce price reductions, qualifying under any of these criteria, which have been referred to the Board. Thus it has, at present, legal powers:

1 to delay an increase, subject to a Prices and Incomes Board reference, for up to one year.
2 Force price reductions.
3 Compel notification and control of dividend increases.

The N.B.P.I. applies the general and specific criteria outlined above to cases referred to it by the government. In some ways its position is analogous to that of the Monopolies Commission, it can neither initiate action nor enforce its conclusions. The N.B.P.I. is a busy board[47] which has grown quickly. It has, on several occasions, interpreted its brief very widely[48] and appears confident of the importance of its role and its ability to play the part. The N.B.P.I.'s reports fall into four main categories, *viz.*:

1 Specific references on a proposed increase in prices or incomes (e.g. Report No. 53, *Flour Prices*, 1968; Report No. 30, *Pay and Conditions of Limbfitters employed by J. E. Hangar and Co.*, 1967).
2 Continuous reviews of incomes (e.g. Report No. 70, *Standing Reference on the Pay of the Armed Forces*, 1968).
3 General Reports (e.g. Report No. 65, *Payment by Results Systems*, 1968).
4 References concerning nationalised industries where (since 1967) the N.B.P.I. is asked to conduct an 'efficiency audit' (e.g. Report No. 56, *Proposals by the London Transport Board for Fare Increases in the London Area*, 1968).

References to the N.B.P.I. have usually been early warnings of proposed price increases, but have also concerned allegations that existing prices are too high. The sifting process has meant that for a reference to be important enough to be worth consideration it has usually been asked to consider an industry-wide price agreement.[49] The N.B.P.I. has been hostile to price-fixing arrangements largely on the basis of a normative judgement that prices should be related to costs. This has resulted in disagreement with a Restrictive Practices Court judgement in the case of cement pricing arrangements.[50] Here the Board reduced a proposed price increase (from 5s. to 2s. per ton) which had been based on a 'profit margin sanctified by the Court'.[51] Other increases have been rejected because of the inflationary pressure which would have been generated. For example, the Board was critical of fixed dealers' margins being applied to goods the price of which had increased as the result of devaluation.[52]

In the case of the reference on bank charges on current accounts,[53] the Board's willingness to interpret the reference and its role in the widest sense meant that its findings on charges (that they were not excessive, but should be related to costs),[54] became incidental to wide-ranging suggestions concerning methods of improving banks' performance.[55] A by-product of the enquiry—the most searching examination of the British monetary system since the Radcliffe Report—was to prompt radical changes in the structure of the industry. Evidence was given that the Bank of England and the Treasury would not obstruct some further concentration of banks. The result was that banks, who had hitherto believed that the attitudes of the 1918 Treasury Committee on Bank Amalgamations still represented the current view, attempted three mergers within months.[56] The Board of Trade intervened under the 1965 Monopolies and Mergers Act, and the final merger was blocked by an adverse Monopolies Commission report. Thus a major structural change resulted, not from the I.R.C., but from a Board charged with operating a largely exhortatory policy primarily concerned with the control of inflation. A Board, furthermore, whose criteria and composition are quite different from the I.R.C. and the Monopolies Commission. Other references to the N.B.P.I. have resulted in enquiries involving a consideration of structure (with a criterion of public interest framed in terms of permissible price increases).[57] As mentioned above, there are powers to enforce the conclusions of a report. In practice the usual procedure is for a report to be followed by discussion between the parties and the relevant government department.

The 1964 Joint Statement of Intent concerned *Productivity* Prices and Incomes; the N.B.P.I. has paid great attention to productivity, partly this has been because productivity agreements have turned out to be the most important of the four incomes criteria[58] but partly it has been the result of the N.B.P.I. interpreting its role as

> 'to try and loosen the relationship between pay within a factory or an industry and the pay thought to be paid elsewhere. The Board has instead tried to substitute . . . a closer relationship between internal performance.'[59]

It has produced reports on productivity agreements[60] and payments by results[61] and its guide-lines for a 'good' productivity agreement have been incorporated into the policy as the criteria to be applied to an increase above the ceiling. It is important to emphasise that positive economics says nothing about whether incomes 'should' be related to productivity any more than they 'should' be related to market forces. A wages/productivity relationship is not logical in the sense that a scientific observation that the world is round leads to deductions on necessary principles of navigation. Once, however, the value-judgement relating incomes to productivity has been made, then incomes policy can be judged as to whether it has been consistent with that goal. No one needs to make up his mind about incomes policy as such, he does need to decide whether he judges that wages should be determined by a perfectly competitive labour market, the present imperfect market or by some other system. In this way the N.B.P.I., by fostering productivity-related pay (the first objective), may be not only helping growth (second objective)—if productivity increases are required then wage increases may be the best way of getting them—but also contributing towards the third objective (social fairness). The third objective is unquantifiable; what evidence exists for success in the second is that there has been an increase in productivity since 1967—but there is no scientific way of likening it with the policy.

In other ways, however, a prices and incomes policy may act against the third objective by aggravating income differences between groups. This may happen:

1 because only a minority of increases are reported on, and some parties pay more attention to the policy than others;
2 because workers, whose earnings are the result of a national agreement, may have incomes strictly controlled whereas 'white collar' workers and executives may evade the policy by an annual price rise, e.g. for seniority;
3 because wages and profits are fundamentally different in that wages unpaid are usually paid to the recipient whereas profits undistributed may be taken as capital appreciation or be distributed at a later date when the ceiling has been raised.

To sum up, prices and incomes policy can never be general as it can never claim to act on all causes of inflation or to control equally all income and prices. Our policy is not the only technique; in the U.S. the President has enforced price control by shifts in government buying, stock pile policies and changes in tariffs.[62] Its enthusiasm for productivity may well be misguided.[63] In the short term its value may lie in its exhortatory qualities.[64]

EXHORTATORY POLICY is very different in mood and spirit to physical policy. It achieves its end, if at all, by the propagation of knowledge or attitudes of mind; incomes policy has contained some element of this in the past as have savings campaigns and National Productivity Years. Exhortations to work harder, save more, spend less or export more have an enervating *déjà vu* aspect that helps to explain their ineffectiveness. No government relies greatly on these techniques but there seems no harm in adding them to the armoury of control weapons. They are almost certainly useless in the short run, but they may have some effect in the long run; it would appear difficult to prove that a given change in a variable like savings, or exports, was caused by a propaganda campaign; no such proof has ever been offered. Any long-run effects are generated by changing attitudes (Export or Die, Beware of the Squanderbug) or by the spreading of information (Quality and Reliability Year).

Although we cannot yet point to the opportunity costs of exhortatory policy, either in resource terms or in terms of the resultant allocation of resources, it is possible to indulge in some *a priori* comments.

First, the policy assumes that altruism enters into utility functions; there is no evidence for this and the assumption looks like wishful thinking. Second, by some criteria, such a policy is immoral, for anybody who complies gains the collective benefit and pays the individual cost, while the non-complier gains the same collective benefit at no cost. Third, there is not much hope unless the estimated cost of non-compliance exceeds the estimated cost of compliance. Fourth and fifth, most of the public must agree with the government's purpose, and the size of the relevant population—say the savers—should be quite small.[65]

MONETARY POLICY has fluctuated in fashion since the war. The I.S.L.M. model leads us to suppose that it will be effective only in some circumstances.

It was once favoured on the grounds that a change in interest rates and the availability of money would lead the price mechanism to reallocate resources.[66] The theoretical difficulty is to see any advantage in the allocation produced in this way, either in a welfare sense that it is 'nearer' the social optimum, or produces an output-mix preferable in some other way.

There are difficulties in visualising quite how monetary policy will produce the level of economic activity preferred by the government. First, there is evidence that investment is not particularly elastic to interest-rate changes.[67] This is not surprising; few investments are likely to be hazarded by a small change in interest rates because few firms work to such a fine margin, because the interest change may be quite a small part of total costs and changes in this cost may be insignificant compared to the uncertainty of the revenues.

Anyway once started it may be difficult and expensive to stop a project which represents a process of investment over some period of time. Such investments are begun with the knowledge that interest changes can alter during that time and the investment decision sometimes allows for this.

Second, those who are affected by the new interest charges may simply turn elsewhere for the funds; for instance, to a share issue. Third, if inconvenienced by the new level of interest rates some firms may simply raise their product prices. In either of these cases, the investment level continues and thus monetary policy is vitiated. Fourth, the workings of the monetary system change, making redundant policies which are based on old institutions and practices. New institutions, such as the parallel money markets, develop and new banking practices emerge. The Euro-Dollar market, for instance, does not follow the traditional approach to assets of maintaining echelons of differing liquidities but simply matches assets against liabilities by their return and their liquidity.[68] These changes blunt the effectiveness of monetary policy, not to mention changes in the economist's understanding of the significance of the supply of money.[69]

These difficulties operate whether we are discussing a decrease in investment in response to higher interest rates or a projected increase to follow lower rates. A final difficulty is that monetary policy assumes a uni-causal approach to investment; either it ignores the marginal efficiency of capital or it assumes that factors determining *m.e.c.* are constant while the interest rate is changed. Neither of these assumptions is impressive or attractive.

Even when a changed interest rate does alter investment, there can be forbidding disadvantages. First, it raises the cost of government borrowing and so taxation which may well be regressive in its net effect, since, whoever pays the tax, the beneficiaries are certainly asset-holders who, on the whole, tend to be the richer part of the community. Second, it attracts foreign funds to the United Kingdom from other international financial centres and this so-called 'hot money' is a distorting, volatile and disturbing element in the payments position—which does not deny that for some purposes it might be welcome.

Third, the effect falls unequally on different industries as they have different capital requirements per £100 of output. No one can believe that, by chance, the favoured ones are important to exports, growth, employment and so on. Fourth, the effect is unequal in that firms are affected unequally according to their debt-structure.[70] Once again, we cannot assume coincidence is on our side. Some firms escape fortuitously because they are not current borrowers while, fifth, some escape by statute because the government gives special credit treatment to those firms for one reason or another.[71] Examples are the Agricultural Mortgage Corporation and the Ship Industry Mortgage Finance Board.

Clearly, monetary policy is a very haphazard technique and there are persuasive reasons for believing it is an ineffective one. It is unlikely that anybody now believes

> '. . . the inescapable conclusion—that the only possible way of avoiding the physical interventions . . . is by relying on the classical techniques (Open market-operations and Bank-Rate).'[72]

Its apparently random results, and apparent ineffectiveness, combined with the poor United Kingdom economic post-war performance, have led to the search for new policy modes such as incomes policy. There is some doubt whether this is the gambler's last throw, the great breakthrough in policy tactics—or just incompetence.

Our last problem in this section is the *money supply*. There has been a habit for some time of regarding those who emphasised the significance of money as eccentrics. However, those days are over; as the account of the I.S.L.M. model showed monetary implications must be taken into account in the theory and policy of macro-economic problems and also, how far the government can control the twin monetary phenomena of the interest rate and the supply of money.

The policy problems concern the price level and the management of aggregate demand. There is little evidence to support a close direct relationship between the money supply and the price level. From the mid 1950's to the early 1960's the money supply (on any likely definition) fell and since then it has changed in roughly the same proportion as the G.N.P.[73] Yet these were periods of inflation. Further, the price level certainly does not change in a day-to-day relationship with the money supply. It is much more likely that the connection between the money supply and the price level is through the level of aggregate demand and its effects on inflation.

On the whole, Keynes played down the role of money from a theoretical viewpoint. As his main emphasis was on the control of aggregate demand it really does not matter much to Keynesian economists whether it turns out that aggregate demand is better managed by fiscal or monetary techniques. Monetary policy was disappointing in the 1950's and fiscal policy has been no different in the 1960's as it has become clear that consumer spending will not respond predictably to tax changes due, for instance, to the presence of wealth effects. The more affluent a society the greater are these likely to be.

If the money supply is fixed, the government has to allow interest rates to move to whatever level will shift public preference from money to income-earning assets, unless it is preferred to face other consequences. If the government attempts to compromise with forms of credit rationing, all that seems to happen is that new sources of credits or forms of 'near-money' are developed. As the government creates legislation to draw these within its ambit so yet newer forms come into being; as with income-tax legislation, the government tends to be one step behind.

Not only does the government have difficulty in controlling money supply and interest rates together, because they are not independent of one another, but also it has difficulties with the money supply alone.

It can control the cash base to the money supply fairly closely but there are variables relevant to the total supply of money with which it has difficulty. First, new institutions develop in the money market; second, these and older institutions change their attitudes about reserve ratios and so the size of the credit multiplier on the cash base; third, the public desire to hold cash alters as well as its desire to hold bank deposits, and fourth, the Balance of Payments surplus or deficit leads to the Exchange Equalisation Account selling or buying sterling and so affecting the domestic money supply.

It is particularly difficult to relate either the theory of the money supply, or monetary theory in general, to practical policy because the theory is in a state of rapid transition and there is insufficient agreement on either facts or relationships.

FISCAL POLICY We have earlier considered the United Kingdom experience in determining consumption by fiscal means and the I.S.L.M. model leads us to believe that its effectiveness will vary from case to case. Here we consider mainly the problems connected with the form of taxation, the level and the size of government expenditure.

Economists usually relate taxes and subsidies to 'taxable capacity', that is the individual's ability to pay taxes. It is normally thought that the diminishing marginal utility of money means that richer people 'should' not only pay absolutely more but proportionately more of their income. This idea of progressive taxation turns on the notion that if the rich pay proportionately more, then their subjective loss of welfare is equal to that of the poor. Thus, by treating men unequally we in fact treat them equally! This is because their tax burden in welfare terms is the same even if it is different in money terms. The taxable capacity approach leads us to favour direct taxation rather than indirect; this is because indirect taxes are on goods and are not increased according to who buys the goods. They are, therefore, basically unrelated to taxable capacity and are also regressive. They are also poorly related to taxable capacity in that they depend on the individual's tastes between taxed and untaxed goods[74] and in no way at all to the person's ability to pay.

What are the facts of the British system? Direct taxes are approximately equal in size (15·1%) to indirect taxes and only slightly higher if direct taxes on corporations are included (17·7%).[75] This is the first reason for believing that the United Kingdom's tax system is only poorly related to taxable capacity. The facts with regard to the progressiveness of the income tax further this impression. In 1966 two-thirds of the population earned less than £1,000 p.a., and, on average, paid 6% in income tax; those earning between £1,000 p.a. and £2,000 paid, on average, 12%. This comprises 95% of the population. *The notion that the United Kingdom has heavy income-tax rates has no more basis in positive economics than the idea that the United Kingdom pays more taxes than other countries.*[76]

It does have high marginal tax rates in that less than 1% of the population pays more than 50% of its income in income tax. Only then does the belief that Britain is heavily taxed—in absolute terms and in relation to other countries—hold good. Why then are these beliefs so widespread? First, such complaints are a form of self-indulgence; second, the appearance is strengthened by the anachronism of a tax structure that proceeds in a few steps to the standard rate; third, the most quoted rate is the rate of unearned income (8s. 3d.) but the most paid rate is the earned-income rate of 6s. 5d;[77] fourth, the 1% highly taxed is a vocal and articulate section of the population.

A different way in which the United Kingdom tax system is unrelated to taxable capacity is that the indirect taxes are narrowly based on a few goods like petrol, alcohol and tobacco and so their incidence is more random than some of the more broadly based continental tax systems. Apart from the excise tax on these three items, there is a wide variety of indirect taxation which amounts to an average rate of 7½% on the amounts spent.

It is difficult to believe that the United Kingdom is highly taxed in any sense, or that its taxes are much related to taxable capacity; it is easy to believe that, since indirect taxation falls most heavily on the poor, and direct taxation on the rich, there is a middle-income bracket who do most of the consuming and are lightly taxed in relation to their income.

The legal vagaries of the British tax system also have consequences of interest to the economist seeking any relationship between the theoretical concept of taxable capacity and public policy.

The income-tax system relies on unequal taxes on unequal incomes in response to the hypothesis of diminishing marginal utility. Since, however, we have no way of measuring utility between persons we also have no way of knowing how progressive the tax system *should* be. It is doubtful whether the British system, with a large income group paying the standard tax rate, is really the appropriate one especially in view of the regressive nature of indirect taxation. The United Kingdom system also allows unequal taxes on equal incomes where the tax-payers have unequal family responsibilities, unequal necessary expenses and unequal tax periods in which to spend the money.

However, all this operates in an anomalous fashion. Every tax-payer is entitled to equal tax relief on his wife and children whatever his need for that relief; there is an elaborate system of recognising some claims for expenses, and not others, on the basis of precedent. Many of these precedents may act in a way that is generally acceptable, but there is some evidence that they can act in a random way that favours those who can employ accountants and lawyers—that is, the better-off.[78] Similarly, while it is sensible to allow those who earn money in an irregular way, more in some years and less in others, to 'spread' the income over a number of years rather than pay as much in a good year as another, who earns the same in that year but on a regular basis, this 'spreading' concession is allowable only to specific occupations such as authors and artists and not to others, in equal need, such as professional footballers or boxers.

A final problem on the nature of British taxes is whether or not they have a deterrent effect. This too is one of the widespread beliefs of our time. Is it a myth or is it empirically based?

There is certainly evidence that people do think there is a relationship between work-effort and tax and, presumably, this is what matters rather than theorists' speculation about utility functions. One survey showed that none of a sample of workers knew what their marginal rate of tax was, that three-fifths over-estimated it, only 6% of managers in the same survey could give correct answers and four-fifths gave exaggerated answers. Very few knew the standard rate of tax.[79]

Whatever the disincentive effects of the United Kingdom's tax system, there are reasons for believing that its effect is easily exaggerated and that the tax systems of other countries have greater disincentives.

If we state the disincentive effect as being that 'an increase in direct taxation will reduce the supply of effort' this seems implausible for the majority of workers who are in no position to reduce their effort or working hours. If the disincentive effect is formulated as that 'a given level of taxation will make workers less ready to work harder or overtime hours' it may be true, but only for a minority.

Second, the burden of direct taxes, as a percentage of personal income, is lower in the United Kingdom than in West Germany, France or Sweden and only slightly higher than in the U.S.; the marginal rate in the United Kingdom for *most people* is lower in the United Kingdom than in most other countries.[80]

However widespread beliefs may be about income tax, there is no clear *evidence* that the United Kingdom's system has serious disincentive effects. The only safe course is agnosticism; the disincentive effect—if it exists at all—is minimal.[81]

We have already noted that the size of the government's budget and its relationship to government spending is significant for a government (or balanced budget) multiplier, and thus for aggregate demand; and its pattern is important because of the effects on regions and on industries. The resultant debt structure, and its management, can raise problems. The government, for instance, is constantly creating and redeeming debts and it is anxious to avoid large transactions that might temporarily affect the securities market and the rate of interest, so it issues bonds gradually to the market to avoid price fluctuations and gradually buys bonds due for redemption so that it is not engaged in sudden large cash purchases.

Laymen sometimes see a particular role for government spending and attribute to it a causal significance in inflationary and balance of payments problems. This is prejudiced nonsense; no particular unit of spending is any more or less 'blameworthy' than any other unit if total expenditure is inflationary, any more than any one brick is different from any other in causing the height of a wall.

However, it may be that government expenditure can be more easily altered than private expenditure (for practical and political reasons) and thus a retrenchment of government expenditure can be an attractive anti-inflationary device. This is quite different from saying it caused the inflation. In such techniques a distinction must be drawn between cuts which release real resources, like cuts in road-building, and cuts which have no such effect, like those in transfer payments.

It is worth noting that government revenue as a proportion of G.N.P. is 35·5% in United Kingdom, but 46·3% (Sweden), 41% (Norway), 40% (Netherlands), 39·4% (France) and 37·5% (West Germany), and it is only less in U.S. (28·3%) and Switzerland (25·4%). This is rather different from the popular opinion.[82]

Two final comments on fiscal policy are in order. There is no consistency whatsoever in what the state provides free (roads), or for a price (electricity) or on an insurance principle (health service). The form of financing matters a great deal as the money price is taken as a measure of the opportunity cost; and on this measure (accurate or otherwise) the consumers base their demand and this helps fix the size of the industry. When the price is a bogus measure then inappropriate volumes of resources are allocated to the industry. This is because the consumer does not know the opportunty cost; all this is manifested in the question 'it [e.g. a road] is free, but is it cheap?' Second, experience in manipulating fiscal weapons to gain some particular level of activity has not been encouraging. Estimates of tax revenues from new taxes have sometimes been woeful[83] although estimates of G.N.P. have been generally accurate.

In general it is difficult to feel that the government has—at the moment—either the knowledge or the techniques to tune the economy finely at all.

THE RECORD:

By some criteria the U.K. *exchange rate* has been established and the goal of the government's economic policy achieved. In 1914 the rate against the U.S. dollar was £1 = $4·86 and more than fifty years later is has roughly halved in value against the U.S. dollar. Most other prices have changed by much greater amounts, so that the external value has depreciated more slowly than the internal value, for domestic inflation has been much faster. When the U.K. left the Gold Standard in September 1931, the rate against the dollar was allowed to fluctuate and by December it was $3·25. From this low point it slowly recovered, thus making U.K. exports dearer and endangering the export position. It was decided that the Bank of England needed to intervene so that inflowing foreign currency would not cause an appreciation of sterling! (This is the exact opposite of present problems, showing how arbitrary is our attribution of merit to surplus countries and blame to deficit countries.) The 1932 Finance Act gave the government the tool of intervention in the Exchange Equalisation Account. Its original purpose was to purchase gold and foreign currency for the government rather than allow incoming funds to drive up the price of sterling. It was also intended to insulate the domestic economy from the effect of international forces not directly connected with the payments position, such as speculative phenomena.

After an uncertain start, the E.E.A. helped to bring some reasonable stability to the international exchanges. From 1934, when the U.S. dollar resumed a link with the price of gold, until the Second World War, the rate against the dollar remained generally within 5% of \$4·86⅔. During the Second World War the E.E.A. was responsible for exchange control and for using gold and currency reserves in the national interest. All privately held gold and exchange had to be sold to the government and most of the gold in the Bank of England Issue Department was also transferred to the E.E.A. The foreign-exchange market closed down and the E.E.A. financed the dollar parity at £1 = \$4·03.

After the 1944 formation of I.M.F. the official reserves needed to be sufficient to moderate day-to-day fluctuations, and to keep the exchange rate within 1% of the I.M.F. rate even in the presence of serious short-run trading difficulties possibly reinforced by speculative flows. *No such adequate reserves were ever built up.*[84] This has been the chief obstacle to the achievement of the United Kingdom's economic policy goals as their smallness has certainly restricted the policy options.

After more payments difficulties, sterling was devalued in September 1949 to £1 = \$2·80. The foreign-exchange markets were gradually opened so that the E.E.A. took a smaller part in day-to-day operations and became the residual supplier and purchaser of foreign currency. It was an internationally agreed goal that exchange control should be abandoned in favour of convertibility at the fixed I.M.F. rates. This was achieved only for non-resident holders of sterling in December 1958. The United Kingdom's short-term liabilities far exceeded her short-run assets of gold and foreign currency holdings (but not necessarily her long-run assets) and so she was especially vulnerable to the I.M.F. system that required short-run difficulties to be dealt with internally rather than by exchange-rate manipulation. These internal policies always included domestic restriction of growth, employment and output. The I.M.F. resources have not been sufficient to provide credit for countries in short-run difficulties so that in the 1960's new sources of credit have been established in the form of inter-central bank 'swap' arrangements. After more payments difficulties, sterling was devalued on November 18th, 1967, to £1 = $2·40.

There have been only two exchange-rate changes since 1937. On the other hand, both changes were of some magnitude and for lengthy periods the sterling exchange rate was under pressure.

If we are to assess the effectiveness with which the government has realised this goal (which is not to attribute any priority to that goal) the comparisons must be with internal price change and with the devaluations of other countries.

In brief, the United Kingdom has devalued at a slower rate than her own domestic rate of inflation and is one of only nineteen countries to manage this. If the comparison is with the other countries devaluation-rates, rather than with their devaluation-inflation ratios, then thirty-five countries have devalued less, thirty-eight have comparable records and twenty-four (including France) have devalued more. Thirteen countries have devalued not at all or less frequently, twenty-four have devalued as often and forty-five more frequently. These appear to be the answers[85] to the question of Britain's performance in stabilising its exchange rate; whether the question is worth asking is quite a different matter and at what cost this performance, such as it is, has been achieved is a different matter yet again.

The ratio of official reserves to external liabilities is shown in Table 1; clearly the post-war reserves have been inadequate for the tasks required of them. These remarkable figures—pre-war greater than 50% and post-war less than 30%—are attributable, at least in part, to the wartime sale of assets and increase of liabilities and post-war payments difficulties, partly caused by the low level of reserves themselves, so that a vicious circle develops, and also by a number of other factors such as domestic inflation, the reserve role of sterling and a generally overvalued currency.

These figures must be treated with the scepticism due to published payments figures.[86] They also contain no reference to long-run assets, such as fixed capital wealth, located abroad but United Kingdom owned, for which no public figures are available. These are generally held to be so large that the United Kingdom's position is one of small liquid assets and larger liquid liabilities, but even larger fixed, rather illiquid assets—perhaps even unrealisable ones.

What is the record in the *Balance of Payments* itself? The answer to this question is ludicrously elusive. This is partly because of difficulties in the concept of a Balance of Payments and partly to the difficulties of statistical estimation. In the United Kingdom it is common to rely on the size of the basic balance—that is the current balance together with the net export of long-term capital. This is a

TABLE 1

End of	*Official gold and currency reserves (£) A*	*Net external liabilities (£) B*	*A as % of B*
1932	243	468	53
1939	545	517	105
1945	610	3,567	17
1946	664	3,636	18
1947	512	3,856	13
1948	457	3,497	13
1949	603	3,669	16
1950	1,178	3,989	30
1951	834	4,031	21
1952	659	3,716	18
1953	899	3,935	23
1954	986	4,077	24
1955	757	3,944	19
1956	799	3,965	20
1957	812	3,771	22
1958	1,096	3,546	28
1959	977	4,078	24
1960	1,154	4,324	27
1961	1,185	4,342	27
1962	1,002	3,769	25
1963	949	3,889	24
1964	827	4,296	19
1965	1,073	4,856	22
1966	1,107	5,149	21
1967	1,123	5,346	21

SOURCE *Bank of England Quarterly Review*, December, 1968, page 389.

relatively new practice started in 1964; previously interest was in the current balance itself. A policy based on a current deficit may be quite inappropriate in the case of a basic deficit. From 1963 to 1966 the basic deficit was £1,200 m. but the current balance about £350 m.; allowances for unrecorded items might reduce the latter deficit to negligible proportions. In such cases, the basic deficit figures can mislead public opinion into thinking that the United Kingdom has an increased indebtedness, that it is failing 'to pay its way'. In fact over those years the United Kingdom had no significant change in its creditor status. Bank of England figures show its overseas assets and liabilities have hardly changed, and it is, in fact, a *net creditor* of £14,000 m. Public and journalistic comment focus on the apparently important basic figures.

The statistical difficulties in estimating the payments position are exemplified by the constant revisions. The current surplus balance for 1966, for instance, was originally shown as a deficit.

Given these two sets of problems, it is by no means clear how far the United Kingdom has achieved, or fallen short, of its goal of a payments surplus. There is an authoritative viewpoint on the post-war period until 1958.

> 'The fact that there has been a substantial surplus on current account during the past ten years suggests there has been no fundamental lack of balance in the United Kingdom's trading position. . . . The repeated exchange crises have not been due to any failure on the part of the United Kingdom to "pay its way".'[87]

This opinion—and that is all it is—was based on a cumulative surplus of £1,000 m. for 1949–58.

The pattern for the 1960's is less clear, for the current account shows large year-to-year fluctuations.

TABLE 2

	Current balance (£m)	*Balance unaccounted for (£m)*
1960	−265	259
1961	4	−25
1962	112	75
1963	111	−73
1964	−399	41
1965	−91	67
1966	15	−10
1967	−404	175
TOTAL	−925	549

SOURCE Conan, A. R. 'Does Britain pay its way?', *National Westminster Bank Review*, February 1969, p. 5.

This accords with the popular image of the United Kingdom failing to pay its way in the world. Even allowing for the whole of the unaccounted balance, there is a cumulative deficit of over £400 million which clearly contrasts with the previous decade.

However, this still does not mean that the United Kingdom has failed to pay its way in some moral sense—only in the technical sense of an inbalance in these items which we choose to include in the payments figures. It is part of the conventional wisdom to base policy on such figures and to reflect gloomily on the national character.

But the matter is not so simple; these figures cannot be used in this way to claim that the United Kingdom cannot meet its bills (to fall into journalistic phraseology). *This is because the deficit, as officially computed, includes debts incurred on behalf of other countries and the United Kingdom fails to earn sufficient to meet all such debts, as opposed to its own debts. This is all that the figures show.* These debts include grants to less developed countries and military defence on behalf of others. Much less obvious is the effect of Britain's commercial policy which subsidises other countries' exports or gives other special advantages. Two examples will suffice: Britain lessened its East of Suez programme for payments reasons and immediately Australia, New Zealand, Malaysia and Singapore had to raise their defence budget; under various agreements the United Kingdom imports wheat, meat, butter, coffee, and sugar at prices higher than would obtain in a free market. Britain's reserve currency role has also helped others and hindered Britain in the attainment of a payments surplus.

We are not saying that these policies of aid, defence and commerce may not be justified in some political or moral way, but simply that they confuse the significance of the payments position.

For what they are worth, we have included in Table 2 some figures from 1960 to 1967.

What is Britain's record in *economic growth*? Measurements of growth rates and of National Incomes are a notoriously tricky business and especially those involving international comparisons. However, the following estimates carry a great deal of authority.

TABLE 3

Country	*National Income growth rate*		*Per capita growth rate*	
	1950–64	*1955–65*	*1950–64*	*1955–64*
Germany	7·1	5·6	5·9	4·3
Italy	5·6	5·4	4·9	4·7
France	4·9	5·0	3·8	3·7
Netherlands	4·9	4·3	3·5	2·9
Norway	3·8	3·9	2·9	3·0
Denmark	3·6	4·8	2·9	4·1
U.S.	3·5	3·1	1·8	1·4
Belgium	3·4	3·5	2·5	2·9
U.K.	2·6	2·8	2·2	2·1

SOURCE Denison, E. F., *Why Growth Rates Differ: Postwar Experience in nine Western Countries*, Table 2–3. Brookings Institution (1967).

These figures are unambiguous. By no stretch of the imagination has the United Kingdom achieved this goal of government policy.

However, the explanation of this performance does not justify the self-flagellation and collective despair in which journalists indulge nor the accusations with which politicians castigate one another. Relatively little of the explanation points to factors within government control or to failings of national character.

The explanation seems to turn mainly in the relatively small U.K. labour reserves in primary industries and in the role of investment. Compared with the United States and the leading West European countries, the United Kingdom had less to gain post-war from an increase in employment, from new levels of education expenditure or from a growth in capital as sources of economic growth. There were a number of post-war special factors, such as weather conditions in agricultural countries and the unbalanced capital facilities in the divided Germany. This 'gave' idle capacity which, in conjunction with new capital, had a similar short-run effect as though it were extra new capital. This favoured countries other than Britain. Britain also had less to gain from the transfer of resources from farming and self-employment to the growth-oriented sectors of the economy. The United Kingdom also had less to hope for from economies of scale as a contributory factor in growth.[89]

To a considerable extent, this group of reasons for slow growth are beyond the reach of the economic policy of any political party. The most general cause of growth in these other countries is the elimination of under-used resources within the economy; but in the United Kingdom there was little slack of this sort to be eliminated. Nor could much really be done about the growth of the labour force; in Italy, by contrast, part-time workers could be transferred to full-time work and, to take another example, Germany just happened to have a favourable age-sex composition in its labour force in terms of large numbers of women in the appropriate age groups as it became more common for women to work.

Investment is a quite separate factor which is critical for economic growth as is possibly shown by Table 4.

The pattern is fairly clear; faster growth rates are related to the proportion of National Income invested. The return on investment is often measured by the Incremental Capital Output Ratio—the number of units of investment necessary to produce one extra unit of output; not surprisingly the higher I.C.O.R.s are associated with the highest aggregate returns on investment. It is not agreed among economists just how important the I.C.O.R. relationship is and there is some evidence that the whole concept is irrelevant and that the most important factor is economies of scale rather than the labour in different sections of the economy and the I.C.O.R.[90]

Whatever the form of the relationship between investment and growth, it is probably important for the government to influence investment if the economic growth rate is to be achieved.

TABLE 4

	Annual output growth	*Annual Output per head growth*	*Investment ratio per cost of G.N.P.*	*Incremental capital output ratio (I.C.O.R.)*	*Return on invest ment*
Japan	10·4	8·8	28·8	2·8	36
W. Germany	6·3	5·0	23·7	3·8	26
Italy	5·7	5·6	21·6	3·8	26
Sweden	5·4	3·9	22·8	4·2	24
France	5·2	4·9	19·2	3·7	27
Denmark	5·0	3·8	18·7	3·7	27
Belgium	3·6	3·0	18·4	5·1	20
U.K.	3·1	2·6	17·1	5·1	20
U.S.A.	3·1	2·0	15·1	5·5	18

SOURCE *D.E.A. Progress Report,* Number 21, page 2 (1966).

Earlier, it was emphasised that economic growth was by no means a foregone conclusion as a goal of government policy, and it is worth highlighting that the United Kingdom's growth rate is only poor when judged against that of other countries. Things look quite different judged in an historical perspective; in the post-war period the United Kingdom's growth rate was higher than in any period of similar length in the nineteenth century.[91]

In the period 1950–66 the National Income increased by 49%, by 38% per person employed and by 37% *per capita*. Things could be worse and in living memory have been.

The discussion can be concluded by showing that if we concentrate on the United Kingdom's National Income per head instead of its position at the foot of most growth leagues, it has the eighth highest *per capita* National Income in the world. In 1968 it was contributing 1·16% of its National Income to developing countries. Feasibly this is as appropriate a criterion as concentrating on comparative growth records.

Aid to under-developed countries is the most under-achieved goal of all if our criterion is whether these countries have benefited to a significant extent. If the criterion is Britain's contribution, relative to that of other countries as a proportion of *per capita* National Income, then, as a matter of fact, as opposed to rights or wrongs, Britain is ranked fifth, as in Table 5.

TABLE 5

Ranked by National Income per head	*Ranked by % of National Income contributed to less developed countries*	*Proportion of G.N.P. contributed*
U.S.	8	0·76
Sweden	13	0·64
Canada	11=	0·66
Denmark	15	0·28
Australia	9	0·71
Norway	14	0·29
France	1	1·70
U.K.	5	1·16
West Germany	7	0·81
Belgium	3	1·31
Netherlands	2	1·49
Austria	11=	0·66
Italy	4	1·28
Japan	10	0·70
Portugal	6	1·14

Note: This table ignores countries in column 1 not contributing to L.D.C.s and also Communist countries for which no figures are available.

One would expect on *a priori* grounds that relatively little has been achieved in the *redistribution of income*. This is because many forms of wealth and income are untaxed, income-tax rates are not particularly progressive and because such a high proportion of taxation is in the form of regressive indirect taxes.

The distribution of income is conventionally measured by the Gini co-efficient. This proceeds as in Fig. 1.

The first percentage of population is recorded on the vertical axis and the percentage of income earned on the horizontal axis, then the second percentage of population and the percentage of income possessed are added giving cumulative totals from the left-hand lower origin. Now, if 1% of the population has 1% of income, 2% has 2% and so on, the functional relationship between them will be the straight line, *OF*. If, however, there is an unequal distribution, then it will veer below *OF*. If 1% have 100% of the income then the

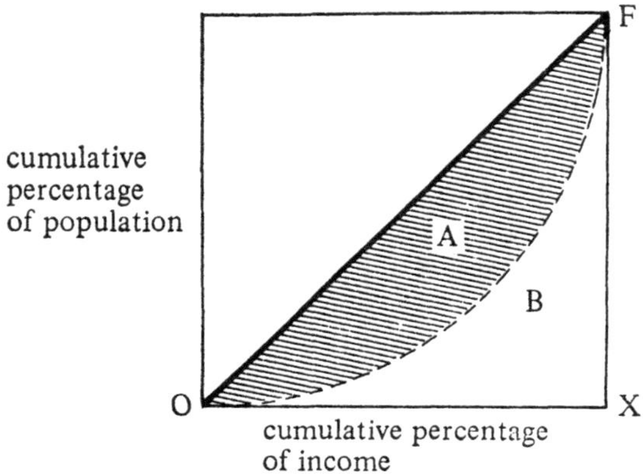

Figure 1

line would follow *OXF*. It is more likely to be similar to the dotted line shown and the co-efficient is the area of the shaded section over the whole area under the 45° line, that is $\frac{A}{A+B}\%$. The co-efficient can vary from perfect equality of distribution (0%) to perfect inequality (100%).

Some post-war coefficients are:

1949	35·31
1954	33·89
1959	33·66
1963	32·24 [92]

There is some trend towards greater equality over time, though whether this scale of inequality is what the government or public requires is quite a different matter. These co-efficients are based on Inland Revenue figures and so ignore the low income groups and are confused by social structure changes whereby married couples move, on marriage, into a higher tax bracket without any gain in income. More insight is given by using C.S.O. figures and family-size patterns to give Gini co-efficients of per capita distribution. The results are startlingly different:

1949	33·72
1954	34·45
1959	35·62
1963	35·78

SOURCE *loc. cit.*

In other words the government has not achieved its goal: *There has been an increasingly unequal income distribution.*

Allied to this is a regionally unequal distribution as shown in Chapter 11.

There is also much evidence of a residual of absolutely low income groups. The Ministry of Social Security in its *Report on the Circumstances of Families* estimated that there were 125,000 families, with two or more children, whose incomes were less than the Supplementary Benefit level recognised by the welfare state. There must also be a number with small or no families on such incomes. A number of ideas are mooted for dealing with this, varying from negative income tax to a National Minimum Wage.

Given that there is no wealth tax, and that estate duties are easily minimised, it is clear that circumstances in the United Kingdom favour an increasingly unequal distribution of income. The kinds of fiscal policy that would reverse this trend are: wealth taxes of a progressive nature, taxes on *inter vivos* gifts, a more comprehensive capital-gains tax and taxes on company assets. It is not a matter of positive economics that these things should be done; it is such a matter that these, or similar techniques, are consistent with the stated goal.

These facts are at a variance with the popular myth of penal taxes on the rich and a mollycoddled poor; but the theoretician will not be surprised, since technical progress, with a labour-saving bias, leads to a decrease in labour's marginal product and so a higher share of the National Income to property-owners—and property is particularly unequally owned.[93]

What is Britain's record in controlling *inflation*? Table 6 shows that there has been a rather steady inflation in Britain since the war and that U.K. governments have not only failed by absolute standards but also by international standards. Britain is ranked nineteenth of forty-five countries and eleventh out of eighteen comparable countries in its record of controlling inflation as shown in Table 6.

The one goal of government economic policy that has been reasonably achieved since the war has been *full employment* as is shown by Table 7, but Chapter 11 makes it clear that this has not been achieved in a uniform manner; some parts of Britain, especially Northern Ireland, have had chronic unemployment by the standards of the rest of the country.

TABLE 6 *Rates of Inflation in Different Countries*

Country	*Index of Value of money (1956=100)*	*%Annual rates of Depreciation 1956–66*
Guatemala	100	0·1
Venezuela	90	1·1
Honduras	86	1·5
U.S.*	84	1·8
Luxembourg	83	1·9
Canada*	82	2·0
Australia*	81	2·0
Greece	80	2·1
Thailand	80	2·2
Belgium*	80	2·2
South Africa	80	2·2
West Germany*	79	2·3
Portugal*	78	2·4
Switzerland*	78	2·4
New Zealand*	77	2·6
Ecuador	76	2·6
Austria*	75	2·8
U.A.R.	75	2·9
U.K.	74	2·9
Italy*	72	3·2
Ireland	72	3·2
Norway*	72	3·3
Netherlands*	71	3·4
Pakistan	70	3·5
Iran	70	3·5
Philippines	70	3·6
Denmark*	69	3·7
Mexico	69	3·8
Sweden*	68	4·0
Japan*	66	4·0
France*	62	4·7
Finland	60	4·9
Jamaica	58	5·2
Israel	58	5·4
India	57	5·5
Spain	49	6·9

TABLE 6—*continued*

Vietnam	46	7·4
Peru	41	8·5
Korea	33	10·5
Columbia	32	10·8
Bolivia	25	13·0
Chile	10	20·6
Argentina	6	24·5
Brazil	2	31·0

SOURCE *Monthly Economic Letter:* First National City Bank, New York, July 1967.

Notes: Countries with an asterisk are United Kingdom's main competitors. Depreciation rates are compounded annually. The value of money is measured by the reciprocal of cost of living index.

TABLE 7 *U.K. Unemployment for selected years (% of labour force)*

1929: 11·0	1959: 2·3
1932: 22·5	1960: 1·7
1939: 12·5	1961: 1·6
1948/50: 1·6	1962: 2·1
1951/3 : 1·7	1963: 2·6
1954: 1·5	1964: 1·6
1955: 1·2	1965: 1·4
1956: 1·3	1966: 1·5
1957: 1·6	1967: 2·4
1958: 2·2	1968: 2·4

SOURCE *Monthly Digest of Statistics*, No. 278 (February 1969), Table 22, and Lipton, M.: *Assessing Economic Performance*, p. 127 Staples (1968).

Notes

1 As in Chapters 3 and 4.

2 See Archibald, G. C. and Lipsey, R. G., *A Mathematical Treatment of Economics*, Weidenfeld and Nicolson, pp. 236–60 (1967).

3 See Chapter 1.

4 See Chapter 8.

5 D.E.A., *The Task Ahead: Economic Assessment to* 1972, H.M.S.O. (1969).

6 Friedman, M., in essay, 'The Methodology of Positive Economics', in *Essays in Positive Economics*, pp. 7–8, University of Chicago Press (1953). This attitude is an economist's commonplace. 'The value of economic theory lies in providing a framework of analysis which can be used by applied economists in interpreting facts about the real world. Stonier, A. W. and Hague, D. C., *A Textbook of Economic Theory*, p. 98, Longmans (1953).

7 Friedman, *loc. cit.*, page 4.

8 Lipsey, R. G., *An Introduction to Positive Economics*, Weidenfeld and Nicolson, 1st edition (1963). It is possible to overplay this disclaimer. A knowledge of economics does not lead to particular value-judgements, but it might lead to well-informed ones.

9 Lubell, H., 'Effects of Income Re-Distribution on Consumer's Expenditures', pp. 157–70, *American Economic Review*, Vol. 137 (1947).

10 National *m.p.c.*s are difficult to calculate as other factors vary during the time period in which income and consumption figures are compared. However, A.P.C.s are available—U.K. 0·952, U.S. 0·940, Sweden 0·912, W. Germany 0·874, Switzerland 0·861, Netherlands 0·857. See Table 2, Chapter 1.

11 Duesenberry, J. S., *The Theory of Consumption and Relative Income*, Harvard U.P. (1949).

12 Dernberg, T. F., *Consumer Response to Innovation in Household Economic Behaviour*, Yale University Press (1958).

13 Friedman, M., *A Theory of the Consumption Function*, National Bureau of Economic Research (1957).

14 Watts, H. R., 'Long-Run Income Expenditure and Consumer Savings', *Cowles Foundation Papers*, No. 123 (1958).

15 Morgan, J. N., 'Factors relating to Consumer Savings When it is Defined as a Net Worth Concept', in *Contributions of Survey Methods to Economics* (ed. L. R. Klein), (1954).
16 Fisher, J., 'Income, Spending and Saving Habits of Consumer Units in different Age Groups, in National Bureau of Economics Research', pp. 75–102, *Studies in Income and Wealth*, Vol. 15 (1952)
17 Klein, L. R., 'Assets, Debts and Economic Behaviour, National Bureau of Economic Research', *Studies in Income and Wealth*, pp. 95–227, Vol. 14 (1951).
18 Dow, J. C. R., *The Management of the British Economy, 1945–60*, pp. 270–5, Cambridge University Press (1965).
19 Dow, J. C. R., loc. cit., pp. 282–5.
20 So, too, can be the rate of interest! See Chapter 7, Note 12.
21 See treatment of monetary policy, pp. 128–31.
22 Meade, J. F. and Andrews, P. W. S., 'Summaries of Replies to Questions on the Effects of Interest Rates', pp. 14–31, *Oxford Economic Papers* (1938). For criticisms, see White, W. H., 'Interest-Inelasticity of Investment Demand', pp. 565–87, *American Economic Review* (1956).
23 Duesenberry, J. S., *Business Cycles and Economic Growth*, McGraw-Hill, Chapters 4 and 5 (1958).
24 Dow, J. C. R., loc. cit., pp. 286–7.
25 Dow, J. C. R., loc. cit.
26 Knox, A. D., 'The Acceleration Principle and the Theory of Investment: A Survey', *Economica* (1950).
27 Smyth, D., 'Empirical Evidence of the Acceleration Principle', *Review of Economic Studies*, Vol. 31 (1964).
28 Dow, J. C. R., loc. cit., pp. 373–9.
29 See Chapter 11, pages 289–90, for their regional counterparts.
30 Indeed, exemption was granted in the 1968 Act.
31 See Chapter 4 for significance of manpower in service industries for economic growth.
32 White Paper on Prices and Incomes Policy, Cmnd. 2639, p. 5 (1965).
33 Prices and Incomes Act, 1966. Amended by Prices and Incomes Acts in 1967 and 1968.
34 Pages 99–100.
35 *Third General Report*, p. 12 op. cit.
36 For a summary of theories and tests, see Smith, D. C., 'Incomes Policy', in Caves, R. (Ed.), *Britain's Economic Prospects*. For a bibliography of empirical work, together with the Board's own attempt to construct a model to enable it to compare the effectiveness of Incomes Policy, see Appendix A, Report No. 77, *Third General Report*, Cmnd. 3715 (1968). Both these measurements have

been criticised by Lipsey, R. G. and Parkin, J. M. in 'Incomes Policy: a Re-appraisal', *Economica*, May 1970. They find: that incomes policy succeeds in reducing *wage* inflation when unemployment is below 1·8%, otherwise it makes inflation worse; that the policies have created an association between wage rises and union aggressiveness where none existed before; that policies have tended to create more unemployment and to be more successful the higher the acceptable level of inflation.

37 See below, pp. 122–3.

38 Productivity changes may come about from factors being used in different proportions as a result of changes in their relative prices, thus a reduction in the price of land could lead to an increase in farm workers' productivity. It is probably these points which led to the qualifications in the criteria for price increases below (e.g. ii), unavoidable increases in capital costs *which cannot be offset* by reductions elsewhere.

39 White Paper, *An Early Warning System*, Cmnd. 2608 (1966).

40 For the significance of this cypher, see page 122.

41 See the N.B.P.I. Report No. 55, *Distributors' Margins in Relation to Manufacturers' Recommended Prices*, Cmnd. 3456, for a critical investigation of some of these relationships.

42 Appendix I, White Paper, *Productivity, Prices and Incomes in 1968 and 1969*, Cmnd. 3590 (1968).

43 3½% up to July 1966. July–December 1966 complete standstill—('Freeze'). January–June 1967 'Severe restraint'—a nil norm with very few exceptions allowed. July 1967–March 1968—Nil norm.

44 Prices and Incomes Act 1966, Chapter 33, Schedule 2, pp. 38–42.

45 Cmnd. 3590 para. 34.

46 N.B.P.I. Third General Report, No. 77, Cmnd. 3715, 1968.

47 Thirty-six reports in the eleven months to July 1968.

48 e.g. bank charges. See p. 126.

49 Solicitors and architects both enforced minimum scale fees. For solicitors the N.B.P.I. recommended that conveyancing fees should bear a different relationship to the cost of the house and should be recommended maximum scales. The N.B.P.I. opposed the monopoly position of architects and felt that a case for public regulation might exist.

50 See Chapter 10, p. 249.

51 N.B.P.I. Report No. 38, *Portland Cement Prices*, Cmnd. 3381.

52 N.B.P.I. Report No. 55, *Distributors' Margins in Relation to Manufacturers' Recommended Prices*, Cmnd. 3456.

53 N.B.P.I. Report No. 34, *Bank Charges*, Cmnd. 3292.

54 This created problems for some banks who at that time were unable to cost the servicing of a current account.

55 e.g. that they should compete for deposits by abandoning common deposit account interest rates.

56 January 1968, Westminster and National Provincial. February 1968, Royal Bank of Scotland and National Commercial Bank of Scotland. February 1968, Barclay's, Lloyds and Martin's.

57 e.g. Report No. 73. *Hoover Domestic Appliances.*

58 See page 124.

59 N.B.P.I. Report No. 40, *Second General Report*, Cmnd. 3394 (1967).

60 N.B.P.I. Report No. 36, *Productivity Agreements,* Cmnd. 3311, (1967).

61 N.B.P.I. Report No. 65, *Payment by Results Systems*, Cmnd. 3627 (1968).

62 Smith, op. cit. It must not be thought that U.K. government policy towards the pricing policy of firms is very strict; in other countries more direct action is sometimes taken, e.g. steel prices in the U.S.

63 Fogarty, M., 'Incomes Policy—Fishing with a line or net?' in Prest, A. R. (Ed.), *Public Sector Economics.* He makes the point that an emphasis on comparability of wages coupled with price control may force out of business inefficient firms whose costs will rise while revenue is unchanged. The N.B.P.I. has seen its role as one of reducing comparability in favour of linking earnings with productivity as a criterion.

64 Evidence of a change in public attitudes to understanding the relationship between inflation, prices, income and productivity in N.B.P.I. Report No. 40, *Second General Report* (1967), para. 21.

65 See Romans, J. T., 'Moral Suasion as an Instrument of Economic Policy', pp. 1220–5, *American Economic Review* (December, 1966).

66 It was also favoured because of its generality and lack of discrimination. 'It is the same for all of us.' This is really only an advantage for those who favour the price mechanism as a method of allocating resources.

67 Henderson, H. O., *Significance of the Rate of Interest*, Oxford Economic Papers, No. 1 (1958).

68 Revell, J., *Changes in British Banking: growth of the secondary banking system*, Occasional Paper No. 3, Hill Samuel (1968).

69 Freidman, M., 'Demand for money: some theoretical and empirical results', *Journal of Political Economy*, Vol. 67 (1959).

70 See Chapter 2.

71 This can be greater in real terms than might appear since the opportunity cost of future capital can be changed by the new gearing.

72 Unsigned article: 'Lessons from the Money Experiment', p. 311, *The Economist* (28 January 1956).

73 Dow, J. R. C., loc. cit., pp. 301–9.

74 See Table 2, Chapter 1.

75 Although they may be defended on the grounds that they allow a

choice (to smoke or not to smoke). They may also reflect a social policy, e.g. smoking is harmful to health.

76 See Chapter 1, p. 12.

77 There is no doubt that most people do not know their marginal rate of tax. See note 79.

78 See Titmuss, R. M., *Income Distribution and Social Change: A Study in Criticism*, Allen and Unwin (1967). A further random element is the way in which only certain bank loans are eligible for tax relief and that the interest on house mortgages is also tax-allowable whatever the taxable capacity of the mortgagee.

79 Brown, C. V. and Dawson, D. A., *Personal Taxation, Incentives and Tax Reform*, pp. 63–6, P.E.P. Broadsheet (1969).

80 Brown, C. V. and Dawson, D. A., loc. cit., pp. 16–34.

81 Brown, C. V. and Dawson, D. A., loc. cit., pp. 66–8.

82 See Chapter 1, Table 2.

83 Allen, G. H., *Fiscal Marksmanship*, Oxford Economic Papers (1965)

84 For details see Table 1 below.

85 See de Vries, Margaret G., 'The Magnitudes of Exchange Devaluation', *Finance and Development*, pp. 8–13, Vol. 5, No. 2 (June 1968).

86 See appendix to Chapter 3.

87 Committee on the Workings of the Monetary System, Cmnd. 827, para. 633 (1959).

88 Source: Conan, A. R., 'Does Britain pay its Way?', *National Westminster Bank Review*, p. 5 (February 1969).

89 Denison, E. F., loc. cit.

90 Denison, E. F., loc. cit.

91 Beckerman, W. and Associates, *The British Economy in 1975*, p. 11, Cambridge University Press (1965).

92 Prest, A. R. (Ed.), *The U.K. Economy, A Manual of Applied Economics*, Weidenfeld and Nicolson (1968), quoting an unpublished Manchester University Ph. D. thesis by T. Stark. Also, Prest, A. R. and Stark, T., 'Some Aspects of Income Distribution in the U.K. since World War 2', *Manchester School*, Vol. 35, 1967.

93 Revell, J., *Changes in the Social Distribution of Property in the Twentieth Century*. The best-known figure is that 1% of the population held 42% of the dutiable wealth in 1960.

Special Note

It is likely that in 1970–73 the institutions and outward form of Prices and Incomes policy will be changed; it is unlikely that the general lines of our analysis will become invalid; it is likely that new examples will become available.

Bibliography

Apart from the articles cited in the footnotes, there are reliable accounts, of U.K. policy problems in:

CAVES, R. & Associates, *Britain's Economic Prospects*, Allen and Unwin, 1968

DOW, J. C. R., *The Management of the British Economy, 1945–60*, Cambridge University Press, 1964

LIPTON, M., *Assessing Economic Performance*, Staples, 1968

PREST, A. R. (Ed.), *The U.K. Economy: A Manual of Applied Economics* Weidenfeld and Nicolson, 1968

Chapter 7

TWO TECHNIQUES OF PLANNING

This chapter discusses the need for economic models in general and then introduces two important tools in approaching economic planning. These latter concepts—together with Cost Benefit Analysis, discussed in the next chapter—are critical in any scientific approach to resource-use. This eclectic approach has been adopted because there are already many accounts available of the whole range of the planning problem[1] and because our concern is with an introduction to economic policy in general rather than to economic planning in particular.

The word 'planning' has emotive content for almost everybody: the precise nature of the response varies with the individual's political prejudices. We are not concerned with evangelism one way or the other, so our use of the word must be clarified. The interest of the geographer in the techniques of cartography is like the economist's in those of planning; the geographer wants to know the true physical realities of an area, similarly the economist wishes to know the economic realities of his economy, those of true costs and benefits. The analogy can be stretched a little further; not only does the geographer have real heights and distances identified for him but he can use them for prediction—he might forecast that a given rise in the level of a river will flood a certain acreage of land. Similarly, an economist might take his data and forecast at least some of the implications of a particular turn of events—perhaps the effect on the demand for steel pipes as a result of conversion to natural gas. Thus, most planning techniques simply give access to information; this seems preferable to ignorance.

The political content of the phrase 'economic planning' can be anaesthetised yet further; every person engages in economic planning of some sort, whatever his political allegiance. Somebody saving towards a holiday, a car, a house or retirement has chosen economic priorities and is trying to optimise his income and spending over time rather than leave it all to chance. Once society requires particular goals, rather than accepting the results of a free market, it is simply a matter of consistency to introduce planning.

A further point in favour of planning—in this sense of orderly procedure consistent with chosen goals—is that a policy aimed at one goal might have an even chance of damaging another so that, for instance, a growth policy would have a one-in-two chance of inconsistency with a second goal. If a third goal is added, the chance drops to one in four, a fourth to one in eight, and so on. Since the United Kingdom has a multi-goal policy the chances of inconsistency are strong and the case for some sort of planning is also strong.

The first characteristic of planning was the use of *information* and the second is that of *deliberate* action instead of relying on haphazard circumstances. Nothing more was meant by the phrase 'scientific approach to resource-use'. Society is concerned in three main ways: the optimal use of resources—micro-economics; the full use of resources—macro-economics; the optimal allocation of resources between current and future consumption—economic growth.

It is a matter of positive economics that the seven goals of government policy are unlikely to be realised without informed deliberate policy. It is a value-judgement to feel that this 'justifies' government intervention; but it is just as much a normative position to be hostile to state action in the economy and to have opted for market forces, and to have no economic policy, than in fact to have an interventionist policy. If it is decided to intervene in the economy, then a return can be made to positive economics, for the question becomes a matter of choosing the appropriate method to achieve a chosen goal rather than of choosing an appropriate goal. The role of the economist is a modest and technical one: it is about the way to try to do something and not about what you ought to try to do.[2]

Before we discuss planning techniques that yield information and have some predictive powers it is worth looking briefly at the nature of economic models. Such a model traces a causal relationship between a variable and its necessary effects. It also, therefore, predicts the consequences of a change in the factor.

The causal factor, *A*, may be an hypothesis or some well-verified data; the effect, *B*, is normally necessarily entailed by *A* and might be a prediction, a believed consequence or a verified one. It could be something quite straightforward, like the relationship between output and costs that normally manifests itself as a U-shaped cost-curve, although this would be rather straining the term. 'Model' more commonly refers to a relationship between a number of variables and their consequences in which a causal connection is posited. Such models can be most formidable and they are commonly expressed mathematically. Occasionally gamesmanship can be suspected, but mathematics is often simply the most convenient language.

> 'There is no particular honorific ranking of theories on the basis of the language used. The scientist chooses his language primarily as a matter of convenience both in terms of the requirements of the problem and of his facility in handling the language.'[3]

Two points remain: first, economists' models are like maps in their intentions but they are like medieval maps in their precision; economists have not yet learnt to specify their real-world functional relationships as closely as they would wish.[4] Second, a few general models are available that are helpful to policy decisions, so choices must be made between different models in formulating an approach to a policy issue. This choice will seldom be on the grounds that one is logically fallacious and another not, it will more commonly be on grounds of the appropriateness of its assumptions and its purpose.[5] In a similar way, geographers choose between maps according to their suitability for the purpose at hand; a map showing London within the United Kingdom will be adequate for one purpose but quite inadequate for a street journey around London for which another map is needed, itself unusable for a journey on the Underground system. Of course, for some purposes the geographers have no maps and the economists have no models, which is to say that many problems are unanswered.

Attention now turns to an analytic technique that provides information that is valuable for policy choices and so for prediction. *Discounted cash flow* is a device to overcome the problems that arise when we choose between alternative investments and do so by comparing their alternative income streams. We measure these benefits and the costs in money terms. And money is a poor measuring rod. This seems anomalous, as we regularly compare the wealth of one person with that of another in money terms; that is, it is suitable if the comparison is at a given moment of time. The point is properly expressed by saying that money is a poor measuring device over a period of time. As we have already seen this is true in a period of inflation when the money measure of a debt remains constant while its real value changes.

Our present point remains true, however, even in a period of price stability, which would resolve the first weakness of money as a measuring device. The point is quite straightforward. Everybody agrees that:

$$£100 < £106 \tag{7(1)}$$

This implies that if an asset costs £100 and yields an income of £106 in a year then it is worth buying as the wealth created (£106) exceeds the cost (£100). What if, in that year, the £100 could have been lent at, say, 7%? Once we apply time subscripts everything falls into place, for:

$$£100_t = £107_{t+1} \tag{7(2)}$$

Expression 7(2) is transitive so

$$£107_{t+1} = £100_t \tag{7(3)}$$

and substituting 7(3) into 7(1) and using subscripts:

$$£100_t > £106_{t+1} \tag{7(4)}$$

The decision is now reversed: the cost exceeds the *present value* of the future income and the asset should be rejected. Thus, sums of money over time cannot be assessed by simply comparing their magnitudes; the money sums must be adjusted for the future by discounting them to present values. This measuring problem only arises in economics. In physical sciences 100° centigrade now equals 100° centigrade in a year's time, but in measuring the value of wealth we need to take into account the time at which the wealth is earned or spent. This is not true in the physical sciences where a unit of measure—acre, ounce, yard—is independent of the time of the measurement.

The discussion of the marginal efficiency of capital has already noted the general formula:

$$P_0 = \frac{P_n}{(1+r)^n} \tag{7(5)}$$

Put technically and precisely,

> 'the discount rate calculation defines a functional relationship that makes outputs at different points in time commensurable with each other by assigning to them equivalent present values.'[6]

This simple idea is germane to modern investment appraisal both in the private and public sector; the idea has been long known in accounting, but its recent rejuvenation is owed to economists.[7] It is a most powerful idea. This idea, involving an application of compound interest, has been used by actuaries for generations and by economists since the late 1940's.[8]

It is important to emphasise that what we are discounting are cash flows and not profits. Thus, readers with some knowledge of accounting will realise that we are discounting 'income and expenditure account' differences and not 'profit and loss account' results. Great emphasis has been placed in accountancy on apportioning costs and revenues both to operations *and to time periods*. This may be justified in the role of the accountant as a provider of historical records; it is a hindrance to the realistic appreciation of the effect of present decisions on future events. Economists, whose Theory of the Firm treats the manufacturing unit as an instantaneous transformer of inputs into outputs, have never had this mental block. This, plus the alleged practical complications of using the techniques, may explain the delayed acceptance of D.C.F. by many accountants. To repeat: it is flows of income and expense when actually incurred, exclusive of imputed costs such as depreciation, which are being discounted. Thus, accountants who apportion cash investment grants to the whole life of the project are missing the vital aspect of a cash grant—that it is available at a given moment in time rather than through a stretch of time. D.C.F. techniques very clearly measure the discounted value of the grant at the time when it is received.

> 'The two main advantages of D.C.F. methods for determining whether a given project is worthwhile . . . may be summarised as follows:
>
> 1 D.C.F. methods take account of the fact that earnings vary over the expected life of a project and that £100 due today is worth more than £100 due in a year's time.
> 2 Investment decisions and taxation can be taken fully into account.'[9]

This helps us to resolve a number of difficulties. We can now choose between two projects, *A* and *B*, which cost the same (£100) and yield incomes that sum to an identical total but with a different *time profile*. Thus, if *A* gives in three years £50, £50, and £50, and *B* gives £100, £25, and £25 we clearly choose *B*. Furthermore, we may even be well advised to choose a project that yields a smaller sum in total if its time profile is favourable: at most discount rates we would have chosen *B* even if it had promised £100, £25, and £23.

A further example of the generality of the idea is that a section of the M4 motorway in Berkshire is to be widened from two to three lanes. Indignant writers to local newspapers claim that it would have been 'cheaper' to build it as a three-lane motorway in the first place. In financial terms, of course, they are quite right. In real terms there is room for doubt.

The problem must be formulated in the following manner: which resource-use gives the greater benefit: a two-lane motorway plus some other asset, say another road elsewhere, at time *n* with a third lane added at time *m*, or a three-lane motorway at time *n* plus the other asset at time *m*? Given that the third lane would not be much used from t_n to t_m, the two-lane motorway is at least worth consideration especially once we admit the idea of discounting.[10] The letter-writers may be correct in their conclusion but they have advanced a wrong reason in looking to naive financial cost.

Another illustration is that it is sometimes suggested that regional policy leads to the re-allocation of resources to inefficient areas, thus foregoing faster growth in the economy as a whole, in favour of resolving unemployment in particular regions. This is probably a reasonable way to put the choice but it is more correct to note that the costs (in growth foregone) are promised in the future. It is not, therefore, a valid attack on regional policy to say that the benefits foregone exceed the benefits gained on a simple undiscounted measurement. It is a matter of simple observation that "$£100_t = £107_{t+1}$" for most people. We have not here offered any rationale of why goods today are preferred to the same goods tomorrow.

Our next concern is not with the grave practical problems of the proper calculating procedures and the modifications necessiated by tax changes[11] but with a conceptual problem that still remains. So far our point has been that an asset is only worth buying if its income exceeds its cost and to make such a comparison we must discount all benefits and costs to comparable, that is present, values. However, there are two possible ways of doing this—the present value approach and the internal rate of return. We must clarify the conceptual differences by resorting to definitions, then illustrate two practical difficulties and then comment on the two different techniques from an economist's point of view.

The present value criterion selects those investments where the sum of all revenue less all costs, each adjusted for futurity by the use of a discount rate, is positive. The *internal rate of return* chooses those investments where the rate of discount that makes the present value of all revenues, less all costs, equal to zero is higher than the appropriate interest rate. These two would come to the same thing in a world with a perfectly competitive capital market and perfect competition in all other markets. *And even in the real world they can come to the same thing.*

The discounted P.V. of an asset will normally decline as the interest rate rises so that Fig. 1 shows a negatively sloped relationship between D.P.V. and i.

The internal rate of return (*m.e.c.*) is the interest rate where the function (*VV*) cuts the horizontal axis, for, by definition, it reduces the D.P.V. of the investment to the D.P.V. of its costs, so that its net yield must be zero. To find the actual D.P.V. we need the firms' discount-rate, say i_{11}, which gives a positive value to D.P.V. of

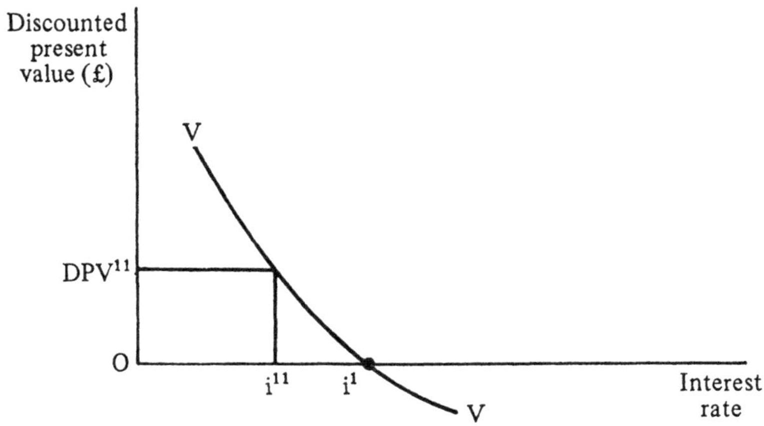

Figure 1

D.P.V.^{11}. The internal rate of return selects this investment because *m.e.c.* exceeds *i*, ($i^{I} > i^{II}$) and so does the D.P.V. technique because the D.P.V. is positive (D.P.V.$^{11} > 0$). But our two criteria are not always mutually consistent.

First, our D.P.V. frontier need not be negatively sloped. A particular asset might earn losses in its early and later years and positive returns in between. If discounted at a high rate, the early losses will be the only appreciable figures and the yield will be negative. If discounted at an intermediate rate, the middle life profits will now have an appreciable magnitude so that the return is positive, while at a lower discount rate the latter years' losses will still have a significant magnitude so that again the project shows a loss. Fig. 2 represents this switch-back effect with a given project giving losses at low and high rates and positive returns at intermediate rates of discount.

This process could be continued as in the broken line section.

There are now two difficulties, the internal rate of return approach is ambiguous giving dual solutions. The internal rate of return is either i_2 or i_{III}.

Second, D.P.V. and internal rate of return are now inconsistent. If the current interest rate is i_{111} then the D.P.V. is positive and the asset should be obtained. But the internal rate of return accepts if *m.e.c.* $> i$. But if *m.e.c.* $= i_1$, then the asset is rejected ($i_{111} > i_1$) while if it $= i_{111}$, then the project is accepted ($i_{11} > i_{111}$).[12]

A second inconsistency is generated when a choice must be made between two mutually exclusive projects. Road and rail transport

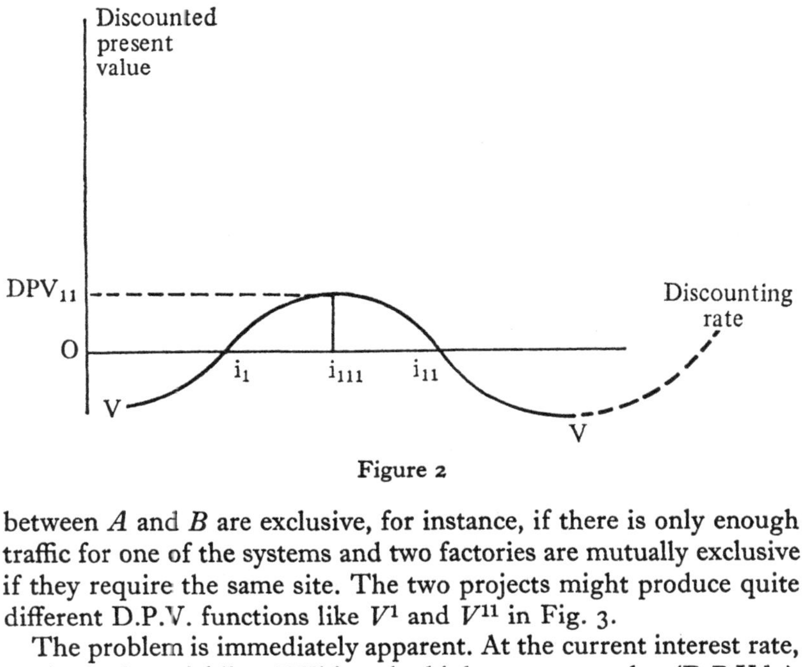

Figure 2

between *A* and *B* are exclusive, for instance, if there is only enough traffic for one of the systems and two factories are mutually exclusive if they require the same site. The two projects might produce quite different D.P.V. functions like V^1 and V^{11} in Fig. 3.

The problem is immediately apparent. At the current interest rate, i_t, the project yielding VV' has the higher present value (D.P.V.^{1} > D.P.V.^{II}) but it has the lower *m.e.c.* ($i^{11} < i^{111}$)!

Once our criteria are inconsistent we need to choose between them. The economist can only offer consistency between ends and means. If we care about futurity, then we choose D.P.V. as our technique, as only it calls for a discount rate representing our relative evaluation of present and future gains and losses. If we care about time profile, then our maximand is a present value and D.P.V. is our criterion. If there is no preference between consumption at different points in

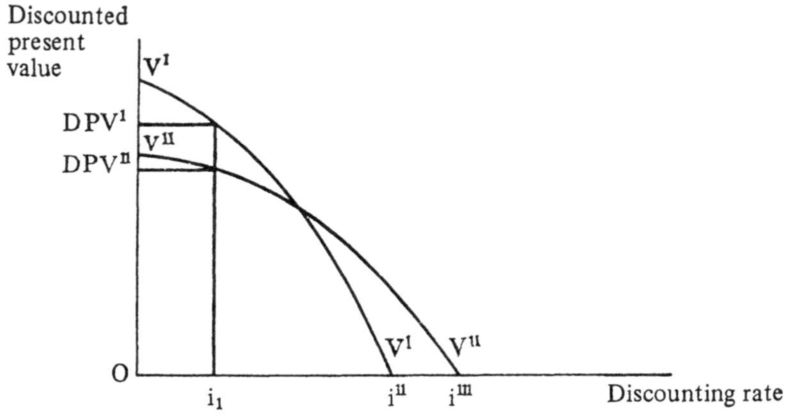

Figure 3

time but, instead, a wish to maximise the stock of assets at the end of the time horizon, independent of timing, then the internal rate of return is our criterion. If our maximand is simply a stock of assets then *m.e.c.* is the consistent criterion. Most people probably do care about the time profile of consumption but Stalinist five-year plans are probably examples of a desire to maximise the total of assets, quite independently of their time pattern. But that is a different matter. The economist tries to offer consistency between ends and means; not choices between ends.

Input-output analysis is a technique which also offers information that helps in policy decisions. It is a specification, or description, of the inputs needed for production of a given output. It can be expanded to include the interrelationships between many products and many inputs. It is, thus, one of the ways in which we can hope to disaggregate the Keynesian model; we have already seen that operating on aggregate variables can lead us into difficulties. There is not, for instance, some point before which an increase in *C*, *I* or *G* always falls on idle resources, and so mitigates unemployment, and after which it falls on employed resources and so generates inflation. There is, in fact, an awkward zone in which there is both real and monetary adjustment. Our problem is to know which injection falls on unemployed resources and which on employed. To do this we must know what are the inputs of industry *Y*, and of industry *Z*, and which are unemployed. This kind of thinking leads, among other things, to regional policy, special tax arrangements for Research and Development and special credit for shipbuilding; because it is felt national stimulation may fall on fully employed resources, general tax incentives will fall on all manner of company activities besides *R* and *D* and easier credit will stimulate industry in general into inflationary expansion.

A second need for disaggregation lies in the tendency for an increase in investment to increase imports. The government wishes to encourage investment for purposes of growth and maintaining employment; if it is to do this without increasing imports it needs to know which investment industries call for more imports than others. Input-output analysis is such a source of information.

There are many ways, such as an algebraic production function, of showing the use of resources and their intermediate relationships. Input-output analysis makes use of a matrix. This is simply a superimposition of vertical columns on horizontal rows so producing a square of cells as below.

Input-Output Matrix

Output industries		*A*	*B*	*C*	*D*	*Z*	*Total*
Input industry	*A*	75	327	1	65	51	1,000
Contributions	*B*	42	72	54	75	107	800
to industries in	*C*	39	107	—	108	634	900
Columns	*D*	76	428	102	27	715	2,000
	Z	83	3	39	523	3	800
TOTALS		1,000	800	900	2,000	1,000	10,000

This kind of device has a number of uses in micro-economics theory which need not delay us; we will give an example in the field of macro-economic planning. If industry *A* wishes to expand its output by £1,000 then it needs an increase of £75 from itself (there is nothing odd here, machine tools are used in the machine tool industry and so on), £42 of output from the *B* industry, £39 from the *C* industry and so on. But for the *B* industry to expand significant calls must be made on the *D* industry, and so on. Do industries *B*, *C* and *D* make calls on imports? Are the domestic inputs already fully employed and where are they located? In such a way the government can start to trace out the implications of expanding industry *A*—for whatever initial reason—and this puts us in a more informed position to choose between expanding industry *A* and some other.

Like most economic models, input-output tables can vary from one to another: each is designed for its own purpose. If the digits in the cells, for instance, are inverse co-efficients then they tell us not that an output of £1,000 from *B* needs £327 from *A* and £107 from *C*. This is quite a different matter. Every £1,000 of aluminium may call for a high proportion of that expenditure on electricity (say $\frac{1}{5}$); this is not at all to say that the same proportion of electricity output goes to the aluminium industry. Conventional input-output co-efficients tell us the importance of the industry in the row to that in the column; inverse co-efficients tell us the reverse.

Such analysis is helpful in the problems indicated, and in identifying bottlenecks in the production flow, and in pointing to mutually exclusive choices (in the short run). An increase in industry *A* (cars) makes calls on *B* (tyres) which calls on industry *C* (petro-chemicals) which calls on *D* (steel). But steel is also needed for the cars. We begin to know whether the projected increase in cars is compatible with the production ability of the steel industry to feed it and its component industries. If the totals do not exceed the production ability of the steel industry itself, it is feasible. If the steel industry is fully employed, then we can look to its other customers to see who can go without in order to increase the car production. And so we begin to know the opportunity cost of the increase in car production and begin to formulate informed priorities about investment programmes for the long run.

Input-output analysis is thus a powerful but simple tool of analysis. There are difficulties, however, for it tends to be inflexible. Firstly, it assumes that products are homogeneous in their nature and in their demand for inputs. A proud car-owner will deny the first and in a world of varying farm fertility it is just not true that a bushel of wheat always needs the same amount of land. The input-output tables fail to tell us that we can escape from some of these strictures by varying the quality of the car, its size and its speed or the quality of the steel. And the industry at present using steel, which is to be denied it, may be able to maintain production by using another metal altogether. If this other component industry is not in full production then the problem is solved. The opportunity cost of extra cars was not a smaller quantity of something else but a change in the form of something else.

Input-output tables also assume fixed production co-efficients that are independent of scale. That is they deny scale economies and claim that a larger scale of output needs the same proportion of all inputs as a smaller one. This is plainly not true. They are only reliable, therefore, if we are taking fairly modest changes in output, say 20%–30%, according to circumstance. They are of little help if we are talking of doubling output.

A further difficulty lies in identifying the product with the industry. A table giving details of the aerospace industry may be misleading about the difficulties of expanding aircraft production unless it shows the significance this now has in the aerospace industry.

These difficulties are not a reason for setting this sort of analysis aside—they are urgent reasons for using it carefully. We are not yet so lucky that we can refuse help. This kind of input-output and inter-industry economics is quite common so that most countries have some form of input-output table. They are available in the U.S., U.K., Germany, France, Japan, Italy, Norway, Spain, Argentina, among others.[13]

Notes

1 Denton, G., Forsyth, M. and Maclennan, M., *Economic Planning and Policies in Britain, France and Germany*, Allen and Unwin for P.E.P. (1968), and Mitchell, J., *Groundwork to Economic Planning*, Secker and Warburg (1966).

2 This is true of positive economics; normative economics can be concerned with the wider range of interesting questions concerning what ought to be done.

3 Cohen, K. J. and Cyert, R. M., *Theory of the Firm*, Prentice-Hall (1965).

4 This point could easily be exaggerated, some encouraging results have been obtained.

5 We have already seen that a multiplier which assumes lagged responses is more appropriate to the United Kingdom economy than one that does not. See Chapter 6.

6 Feldstein, M. S., 'The Social Time Preference Discount Rate in Cost Benefit Analysis', *Economic Journal*, LXXIV, p. 361 (June 1964).

7 Its chief advocate in the U.K. has been Alfred, A. M.; Turvey, R. is largely responsible for its adoption by the public section, v. Essay by Peston, M. H., in *Public Sector Economics*, (Ed.) Prest, A. R., p. 129, Manchester U.P. (1968).

8 e.g. Dean, J., *Managerial Economics*, Chapter 10, Prentice-Hall (1951).

9 N.E.D.C., *Investment Appraisal*, p. 3, H.M.S.O. (1967).

10 The authors have no knowledge that this was the approach behind the two-lane decision. It may have been in fact based on traffic estimates that predicted no need for a third lane, as is suggested by the fact that the bridges are not easily widened for a third lane.

11 See Alfred, A. M. and Evans, J. B., *Discounted Cash Flow*, Chapman and Hall (1965) and N.E.D.C., *Investment Appraisal*, H.M.S.O. (1967).

12 The appropriate interest rate will differ from case to case as there is no perfect capital market. The interest rate at which a firm borrows could be considered as the average of its various debentures and loans or as the interest rate for the marginal project under consideration. Attention should also be given to the future costs

of the changes in gearing. Merret, A. J. and Sykes, C., *Finance and Analysis of Capital Projects*, Longmans (1963).

13 The best-known sources are:

Leontief, W. W., *The Structure of American Economy 1919–39*, Oxford University Press (2nd edit.) (1951).

Leontief, W. W., *Studies in the Structure of the American Economy*, Oxford University Press (1953).

Chenery, H. B. and Clark, P. G., *Interindustry Economics*, J. Wiley and Sons (1959).

Stone, R. (Ed.), *Programme for Growth*, Vol. 3, Chapman and Hall (1966).

Bibliography

BARKER, T. S. and LECOMBE, R. J. R. C., *Economic Planning for 1972: An Appraisal of 'The Task Ahead'*, P.E.P., 1969.

SHONFIELD, A., *Modern Capitalism*, O.U.P. paperback, 1969.

WRIGHT, M. G., *Discounted Cash Flow*, McGraw-Hill, 1967.

Chapter 8

THE NATIONALISED INDUSTRIES: GOVERNMENT OWNERSHIP OF THE FACTORS OF PRODUCTION

This chapter deals with some of the economic problems of the nationalised industries; such industries present problems which are important both because they are quantitatively significant in the economy, for decisions taken within these industries can have far-reaching effects outside of them, and because they are the most highly developed form of government intervention in the economy.

> 'The nationalised industries are of the greatest importance to the economy. Their net assets are valued at £9,500,000,000 and they invest annually around £1,300,000,000 a year over half of which is financed by the Exchequer. In comparative terms their annual investment is equivalent to the whole of that of manufacturing industries; they contribute about 10% of the gross domestic product and they employ around 7% of the total labour force. In Exchequer terms a decline of only 1% in the earning power of the industries as a whole means an increased £90,000,000 per annum to be found by taxation or exchequer borrowing—approximately 6d. on the standard rate of income tax.'[1]

The government influences a great many industries, but in the case of the nationalised industries it completely controls them; the government finances, to some extent, many industries but in the case of the nationalised industries it is wholly reponsible for their finances. They are, therefore, inviting to the interest and expertise of economists who have, as a whole, not been slow in taking the opportunity. As might be expected their endeavours have been attended by some false claims but the intervention of economists in these problems had had its advantages. These problems are politically controversial and intellectually difficult but some progress has been made in separating the normative from the positive and, also, in formulating the principles of welfare economics into appropriate questions. In recent years, although difficulties remain, there is at least as much light as there is heat.

The term 'nationalised industry' can cover many forms of public enterprise from a deliberately created national authority to a quite local body started on the initiative of a local authority. Economists, as such, have very little to say about what is the proper form for a nationalised authority; we need only note that such bodies may be deliberately created by Act of Parliament, like B.O.A.C., or may be in the form of government holdings of the shares of a joint stock company, like B.P., or, again, may be in the form of a government ministry, like the G.P.O.[2] It may be of great importance to lawyers, sociologists or political theorists, what form nationalised authorities take; the economist need not be embarrassed by his professional agnosticism on these points[3] but instead, comforted by the wide applicability of the economic principles which have now been developed.

These principles seem to apply equally whatever form the public authority takes. The different ways in which they are applied follow from the political constraints, not from any limited nature on the part of economic principles. For our purpose, a nationalised authority is a body which has a private existence, but public responsibilities, thus distinguishing itself from joint stock companies, which are private bodies with private responsibilities to their shareholders, and from government ministries, which are public bodies with public responsibilities. The most common form for the nationalised industry is now the public corporation, so that it does seem that uniformity is now coming to their legal nature; there is uniformity too in the relevant economic principles, which hold good whether we are discussing a nationalised corporation, a government department engaging in commercial activity,[4] or a public library run by a town council.

The major economic problems of nationalised industries concern their investment programmes and their pricing policies.[5] Although it is convenient to separate these two for pedagogic purposes, they are in fact interdependent since a different attitude can be taken to a proposed investment if a different pricing policy is considered for the goods or services generated by the programme. Apart from detailed discussions of these two problems, the economist also has something to contribute in getting the nationalised body to frame its questions in the best manner. This means carefully identifying the organisation's goals so that any conflict between its public responsibilities and, for instance, its commercial desire to gain a profit is quite clearly seen. It is then the responsibility of the government to clarify to the nationalised industry just what is to be maximised and to identify the constraints within which it has to operate. The government must decide what is its maximand; whether it wishes to maximise conventional profits, output, employment level or whatever and within what constraints—which might be a given share of the nation's revenues, a given demand on imports or whatever.

At first glance, the investment principles relevant to nationalised industries seem quite clear. Capital must be allocated between alternative uses so that the marginal return in each use is equal, otherwise it is possible to re-allocate the given investment, that is without changing real opportunity costs, to advantage. Clearly, if the last million pounds spent in one coalfield gave a return of 7% and the last million in another gave a return of 5%, investment should be increased in the first by withdrawing it from the second thus reducing the incremental return in the first coalfield, while in the second, from which investment resources have been removed, the incremental return is increased until the returns are equal in both cases. Now this so-called optimality rule is a very useful basic guide but in fact it is impossible to apply it in a general fashion. The first reason for this is that no uniform cut-off rate is, in fact, available because it is impossible to measure the returns from some forms of government investment. There is no measurable return from, for instance, investment in police stations, to be compared with, for instance, the return from investment in motorways. This means that the optimality rule, which would give marvellous results if applicable, has in fact to give way to a more rule of thumb approach. Second, the government has to resort to sub-optimisation; this means that, on largely political considerations, it decides on the size of budgets which are available for the various government ministries because there is no reliable scientific way in which the government can compare the amount of resources it should devote to transport with the amount it should devote to scientific research. Once these budgets have been decided, it does then become possible to apply the optimality rule in most cases. The government can thus allocate parts of its transport budget between different claims thereon, but it is at a loss when trying to decide on scientific principles what total sum should be allocated to transport.

We will have to resort to this approach so long as there is no way of quantifying the returns from some government activities such as the building of police stations, or sewage works, and while administrative talent is limited so that it is impracticable to centralise all decisions. The transport ministry will have to continue to allocate sums in given budgets to particular activities, say railways and roads, just as the managers of departments within companies have to work to budgets which constrain the policy options open to them. Any evidence that there is a higher incremental return from expenditure on advertising than on production is irrelevant to the operation of a given budget, but relevant to the size of future budgets.

It is now possible to bring together two problems which we have come across in earlier chapters. Most of the difficulties of investment in nationalised industries, and to a lesser extent those of pricing policy, originate from the inefficiency of money as a measuring device. Micro-economics makes it quite clear, first, that, in normal circumstances, the money prices are bogus measures of the true costs. Investment analysis makes it clear that, second, not only will money prices seldom represent opportunity costs, but also a given money price itself represents quite different values, either as costs or benefits, at different moments of time. The fact that we do care about futurity, the time profile of costs and benefits, necessitates the discounted cash flow approach. Only this method recognises that a given sum of money has a different value according to the time at which it is gained and spent. A sum of money cannot be given a value independently of its temporal characteristic.

Both these problems become manifest in the case of nationalised industries. The managers of nationalised industries need to use the present value approach to their investment decisions but they face different problems to their colleagues in the private sectors. This is because they have public reponsibilities rather than private ones and, therefore, they are obliged to identify not only those costs for which they are commercially responsible, that is those costs to which they can be held in court, but also the true opportunity costs of production and these may be quite different from the money costs. There is a parallel problem in the case of valuing the production of nationalised industries; in appraising the value of particular investment projects they must address themselves not only to the charges they can make for the goods and services produced, but also to any other benefits produced for which no charge can, in fact, be made. These obligations are forced upon them by the nature of public enterprise; they are difficult to execute because of the inefficiency of the price mechanism in attaching money prices to either costs or benefits.

> 'Significantly costs and benefits can occur which are outside the financial concern of the industry and it is the special responsibility of the government to ensure that these social factors are reflected in the industry's planning.'[6]

Most of these costs and benefits will be externalities—air pollution, noise-levels, scenic effects, changed traffic patterns and so on.

This whole problem is conveniently recognised once it is realised that to demonstrate that something is commercially unprofitable is not *the same as demonstrating that it is uneconomic.* This can be because the money prices may grossly exaggerate the real costs which are always opportunity costs rather than the money prices, and because the total revenue is not always an accurate measure of the total benefit produced by the public enterprise. Private enterprise, quite properly, addresses itself to money costs and money benefits, since these are the ones for which they are legally responsible, and it is the difference between these which can represent any profit at the disposal of the shareholders. Conventional book-keeping is designed to keep a proper record of the money flows into and out of the firm, to meet the obligations laid down by the Companies Acts, to safeguard the shareholders' interests and to identify and correctly measure their profits. It is, however, quite inappropriate to apply the same techniques and the same criteria to public enterprise; concern is now with what is economically worth while rather than with what is commercially worth while and these two are seldom the same thing. Those critics of the nationalised industries who point to the losses sometimes made by them are in fact using quite misleading criteria; it is as if one were to apply the rules of Latin grammar to the construction of an English sentence. These comments must not be construed, however, as an attack on conventional accountancy or book-keeping; these techniques are appropriate to a particular set of problems and questions, the point is that the problems and policies of nationalised industries need their own techniques.

To take a well-known example, the building of the Victoria Line in the London Underground system will result in a severe book-keeping loss, but, nevertheless, this information is wholly irrelevant in deciding whether or not to go ahead with this project.[7] The London Transport Executive need only concentrate on two problems; first, do the economic benefits outweigh the economic costs, second, if this is so, does the rate of return on this investment exceed the rates of return on an alternative investment available. The difference between the investment criteria for public enterprise and for private enterprise is that both need to use a discounted cash flow approach but public enterprise needs to discount not only the money costs and the money benefits but all economic costs and all benefits.

Cost benefit analysis answers these problems; it has the conventional approach of investment analysis in insisting on a present value technique but, in addition, it seeks to measure true costs and true benefits.

In cameo this is the argument: private costs and benefits are a subset of social costs and benefits and since nationalised industries are concerned with maximising social benefit they must refer to the whole set of costs and benefits. A surplus or deficit in the private subset *carries no implications whatsoever* that there is a similar surplus or deficit in the social calculus. Thus the Victoria Line runs at a commercial loss but at a social surplus, while the Concorde may fly at a commercial profit but at a social loss.

It soon becomes apparent that the techniques of cost-benefit analysis are based wholly upon economic principles. There are six quite separate sets of problems; firstly, all the costs and benefits must be identified, second they must be measured, third an appropriate interest rate must be chosen, fourth any constraints must be acknowledged, fifth, it is necessary to select some appropriate investment criterion, and sixth, some account must be taken of uncertainty.

1 The *identification* of the costs and benefits brings three problems. The first is a matter of definition; costs are defined as the time stream of consumption foregone, both immediate consumption and future consumption from alternative investments foregone, while benefits are defined as the time stream of benefits generated.

A second important and practical problem is that the scope of the project should be explicitly defined. This brings us to a further reason why cut-off rates are inapplicable in viewing the total government investment programme. Most investment programmes are not open to a marginal analysis; this is because they are often in the form of indivisibilities, that is we cannot sensibly talk about building half a Channel Tunnel, it is the whole thing or nothing at all. Even in those investment programmes which are open to some incremental adjustments, in practice, only two or three of the alternative levels of investment available will be seriously investigated. So it is most important that the investment project under discussion must be clearly defined in the sense of which costs and which benefits are to be included. This may seem inconsistent with the earlier insistence on including all economic benefits and costs. However, there are good reasons for wishing to draw the line. It is sensible to look at the side effect of an investment project and it may also be sensible to look at the side effects of these first side effects; but this process can be continued almost indefinitely; it becomes necessary to acknowledge that some of these side effects although finite are so insignificant as not to justify the time and effort of calculating them, it becomes impractical to consider them. In parenthesis, cost-benefit analysis is sometimes inappropriate to a particular investment project simply because of the size of side effects; it is feasible that a large irrigation scheme in a poor, under-developed country could so change the whole spectrum of prices that its consequences are immeasurable. Thus investment appraisal is sometimes inappropriate because of the sheer size of the project and its consequences and, in other cases, the technique need not be taken too far because the consequences become too small to be seriously worthy of consideration.

An example of this latter point is that the Victoria Line calculations did not try to value any change in accidents on the Underground. In fact, accidents on the London Underground system are very few but they are frequent on the roads, so the analysis of some road improvements does include a value for the changed accident rate.

A third problem in identifying the true costs and true benefits is associated with the notion of externalities. Cost-benefit analysis confines itself to changes in the physical production possibilities, it ignores side effects on prices as these are rent effects and not opportunity costs. Thus, if houses at the terminus of the new Victoria Line changed in site value this consequence will be ignored; this is not to say that the money price change is unreal and it is not to say that the owner of the property does not benefit, it does say that society is no richer and no poorer because it owns no more and no less property than it did before the construction of the Victoria Line. All such rental effects must be excluded from a correct calculation of both the costs, such as a rental element in factor prices which disguises the true costs, and in product prices such as the changed land values above.

2 Our second main set of problems concerns the *evaluation of these costs and benefits* once they are properly identified. The first point is that the relevant prices are comparable prices and this in fact means constant prices; it is normal to choose present prices. This is a further manifestation of the fact that a given sum of money represents a different amount of welfare at different moments in time. Thus it would be silly to value an investment which gave a return of £100 in each of the first two years of its life and £200 in the third and final year of its life at £400. It would be even sillier to justify the investment because the cost, incurred before the start of year one, was less than £400. It is also necessary to use constant prices in order to obviate the difficulties of inflation.

Second, prices which have been derived in imperfect markets, whether factor markets or product markets, are irrelevant to the investment decision as they give a false guide to the cost of production or the value of output. Thus, if 100 building workers are attracted to the Victoria Line, and they are paid £40 per week, it is ludicrous to suggest that the opportunity cost of the Victoria Line is £4,000 worth of council houses foregone per week. If they were previously paid £20 per week then £2,000 worth of council houses are foregone per week, the difference being a rental effect on the factor price of building workers.

Third, taxes and subsidies distort money prices and we are concerned not with money prices but with opportunity costs and true benefits so they too must be allowed for. Thus, if a motorway reduced the amount of petrol used in a journey from *A* to *B* this is indeed a benefit, but it is absurd to multiply the number of gallons saved by the current market price of petrol and to conclude that that is the value of this particular benefit. The community has saved so many gallons of petrol and these must be valued at their opportunity costs, that is less any tax. A similar argument applies if petrol is an input. The opposite would be true of any particular project which lessened the use of a subsidised factor.

A fourth point is that if the factors of production would otherwise be unemployed then the opportunity cost of their use in the investment project is, in fact, zero so that it would be quite inappropriate to include wages, rent or interest paid to factors of production otherwise out of work. In such cases, the true opportunity cost is zero and this must be quite explicit in any decision to invest or not. Just as the existence of unemployment tends to lead to an overstatement of the social cost of an input so, also, the existence of the multiplier can easily lead to an underestimate of the benefit gained from a particular project. It would, however, be really difficult to calculate all the consequent changes in employment, output and income generated by the multiplier process from one original investment so that, in fact, the normal procedure is simply to take into account the immediately consequent changes in investment in employment and output. This is justifiable in practice rather than in principle.

A fifth difficulty occurs with the case of collective goods. These have no market price, as is the case with roads or with street lighting. Whether these are used as inputs, or are in fact the outputs of the particular investment project, it becomes exceedingly difficult to attach to them any money value at all, quite apart from the problem of whether it correctly measures the cost or benefit. It is, however, clear that in discovering the total demand for a collective good, the appropriate thing is to add together the individual demand curves for the product vertically, rather than horizontally, in order to discover the market demand curve. In finding the market-demand curve for a conventional good, it is correct to sum the individual demand curves for that good at different prices horizontally in order to discover the market demand curve at the different prices. If, however, this were done for a collective good, such as the Forth Bridge, it would lead to the conclusion that the community required thousands of Forth Bridges at 2s. 6d. each, when in fact it requires one Forth Bridge which can be crossed for a toll of 2s. 6d. thousands of times.

A sixth and final difficulty concerns any intangible effects of an investment project such as scenic effects, deleterious or otherwise. There is seldom a reliable way of putting any value on these, whether they be costs or benefits; usually it is possible only to acknowledge that they do exist and take this into account in a marginal decision. Any such decision would, of course, be unscientific; one example of a possible quantification is the sound-proofing on buildings necessitated by an airport project. No quantification is obvious in a case such as the scenic effects caused by the Albert Memorial, nor even whether it is a cost or a benefit. Most such social investments are costs to the generation that builds them and benefits to succeeding generations. The Albert Memorial would appear to be the reverse case.

It is worth noting at this point that when the money price of an input does not show its true opportunity cost either because of market imperfections, or taxes and subsidies, or because it would otherwise be unemployed, then the economist must seek some money price which he can write down in his cost-benefit analysis which does correctly represent the opportunity costs. Such prices are called shadow prices and they normally correspond to the marginal cost. In this way the economist hopes to manœuvre his way out of the difficulties presented by the non-optimal operation of a free-market mechanism.

3 After considering the problems of identifying and measuring costs and benefits in their correct fashion, attention must now be turned to *the choice of an interest rate at which these costs and benefits must be discounted.* It has already been seen in Chapter 7 that, because of our concern with futurity, all future sums of money, whether costs or benefits, must be discounted to present values; and furthermore that the appropriate method is to resort to present values rather than the internal rate of return.

However, additional difficulties arise once we seek the rate of discount appropriate to the community as a whole. The conventional textbook account asserts that an investment programme is optimalised when true costs, in the form of consumption foregone over a period of time and expressed in present values, are less than or equal to the true benefits, in the form of a new time stream of consumption goods also expressed in present values. It asserts that an investor will consider the time stream of consumption available to him if he does not make any investment at all and compare that with the time streams of consumption available to him from the alternative investments under consideration; he chooses those investments where the value of the consumption time stream exceeds that of allocating resources to consumption rather than investment. This is formally correct but it is not always useful for the investment programmes of nationalised industries. We would need a single interest rate that measured the social rate of time discount and also the productivity of capital. It is now recognised that, in a mixed economy, with market imperfections and multiple interest rates, no single discount rate can do both these things.

Two types of discount rate have been suggested: 'Social time preference' (S.T.P.) and 'social opportunity costs' (S.O.C.). A social time preference function gives current values to future consumptions; it is a normative function reflecting society's evaluation of the relevant desirability of consumption of different points of time. The social opportunity cost is a measure of the value to society of the next best alternative use to which funds employed within a public project might otherwise have been put. In a perfectly competitive world the opportunity cost of these funds could be represented by the market interest rate; *but in our economy no single interest rate of return can fully measure the* S.O.C. *of funds*. The search for a 'perfect' formula to describe S.T.P. is doomed to failure—it has to be normative, taking account of social and public policy.

Classical theory considers the interest rate to be a price induced by the productivity of capital and required as payment for postponing consumption. Although the emphasis of economic theories has shifted from this idea, that the interest rate brings into equilibrium real savings and investment schedules, to the loanable funds and liquidity preference theories which emphasise the non-real, monetary nature of interest rate determination; policy-orientated discussions of the role of the interest rate must avoid the notion that the interest rate in a perfectly competitive market would correctly measure opportunity costs, equate the social productivity of capital and social time preference and yield a Paretian optimum.

Such an interest rate might appear useful for public decisions because it would be the price that guided private investors to maximise their welfare over time. In fact this is not the case. This is because the Second Best Problem makes it clear that perfection in the capital market need not improve the community's welfare. Second, this is because to correctly optimalise future consumption it is necessary to know future income; such information is just not available. Third, the perfectly competitive capital market generates an interest rate that measures private costs and benefits and not the social ones. It is, therefore, quite inappropriate for problems of public investment.

There is yet a fourth difficulty in moving from the individual private investor, and a theory appropriate to his problems, to the problems of public investment. Let us consider two possibilities of investing £100 in which one investment repays £200 after twelve years; the other repays £25,000 after a century. Both returns are approximately 6%; a private investor might be indifferent between the two options because he could sell his investment whenever he wished; in fact, he could borrow against the future output of the project. But society as a whole cannot sell or borrow in this way; it must evaluate the alternative investment in terms of their specific time profile. If society's time-preference discount rate is more than 6%, £200 after twelve years is preferable to £25,000 after a century; if society discounts consumption by less than 6% the £25,000 is preferable. The problem arises because of the differences between private and social investment; a private investor can sell his asset to another investor but society cannot sell the Forth Bridge.

We may feel, then, by way of summary, that the interest rate, even on a perfect capital market, is inappropriate for evaluation of public investment projects. This is because of the differences between social investment and private investment and also because the Second Best Problem indicates that equating prices and marginal cost in one market, in this case the capital market, does not necessarily improve the welfare of the community.[8]

It becomes necessary to choose a rate which reflects the government's *judgement* of the relative social welfare of consumption at different moments in time. In other words, the economist has no specific scientific technique to offer which will enable the government to faultlessly distinguish between the different projects. In the end, the government is forced back on its own value-judgements; the economist can, however, fufill a useful purpose in indicating to the government when the goals of the government are inconsistent with particular techniques. If, for instance, it is the goal of the government to turn a nationalised industry at this moment making a commercial loss, into a commercially viable enterprise, then any argument about the choice of internal rate of return or present value approach becomes wholly irrelevant. Thus, if the government had to choose between two investment projects in such an industry, which had a deficit of £9 m., where project 'A' offered £10 m. in year one and £5 m. in years two and three, and project 'B' offered £6 m. in year one and £20 m. in years two and three, it would be quite inappropriate to apply either internal rate of return or present value approach to these problems. There is no problem; the government clearly chooses project 'A' simply because this project enables it to realise its goal, which is to turn the enterprise into a profit-making concern in the shortest period of time and not to compare the values of the time profile of the consumption generated over the whole life of the capital asset. In other words, a discounting approach is inappropriate if the maximand is independent of futurity; however, there can be few such cases.

Just as the S.T.P. rate itself is in fact a value-judgement so, also, what is a well-chosen S.T.P. rate for a given community at a particular moment of time, need not hold good for other moments of time. It is to be expected that the S.T.P. rate changes over time in response to changes in economic growth, the proportion of income being consumed, the rate of population expansion and the private time preference rate.

All that we can ask is that public investment decisions reflect as closely as possible the social opportunity cost of the funds used and of the real resources foregone; this is best done by using a shadow price that reflects social time preference, as near as this is known, and the productivity of funds in private investment. We will later see that something very like this is indeed practised in the United Kingdom.

4 Having seen the problem of identifying the costs and benefits and the abitrary nature of this solution, having realised the technical difficulties of correctly evaluating these costs and benefits and the arbitrary nature of any solution to the difficult problem of choosing an appropriate interest rate, discussion must now pass to the difficulties presented by the existence of *constraints upon the alternatives open to a nationalised authority*. These constraints may be physical, legal, administrative, distributional, employment or budgetary in nature. It will suffice to take the last two as examples rather than give a tedious account of each one in turn, as the principles are, in fact, uniform. An example of a budgetary constraint is the practice already noticed in another context of allocating a budget of a fixed value to a

public authority which it then has to allocate as best it sees fit. Now sometimes the public authority may be able to show that if it were allocated a greater sum it could, in fact, achieve higher returns; an example is that the L.T.E. was able to show that if it built the Victoria Line in a shorter time than was in fact used, by investing a greater volume of funds in the early years of the project, it would be able to show a greater return on capital. This was technically one of the alternatives facing the L.T.E., but, in practice, a budgetary constraint put it out of sight. This was because the government had taken a prior decision about the volume of funds to be allocated to the L.T.E. and to alternative uses over those years. An employment constraint existed when B.O.A.C. had to optimise expenditure on airliners provided employment was maintained in the British aircraft industry.

5 Following the problems of identifying and measuring costs and benefits, choosing a discount rate and recognising contraints, there is now the problem of *choosing investment criteria*. In the previous chapter we saw that the economist can only offer consistency. Given that society considers not only the magnitude of a project's return but also its time profile, the normal procedure is to select all schemes where the present values of benefit exceed the present value of costs.

6 *Our sixth problem concerns uncertainty*; we would like our investment appraisal to take note that all the costs and revenues so solemnly discounted are estimates. To the economist, 'uncertainty' is a state of affairs where information about the probability of future events is incomplete. A range of flood-control benefits can be forecast, for instance, but there may be extreme flood occurrences in the future which are not predictable from the available information on past floods.

The economist cannot offer a reliable scientific solution to these problems but only encourage awareness—an awareness that to take no action has the benefit of no resources foregone in dealing with the problem and the unknown cost of future events which hazards the project's viability in its present form. It may prove to have greater costs than benefits or it may be that it could have shown an even greater positive return if a slightly different decision had been taken.

'Risk', to the economist, is the state of affairs in which a probability distribution can be assigned, in this case, to the costs or benefits and a new stream of costs and benefits results upon which the investment decision is taken. These objective probability distributions can be built into the calculations, in an admittedly crude fashion, by using contingency allowances in the costs or benefits, or, by appraising the project's viability on an economic life shorter than its expected physical life or, again, by raising the discount rate.

In conditions of uncertainty, however, as opposed to risk, there is no guide to rational behaviour. Just as a gambler may cheerfully base his policy on guesswork, so investors may be willing to base their policy on subjective probability distributions. The economist cannot support this but, then again, he has nothing better to offer.

Cost-benefit analysis clearly carries a number of grave difficulties, but its great advantage is that it is often a practical proposition, that it forces us to ask sensible questions and that it forces us to face the problem of quantification from which public authorities were long able to escape on the plea that no suitable methods were available. Any summary of the importance of cost-benefit analysis has to start by seeing it as essentially a practical technique; it will not maximise the community's welfare or in any way take us to the constrained bliss point. It is designed to give answers, which, while not perfect, are operational and reliable to important questions of fact. Second, it should be remembered that it is inappropriate for very large investment decisions relative to the economy and that it does not measure at the margin small changes in costs or benefits. Third, it forces us to recognise that we must make a value-judgement over the interest rate at which we choose to discount costs and benefits in our investment appraisals. It is better to know that the economist operates within a political environment than to delude ourselves otherwise. It is even better, once this is recognised, to make sensible policy decisions within the rules laid down by the government on behalf of the public. The matters are in perspective when the results of cost-benefit analysis are seen as sensible approximations upon which policies can be based; it is out of perspective if it is seen as an academic toy or as a way to optimal resource-use.

Cost-benefit analysis stands in much the same position as medical science to witch-doctoring. Cost-benefit analysis does not give us perfect answers to investment any more than doctors can give us all the answers to medical problems. It does offer workable answers in the place of ignorance and mysticism and, above all, it forces us to ask the right questions.

One final point remains to be made; there is a great *theoretical* difficulty in cost-benefit analysis in that when a money value is attached to the benefit from some capital project, say £1 m., and a money value is attached to the costs, say £900,000, we are in fact assuming that these sums of money represent the same things to the losers and the gainers under the project. It is one thing to escape from ambiguities of money as a measuring device, by using shadow prices as accurate measure of opportunity costs and present values to escape from the inadequacy of money in measuring value over a period of time; it is quite another to pretend that a given sum of money, of whatever size, represents the same amount of welfare to different people. It cannot be scientifically proved that this is nonsense but it certainly cannot be shown that it is correct; on the whole, by reference to introspection, most people think that a given sum of money represents a different volume of welfare according to the person who has that sum of money. The features which would lead to different people attaching different welfares to a given sum of money would be their temperament, their holdings of money, their expected future income and so on. So the great theoretical weakness of cost-benefit analysis is that it assumes a constant marginal utility of money; nevertheless, we cannot escape the grave problems of investment appraisal and cost-benefit analysis has brought a more sensible approach.

Attention must now turn to the problems involved in the *pricing policies of public authorities*. The three main pricing strategies open to a public authority are marginal costing, average costing and multi-part tariffs.

It is convenient to start with the case for marginal costing. The premise is that the community wishes to allocate its resources to the maximum advantage; it has to try this, not by looking directly at opportunity costs, but by looking at money prices, and if these money prices are to be a true guide to the opportunity costs then they must equal the marginal costs of production. Only when money prices equal marginal costs do they equal opportunity costs. We have thus a convenient rule to guide the pricing policy of public authorities; they discover the marginal cost of output and set price equal to that marginal cost and thus optimise the output level of their industry. Only in this way will the output the community demands at a given price be chosen by reference to a true measure of the opportunities open to society.

This principle has generated a great deal of hostility, some from theoreticians and some from practical men who feel that academic analysis is a waste of time, who often feel that relating price to cost encourages 'inefficiency' by not acting as a spur to reduce the level of costs.

It is important, first, to see the book-keeping consequences of marginal costing, for, given that many people are still convinced that it is the duty of a nationalised authority to run at a profit or at least to break even, these consequences have generated much of the opposition to marginal costing. They are easily illustrated in Fig. 1. If output is at Q_1 and the price is fixed equal to marginal cost at that output, then the price becomes P. But the average cost at that output is C, and thus the firm is immediately involved in losses of P, C, R, S at the output OQ_1. That is, marginal costing always leads to a deficit in falling (average) cost industries. On the other hand, in rising cost industries it always generates a surplus. If output is at Q_2, and the price is fixed equal to marginal cost at that output, then the price becomes P_2 and the enterprise is immediately earning the surplus P_2, R_2, S_2, C_1.

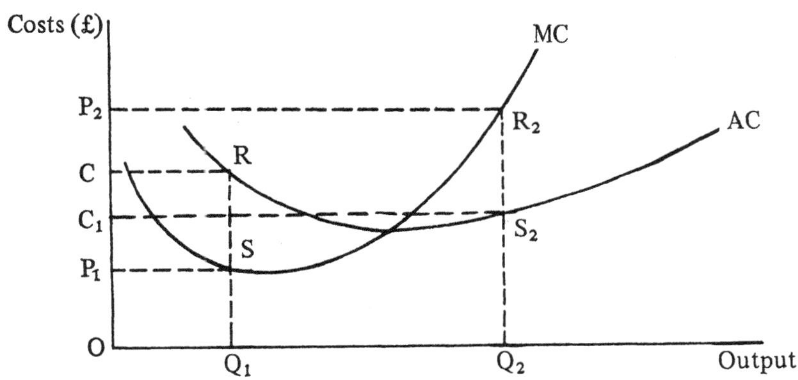

Figure 1

Our first difficulty then is that marginal costing, except for the unlikely case of an output at the nadir of the average cost curve, always involves an industry in a chronic surplus or deficit. As it happens, most nationalised industries have very large fixed costs, such as the railways, the airlines and energy industries, and, therefore, they do tend to be falling cost industries and thus, under this scheme, would be deficit industries. As far as some people are concerned this is quite sufficient to close the case against marginal costing; it always leads to a deficit in falling cost industries and some people still believe that these kinds of book-keeping profits or losses are the only appropriate ones for nationalised industries and that they are a criterion of efficiency. As we have shown they are, in fact, taking over from one sector of life a set of principles appropriate only to that sector.[9]

Average costing, on the other hand, always leads a public body to balance its books. This is a simple matter of an identity; total revenue must always be the price × output, total cost must always be average costs × output, since price = average cost and they are both multiplied by output, then total revenue and total cost must always be identical, thus an average-cost pricing body always breaks even.

There are, however, many other problems of acute interest to the theoreticians. Firstly, marginal costing only meets the necessary conditions for optimality and does not guarantee the sufficient conditions. It runs against the difficulty of the Theory of the Second Best which says that to meet necessary or, indeed, sufficient conditions in one sector of the economy does not necessarily raise the welfare of the community.

There are also serious practical difficulties of calculation; first, what account is to be taken of the passage of *time*? Clearly all costs and benefits must be expressed in present values; but there is another difficulty—many of the assets of public authorities were in fact built many years ago. Are we to consider short- or long-run costs? Is, for instance, the Gas Council seriously to include in the costs of natural gas taken from the North Sea any use made of assets which were installed thirty, forty or fifty years ago in the national network of gas pipes or office buildings which are still being used?

This brings us to the problem of *interdependence*; it is naive to calculate the marginal cost of coal extracted from a new pit in a way that ignores other assets, which are part of the system whereby coal from this new pit is finally distributed.

A further practical difficulty comes in identifying the marginal unit produced where there are *indivisibilities*. If an extra passenger is crowded on to a train there may be zero extra costs incurred so that his marginal costs, and thus his price, 'should' be zero. This is in striking contrast to another passenger for whom a whole new carriage has to be attached to the train or, for that matter, a whole new train runs; in such cases the marginal cost is the cost of running the extra coach, or train, and thus the price for that passenger would be absurdly high. Any figure produced for marginal cost must therefore involve some element of arbitrariness. Cost accountants do have sensible well-established precedents for dealing with these sort of problems but it must always be remembered that they are simply conventions and not accurate scientific measures of the marginal cost.

These kinds of difficulties have led people to heap much abuse on marginal costing principles. It must be recognised at once that these kinds of points do *not* help us at all to choose between marginal costing and average costing, for every single point could be made in exactly the same way against average costing. Though these difficulties are real they are no guide in choosing between the alternative pricing policies.

Since we can expect marginal cost pricing to generate either surpluses or deficits we immediately have a problem of cross-subsidy. Public authorities have to pay their bills and so any deficit must be made good, this is most often done from tax revenue. This means that in fact the general public is subsidising some of their members, not according to their needs for subsidy or the taxable capacity of the tax-payers, but simply according to whether or not they are customers of this particular body. This means that there are random cross subsidies between members of the community which have no basis in taxation and that a redistribution of income is taking place which may be at variance with the aims of the government. Under such a system, for instance, quite rich people using some particular railway service may be subsidised by the rest of the community who do not use that service simply because they cannot afford the fares. This is an anomalous and ironic situation.

Similarly, if there is a surplus due to marginal costing, identical problems arise; in early stages these surpluses may be allocated to investment programmes, but if they prove to be chronic in nature then eventually they must be returned to the Treasury, which means that the pricing policy of a particular industry has in fact become a taxation policy, whereby people pay for the goods or services they receive from the public authority and also pay other sums of money into the public purse without any reference to their taxable capacities. Thus, either a decreasing cost industry with its deficits or an increasing cost industry with its surpluses, involves a ludicrous system of random cross-subsidies.

When attention passes to the average costing principle similar practical problems immediately arise. Average cost pricing is the principle that 'every tub must stand on its own bottom'; that is that the activity must pay for itself, or, in another form, that each separate activity of the public body must pay for itself. Difficulties of identifying what is the true cost will, in fact, also arise in this case; there will also, as in the marginal cost case, be difficulties over whether historical or replacement costs should be used in depreciation. Thus resorting to the 'common sense' policy of average costing will solve none of our practical problems at all.

It also generates its own range of welfare problems. These too take the form of cross-subsidies; thus we might find the average cost of railway passenger transport by finding the total number of passenger miles travelled in a year, and dividing that into the total costs of operating the railway for that year, and thus finding an average cost per passenger mile and then fix all railway fares by charging a fixed price per mile. If we do this it is perfectly possible that a train crossing some remote part of Scotland or Wales with one passenger will earn a revenue of a few shillings, and operate at a loss, and it must involve cross-subsidies from passengers on the fully used lines to those on the less used lines. What is more, these cross-subsidies bear no relation at all to the passengers' need for subsidies. The subsidy occurs not because of need, and it is paid not because of ability to pay, but simply, in both cases, because of place of residence. This seems an haphazard way to run a social benefit system. Our goal must be to find prices that truly reflect costs—with exceptions for clearly recognised social reasons and for excess capacity cases.

> 'It is therefore important that, while covering overall accounting costs wherever possible, pricing policy should be devised with reference to the costs of the particular goods and services provided. Unless this is done, there is a risk of undesirable cross subsidisation and consequent misallocation of resources. The aim of the pricing policy should be such that the consumer should pay the true costs of providing the goods and services he consumes, in every case where these can be sensibly identified. There are of course some exceptions to the general rule. In some cases there would be good commercial reasons for charging prices which differ from costs. In others it may be simply practical to cost separately relatively minor operations, in a few cases, cross subsidisation will be justified by statutory requirement or by wider economic and social considerations. But—these cases apart—to cross subsidise loss-making services amounts to taxing remunerative services provided by the same undertaking, and is as objectionable as subsidising on general taxation services which have no social justification. Another reason for charging prices different from costs may arise where there is persistent spare capacity, either for relatively long periods or at certain times, places or seasons. This capacity is unlikely to be used economically unless charges adequately reflect difference between the costs of meeting additional demands where spare capacity exists and the higher costs where additional capacity has to be provided to meet demand. Thus where there is additional demand which could be met without major investment in new plant, it is desirable that prices should be reduced if this would stimulate demand—if necessary to the level where the escapable costs of particular services are just covered.'[10]

However, our great difficulty, both in marginal cost pricing and in averaging cost pricing remains the Second Best Problem. Even if, by some deft manipulation, we could ascribe a price to the product of a nationalised industry which correctly measured its cost to society, we would still be left with the problem that we would have no way of knowing whether or not this improved the world. For we no longer believe that meeting one of the optimality conditions necessarily moves us any nearer the Paretian optimum.

Apart from the possibilities of average and of marginal cost pricing a further possibility is that of discriminating monopoly; in this context this means a two or multi-part tariff. Examples currently in use in Britain are the G.P.O. telephone charges and some gas and electricity charges. The idea behind this procedure is that one part of the tariff should measure that part of the fixed costs which needed to be incurred for a particular consumer; the other part, or parts, of the tariff shall measure that part of the variable costs which were necessarily incurred on behalf of the consumer in some particular use which he made. This has the appearance of neatness and fairness; unfortunately, it is difficult to see that it solves any theoretical or practical problems whatsoever.

In practice, however, multi-part tariffs are, and are likely to be, the most common form of nationalised industry pricing.

> 'Not all costs can be allocated to specific services or activities and some industries, where the area of unallocable costs is large may find difficulty in going all the way towards a pricing structure which accurately reflects these costs of particular services while at the same time covering total costs. Two part pricing is a device commonly implied to reconcile the two objectives, and in other cases a sufficient incentive to attract customers to areas where costs are lower, might be provided in making prices proportional to the cost of the margin but at a level sufficient to cover total cost.'[11]

> 'Most targets have been expressed as a rate of return and on the undertakings assets—though other methods of expressing them are not ruled out because they allow for differing social and non-economic obligations and because they also reflect the difference of composition and valuation of the industries' assets (i.e. the fruit of both investment decisions and performance in the past), the targets are not the same for each industry. They do however, supply a framework in which the industries can consider that overall policy for pricing and borrowing. Nevertheless, although there seems to be a general agreement that targets have served a useful function

the workings of the system have been criticised. In particular, important though it is that nationalised industries should cover their costs and at a satisfactory rate of return for their investments this is not by itself sufficient to ensure that resources are used to the best advantage. In the first place it has been argued that industries (whether publicly or privately owned) with considerable monopoly power can achieve satisfactory results simply by raising their prices, whether or not they are using resources efficiently. Second, it has been argued that an industry may be able to show satisfactory results overall while continuing to provide some services below their true cost and others above cost. But if one objective is to achieve an efficient allocation of resources it may be as objectionable to subsidise big loss-making services by what amounts to a tax on consumers of other services as it would be to subsidise for the general taxation services for which there is no special justification. Third, there may be a spare capacity at certain times, places or seasons sometimes for a relatively long period; this cannot be used economically unless charges adequately reflect the difference in cost between meeting new demand where capacity exists or on higher costs where additional capacity has to be provided to meet demand.'[12]

Thus although multi-part tariffs offer no great solutions to our practical problems, they may be helpful if we wish to attract consumers at particular times (e.g. G.P.O. or British Railways off-peak tariffs) or if we wish to appropriate consumer's surplus (or, to put it more crudely, charge what the traffic will bear). The point is put in Fig. 2. This shows a market price, determined in the normal way, of P_1. But the demand function means that the unit Q_2 would have been brought for P_2 although only P_1 was paid. In other words, that unit was worth more to the consumer than was paid and this is called surplus welfare; the total welfare is the area under the demand curve, A, B, Q_1, O, and the total consumer's surplus is A, B, P_1. Now a multi-part tariff could be an attempt to assign different prices to customers according to the different costs incurred on their behalf, or, an attempt to attract custom, or an attempt to balance the costs and revenues of the entire operation (which is invalid for the reasons advanced in the Treasury memorandum) or, lastly, an attempt to relate price not to the costs attributable to a particular customer but to the welfare generated for each customer. Most such systems do not require individual prices for each customer but allocate customers into a number of groups with a different price for each group. It is doubtful if many people would share a value-judgement that monopolists should act consistently in this manner.

If we now indulge in a bird's eye view of the argument so far, we are forced to the conclusion that, once again, economics is better at asking questions than it is at answering them. However, there is not too great a need for modesty; to ask at least some of these appropriate questions is a distinct advance on the mumbo-jumbo of the layman. It is all too easy to claim that the value of economics lies in promoting a certain attitude of mind when that claim is made to people who do not have that attitude of mind.

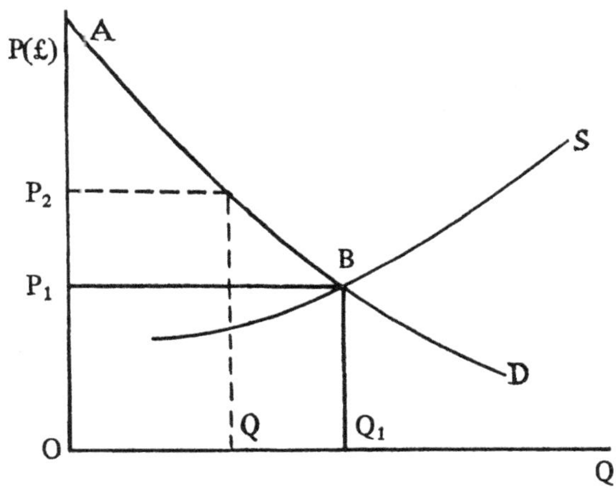

Figure 2

Turvey provides three positive contributions which the economist can make to nationalised industries and indeed to public service in general;

> 'one is forecasting, another is background economic research and a third, which may be developing into an accepted area of professional competence, is cost benefit analysis.'

When defining the work of an economist in the public service his answer is 'they sit on committees and write minutes'. However, the work is not easy:

> 'explaining the welfare economics argument for marginal cost pricing to a group of officials is quite a problem when their desire to abandon the subject grows exponentially with time, when one of them is a fervent postaliser [sic.] and the Chairman is a firm (but sub-conscious) adherent of the labour theory of value.'[13]

Whatever the principles, attention must now be given to the actual practice of nationalised industries in Britain.

The White Paper on Economic and Financial Obligation of the Nationalised Industries, 1967,[14] announced four important new principles in the operation of these industries. Firstly, all investment was to be appraised by D.C.F. principles; secondly, all nationalised industries should use the same discount rate; thirdly, this discount rate should be 8% as this is broadly consistent with the average rate of return in real terms looked for on low risk projects in the private sector in recent years.[15] Fourthly, prices need to be reasonably related to cost at the margin.

Although there might be some technical argument amongst economists about how these principles were to be applied, it is likely that the majority of economists welcome these procedures as being an important step forward in a rational approach in the running of British nationalised industries. They are also an encouraging sign of the usefulness in the real world of economic theory.

There are possibly two points which need to be emphasised. First, a figure such as 8% may be reasonable at one time and not at another. It must be emphasised that the White Paper itself makes it clear that the stated return of 8% is not expected to be the figure for all time in all circumstances; it is the figure chosen at this moment in this important change in the running of nationalised industries. The reason that 8% may be an appropriate figure, at one time and not at another, lies in the changing conditions. Alfred's example is that the comparison between nationalised industries and the private sector is based on the tax system before the introduction of corporation tax. Now that income tax and profit taxes have been replaced by corporation and dividend taxes, the sums which the private sector now has to earn in order to produce a particular return have now altered. As a result the required return for state investment to match is now 10% approximately and, if we allow an inflation of 2%, it raises the figure to nearly 11%. It is clear that (irrespective of the exact figures involved), if the private sector has to alter the gross return necessary to achieve a given net return, then the state industry too must alter its target.[16]

> 'The Treasury recommended that nationalised industries should use discounted cash flow techniques for appraising new investments. These techniques were chosen after long discussion with Departments, the industries and experts and academics in industrial circles. They enable comparisons to be made between alternative projects the receipts and outlays attributable to which

are expressed in terms of present values by the use of a rate of discount. This rate sets the minimum return to be expected from a project at a level intended to ensure as far as possible that the industries do not use resources which would be more efficiently used elsewhere. There is room for argument about precisely what the rate should be at any particular time, but it is clear that all the industries using the same methods of appraisal should adopt the same test rate.

'. . . Some nationalised industries have been using for some time the discounting cash flow techniques at a test rate of around 8%, following discussions about the applications of these methods to the particular circumstances of individual industries, the Treasury recommends that nationalised industries use a common test rate of 8%, which it considers to be right at the present time in view of the economic considerations in the economy as a whole.'[17]

A further possible qualification is the decision to calculate the returns of the state industries on a non-tax basis. Now the purpose of taxation is not simply to gather revenue: it is also to discriminate between, for instance, different locations. If state investment is on a non-taxed basis, then the nationalised industries are insulated from the effects of this taxation and so the purposes of this taxation are nullified. It is seldom a good idea that the left hand does not know what the right hand is doing. It is true that the government can get over this difficulty in the case of really big investments; the sighting of a large steelworks, or an aluminium smelter, can be adjusted in order to be consistent with the government's regional policy and in this case the non-applicability of the discriminatory taxation is unimportant. However, there is no safeguard in the case of much smaller investments where the purposeful discriminatory effect of taxation policy is vitiated.

However, it would not do to return to a simple after-tax basis for the nationalised industries because of the accidental nature of tax liability. For instance, the Electricity Council have collected enough investment allowances and British Rail enough losses to mean that they have no tax liabilities. This leads to a decision on present and future costs and benefits, being influenced by past events. Since we wish to avoid the random nature of tax liability in this case, and also the nullification of tax policy in the previous one, it seems that we must resort to some criterion whereby we consider for each state industry investment project the net (after tax) return calculated on a hypothetical basis of each project subject to the same conditions as a typical profitable private industry undertaking the same project.

The problems of nationalised industries show clearly two characteristics of contemporary economics. First, one of the roles of the economist is to seek out inconsistencies between goal and techniques. Second, progress is being made, in the immediate pre-war period the economist's discussion of nationalised industries—mainly of marginal costing—seemed fit only for the ivory tower. This is much less true now.

The economist is able to show the inherent inconsistencies in an attitude to nationalised industries. On the whole—through the marginal cost-pricing rule—we seek to maximise economic welfare but this is nonsense as the application of marginal costing in one sector of the economy need not improve society's welfare at all. Second, we are not even consistent with the implications of marginal costing as we set nationalised industries profit targets instead of being willing to accept the consequent losses in falling cost industries.

Another set of difficulties arises if we seek pricing rules for the public sector which lead to a Paretian welfare maximum, for the resulting rules are complex and make great demands on information about demand functions.[18] This leads us towards a more piecemeal approach which acknowledges the (somewhat non-rational) constraints set by the government.

However, the constraints in the form of profit-targets do have purposes which—by and large—economists do not accept. First, they are seen as goals, the achievement of which will give an optimal size to the industry—and so to the allocation of scarce resources. *They just cannot do this* because allocative efficiency refers to marginal *social* costs and a given profit target can be consistent with a wide pattern of output levels, none of which need be optimal. They serve no welfare purpose at all and are positively harmful in distorting the pricing problem.

A second purpose of profit goals is to stimulate managerial efficiency. Do they fulfil this role any better than the welfare role? It is a clear defect of pricing rules that refer to average or marginal costs, that they contain no initiative to reduce costs levels per unit of output. If it could be shown that higher profit targets did lead to lower cost levels where a marginal pricing policy was followed, then such targets would have a clear role to fulfil. No such evidence is available. Thus, one of the reasons for giving nationalised industries profit targets is quite mistaken and the other is as yet unproven.

There are, thus, still as many unanswered problems in the investment and pricing policies of nationalised industries as there are solved ones.

Appendix A

NATIONALISED INDUSTRIES: FINANCIAL OBJECTIVES

Industry	*Objective*	*Period covered*
Electricity Boards (England and Wales)	Average 12·3% gross (A)	1962-3–1966-7 (E)
South of Scotland Electricity Board	Average 12·4% gross (A)	1962-3–1966-7
North of Scotland Hydro-Electric Board	(See footnote C)	
Gas Boards	Average 10·2% gross (A)	1962-3–1966-7 (E)
Post Office	8% net (B)	1963-4–1967-8
British Overseas Airways Corporation	Currently being negotiated	
British European Airways	6% net (B)	1963-4–1967-8
British Railways	Have the statutory obligation of reducing their deficit and breaking even as soon as possible	
London Transport Board	(See footnote D)	1963–7
National Coal Board	To break even after interest and depreciation, including £10 m. a year to cover the difference between depreciation at historic cost and replacement cost (F)	

A target for the British Airports Authority will be discussed shortly.

Notes

A Before interest and depreciation.

B Before interest but after depreciation.

C As an interim measure the N.S.H.E.B. agreed to apply such tariff increases as would give a similar percentage increase in revenue as the tariff increases applied by the S.S.E.B.

D L.T.B.'s objective was to earn an average balance of revenue of £4 m. a year, after interest and depreciation at historic cost. This was equivalent to 5% net. L.T.B.'s target is, however, in abeyance in view of the Board's financial position.

E The Minister of Power announced on 19th December 1966 in answer to a Parliamentary Question (O.R. Cols. 232–3) that the objectives of these two industries would continue in 1967/8.

F The N.C.B. were relieved of their objective temporarily in April 1965, but this has now been revived and will continue in 1967/8.

SOURCE *Nationalised Industries: A Review of Economic and Financial Obligations*, H.M.S.O., Cmnd. 3837, 1967.

Appendix B

A convenient example of the power of cost-benefit analysis is given below:

TABLE 2 *Estimating social benefit of constructing an underground railway in London*

	Trend assumed	*P.D.V. (6%) £ m.*	*P.D.V. (4%) £ m.*	*P.D.V. (8%) £ m.*
(A) *Costs* (other than interest charges)				
Annual working expenses	0	16·16	25·07	11·14
(B) *Traffic diverted to Victoria Line*				
(i) Underground:				
value of time saved	0	4·32		
value of comfort and convenience	ϕ	3·96		
(ii) British Railways:				
value of time saved	1½%c	2·93		
(iii) Buses:				
value of time saved	0	6·58		
(iv) Motorists:				
value of time saved	1	3·25		
value of operating costs saved	1	8·02		
(v) Pedestrians:				
time saved	1½%c	0·28		
SUB-TOTAL		29·34	45·30	20·35
(C) *Traffic not diverted to Victorial Line*				
(i) Underground:				
cost savings	0	1·72		
value of comfort and convenience	ϕ	5·72		
(ii) Buses:				
cost-savings	0	7·38		
(iii) Road-users:				
time savings	0	21·54		
Costs savings	0	8·93		
SUB-TOTAL		45·29	66·41	32·03

(D) *Generated traffic*				
OUTER AREA				
(i) Time savings	1½%c	1·37		
(ii) Fare savings	1½%c	0·90		
(iii) Other savings	1½%c	5·36		
CENTRAL AREA				
(i) Time savings	1½%c	0·80		
(ii) Fare savings	1½%c	0·41		
(iii) Other savings	1½%c	2·90		
SUB-TOTAL		11·4	18·65	7·91
(E) Terminal scrap value		0·29	0·82	0·10
(F) Total benefit (B+C+D+E)		86·16	131·8	60·39
(G) Net current benefit (F−A)		70·00	106·11	49·25
(H) Value of capital expenditure		38·81	41·14	36·68
(I) Net benefit (G−H)		31·19	64·97	12·57
(J) Social surplus rate of return		11·3	11·6	10·9

Notes

1 Present Day Values as Year 2 values discounted at rate shown at top of column.

2 Trend assumed to be 5% for fifteen years and then 2%.

3 Social Surplus rate of return as total benefits less total costs (other than interest charges) as return on capital investment averaged over whole period of construction and operation.

4 C assumed compound rate.

5 ϕ assumed to fall to 0 at end of fifty years.

6 These calculations assume a construction period of five and a half years and fifty years of operation.

SOURCE Foster, C. D. and Beesley, M. E., 'Estimating Social Benefit of Constructing an Underground Railway in London', J.R.S.S. Series A, p. 49, Vol. 126, 1963.

This table illustrates a number of important points. First, the choice of discount rate produces quite different sub-totals though, as it happens, the Social Surplus Rate of Return is always positive between 4% and 8% which was the likely range of discount rates at the time of the decision. Second, the importance of identifying all the beneficiaries is made clear: the largest group of benefits is to travellers not on the Victoria Line at all, of whom private motorists are the most significant. Thus those who benefit most from the Victoria Line cannot be directly charged as they are not using the line themselves. Third, an example is provided of the arbitrary limiting of the size of the project by the assumption of the life of the Victoria Line. Fourth, only cost benefit analysis, by identifying and measuring all costs and benefits, casts favourable light on this project; conventional book-keeping, by looking only at a subset of costs and benefits, predicts a loss on the Victoria Line of £2·14 m.p.a. and a total loss to the London Transport Executive of £3·12 m.p.a. (the last figure compares the revenues and costs for the Victoria Line itself; the second figure allows for the fact that without the Line some L.T.E. customers would have to make a longer journey and could have been charged higher fares).

Notes

1 House of Commons Select Committee on Nationalised Industries 1966–7, Minutes of Evidence, Treasury Memorandum, 440–VIII, p. 278, H.M.S.O. (1967).

2 The G.P.O. is one of the oldest nationalised industries; it took the form of a government ministry when there was little experience of any other form. It was changed into a nationalised corporation in 1969.

3 The economist can be a little more positive about the form when faced with opponents of nationalised industries who claim that they are 'inefficient' because they are 'too big'. Organisational problems of large scale production are met by most large concerns, including those privately owned, and they are susceptible to the techniques of scientific management. They are a symptom of size not of the form of ownership. Large scale production can bring opportunities for efficiency in its true sense—the input required for a unit of output.

4 e.g. the sale of government-surplus goods.

5 We are devoting our limited space to economic principles rather than the details of particular industries, the administrative structure, and so on, which has already many accounts.

6 *Nationalised Industries, A Review of Economic and Financial Objectives*, p. 4, H.M.S.O., Cmnd. 3437 (1967).

7 See Appendix B.

8 Felstein, M. S., 'The Social Time Preference Discount Rate in Cost Benefit Analysis', p. 360–79, *Economic Journal*, LXXIV (1964) is a most authoritative account of these problems.

9 The question of using price as a spur to efficiency is referred to later.

10 *Nationalised Industries: A Review of Economic and Financial Objectives*, p. 8, Cmnd. 3437 (1967).

11 *Nationalised Industries: A Review of Economic and Financial Objectives*, p. 10, Cmnd. 3437 (1967).

12 House of Commons Select Committee on Nationalised Industries 1966–7, Minutes of Evidence, Treasury Memorandum, p. 282, 440–VIII, H.M.S.O. (1967).

13 Essay in: Alexander, K. J. W., Kemp, A. C. and Rybczynski, T. M. *The Economist in Business*, Blackwell, p. 153–75.
14 H.M.S.O., Cmnd. 3477 (1967).
15 Merrett, A. J. and Sykes, A., 'Return on Equities and Fixed Interest Securities 1919–66', *District Bank Review* (June, 1966).
16 Alfred, A. M., 'The Correct Yardstick for State Investment', *District Bank Review* (June, 1968).
17 House of Commons Select Committee on Nationalised Industries 1966–7, Minutes of Evidence, Treasury Memorandum, p. 280, 440–VIII, H.M.S.O. (1967).
18 Rees, R., 'Second Best Rules for Public Enterprise Policy', Vol. XXXV, August 1968, *Economica*.

Bibliography

THEORY

PREST, A. R. and TURVEY, R., 'Cost Benefit Analysis: A Survey', *Economic Journal*, LXM, 1965 (reprinted in *Surveys of Economic Theory*, Vol. 3, Macmillan, 1966)

ECKSTEIN, O., 'A Survey of the Theory of Public Expenditure Criteria in Public Finance'; Needs, Sources and Utilisation, *National Bureau of Economic Research Conference Volume*, Princeton U.P., 1961

PEARCE, D. W. and STURMEY, S. G., 'Private and Social Costs and Benefits', *Economic Journal*, Vol. LXXVI, March 1966

TURVEY, R., 'On Divergencies between Social Cost and Private Cost', *Economica*, Vol. XXX, August 1963

BUCHANAN, J. M. and STUBBLEBINE, W. C., 'Externality', *Economica*, 1962

HENDERSON, P. D., 'Notes on Public Investment Criteria', *Bulletin of Oxford Institute of Statistics*', 1965

FELDSTEIN, M. S., 'The Social Time Preference Discount Rate in Cost Benefit Analysis', *Economic Journal*, LXXIV, 1964

TURVEY, R. (Ed.), 'Public Enterprise', *New Penguin Economics*, Penguin, 1968.

THEORY AND ANALYSIS

PREST, A. R. (Ed.), *Public Sector Economics*, Manchester Univ. Press, 1968.

HANSON, A. H., *Nationalisation: A Book of Readings*, Allen & Unwin, 1963

ROBSON, W. A., *Nationalised Industry and Public Ownership*, Allen & Unwin, 1962

White Paper *The Financial and Economic Objectives of the Nationalised Industries* (Cmnd. 1337), 1961

White Paper on Nationalised Industries: *A Review of Economic and Financial Objectives*, Cmnd. 3437, 1967.

House of Commons Select Committee on Nationalised Industries 1966–7, *Minutes of Evidence*, 441-VIII, 1967.

REID, G. L. and ALLEN, K., *Nationalised Industries*, Penguin Modern Economics, 1970

Chapter 9

GOVERNMENT INTERVENTION WITHOUT THE EXERCISE OF DAY-TO-DAY CONTROL

In this chapter we are concerned with three examples of intervention where the government has set up institutions with defined objectives, provided them with some finance, but left them to operate without any direct control. These areas of intervention are:

1 Changing the structure of industry (the Industrial Reorganisation Corporation).
2 Intervening in the capital market (the Agricultural Mortgage Corporation, the Industrial and Commercial Finance Corporation and the Finance Corporation for Industry).
3 Intervening in the provision of finance for a particular purpose (the National Research Development Corporation).
A section of the chapter is devoted to each.

Two general points need to be made at this stage. Firstly, the relative importance of the finance and the expertise which each institution offers varies with each case. Secondly, the institutions used as examples would not consider themselves part of the government 'sector' of the economy. Nevertheless, they represent intervention, in our sense, since they were created by government via legislation and were not born in the private sector.

SECTION I

CHANGING THE STRUCTURE OF INDUSTRY

The Industrial Reorganisation Corporation

The I.R.C. was created in 1966 as an organisation which certainly contrasted with, and perhaps complemented, the Monopolies and Mergers Act, 1965.[1] Basically, it consists of a Board of ten prominent business men, free from any direct government control, provided with capital of £150 m. to be used in the promotion of mergers and aid to individual companies.

> 'The Corporation may, for the purpose of promoting industrial efficiency and profitability and assisting the economy of the U.K. or any part of the U.K. . . .
> (a) Promote or assist the reorganisation or development of any industry; or
> (b) if requested so to do by the Secretary of State establish or develop, or promote or assist the establishment or development of any industrial enterprise.'[2]

The objects of the I.R.C. are to change the structure of industry; the following quotations outline the official view as to why this is necessary:

> 'British industry faces the problem of the small size of many of its production units compared with those in the United States and some other competing countries. The lowering of international tariffs . . . means the intensification of international competition. British industry must be organised so that it can not only face but take positive advantage of this competitive situation. The scale of operations is very important to competitive survival. . . .'[3]

The case for changing industrial structure rests on a belief in the ultimate necessity of having larger business units. Before discussing why it might be necessary to intervene in the market to bring about this result, we will examine critically the major arguments used in support of this belief. It must be repeated that the economic content of arguments against (a), (b) and (c) below is, as usual, general. General presumptions may be, of course, inapplicable in a particular case and the I.R.C. is designed to deal with individual cases.

1 That large firms benefit from economies of scale. In Chapter 10[4] we will mention this argument and now point out two important distinctions, firstly, between plant and firm economies; since large firms may be composed of small operating units which have already exhausted plant economies. Secondly, the distinction between real economies (where the physical input-output ratio improves) and pecuniary economies (where the physical ratio remains unchanged but inputs may be obtained at a lower price). In the latter case the benefit accrues to the firm and there is no (real) benefit to society.[5] What is not so clear is the basis for arguing that in general British industry is seriously out of line compared with other countries. As is shown by the sample below, British plants are smaller than those of

the U.S. but considerably larger than those of countries often considered to be formidable competitors.

Size of twenty largest plants, measured by employees. U.S. = 100

U.S.	100
U.K.	77
France	19
Japan	17
Italy	15
Canada	25

SOURCE Bain, J. S. *International Differences of Industrial Structure,* Yale University Press 1966, 35.

The survey covered up to thirty-four industries in each country during the early 1950's.

2 That larger firms are more effective producers of research and development output. This topic will also be dealt with in Chapter 10, which points out that there is little statistical evidence for this view. These measurements refer to the quantity of R. and D. input or output. Research also shows that large industrial research laboratories are likely to be minor sources of major inventions[6] and that the largest companies in an industry may be among the slowest to take up an innovation.[7] Nevertheless great stress is placed officially on the importance of mergers to promote technological advance.

> 'In the past technological advances have derived in part from Government investment in defence and space but this is an expensive way of getting these benefits and it does not get down to the fundamental problems—the rationalisation of key sectors of industry and the development of new ideas.'[8]

3 The National Plan emphasised that larger firms will be needed to survive against increased international competition. This argument was used before the Monopolies Commission in the G.K.N.-Birfield Merger. Analytically, this is no more than a special case of advantages from large size but it does point to the distinction between absolute size and size relative to the market. Specific international advantages from a merger, the rationalisation of the over-seas selling organisation, were a major point in the case for the B.M.C.-Leyland merger.

Next, in considering the case for an I.R.C., we must ask why it is felt necessary to intervene in the market. If *internal* growth and decline by a company is unchecked by special legislation (except for monopoly legislation) why intervene in the market in the case of *external* growth? After all, the recent increase in mergers started before the I.R.C. was born, why not let the structure of industry initiate its own changes?[9]

Intervention may be based on a belief that the market is an inefficient mechanism in this respect. If we seek to encourage the extension of control exercised by the more efficient groups of management and if we rely on the capital market to bring about this result, it is vital that the results of efficient management should be reflected in share prices. If efficient management is not shown up in this way but is obscured by other factors (e.g. speculation about future market conditions, profits inflated by monopoly) then there can be a case for 'expert' intervention. The I.R.C. emphasises good management,[10] especially since it is held that some financial combinations have not resulted in the redeployment of assets to gain advantages (a) and (c) above.[11] On the other hand, good management may mean an outstanding manager who is, by nature, a transient asset to a firm.

Financial journalism emphasises that a merger or takeover process allows shareholders to evaluate management and shift assets accordingly. A necessary condition for such an evaluation process is that the bid must be contested, since otherwise neither the information about both companies is made available, nor is a choice made. Unfortunately this is not a sufficient condition. The triumph of News Ltd over Pergamon Press for the News of the World Ltd in 1968 was an example of a case where insufficient information was available to shareholders for a rational judgement to be made. Furthermore the activities of committed merchant banks hampered and restricted the choice which was ultimately made on non-rational personal grounds anyway.

Furthermore, it can be argued that the possibility of taking-over or being taken over may lead to bad decision taking. Thus the subsequent profitability (and thus share price) of several companies taken over has fallen considerably compared with the forecasts made at the time of the merger. In other cases firms may have deliberately cut down on expenditure such as R. and D. in order to increase profitability and provide resources to be used in merger activity.

Finally, it may also be argued that due to imperfections in the market (e.g. sales protected by product differentiation, reluctance by entrepreneurs to relinquish control) the process takes too long and that a catalyst is necessary. This rests on a subjective judgement that the process is too slow. It also implies that resources are better devoted to intervention by the I.R.C. rather than, for example, more vigorous attempts to eradicate the causes of the problem.

A final feature of the I.R.C. is that it has been given criteria external to those of firms themselves. Thus it gives priority to schemes which will quickly increase exports or reduce imports. It takes regional policy into account and places particular emphasis on schemes to ameliorate unemployment caused by plant closure.

The case against intervention by I.R.C. may be summarised as:

1 That mergers, for reasons already put forward in this Chapter and Chapter 10 should not be encouraged.
2 That in addition mergers between firms in the same industry (which are likely to be the type bringing economies of scale) involve a concentration of market power and that monopoly or oligopoly market structures are undesirable (see Chapter 10, pages 222–33).
3 That it is inevitable that the I.R.C.'s work will be discriminatory. It cannot consider all possible mergers and thus some firms may have the opportunity of public funds denied to others.[12] To the economist, this may be merely a case of allocating scarce resources; to the businessman it may represent unfair competition.

We now turn to a consideration of the activities of the I.R.C., which have fallen into three main types.

The major activity so far has been the promotion of mergers and reorganisations. By the latter is meant the transfer from company to company of part of one firm's activities. Thus parts of Elliott Automation and E.M.I. have been transferred to Nuclear Enterprises resulting in the doubling in size of the last company. In the weakest form this intervention may be no more than informal confidential discussions between companies and the I.R.C. These may be initiated by either party. A stronger form of intervention is the case where the I.R.C. brings firms together to initiate a merger which it may, or may not, support by financial help. Thus the G.E.C.-A.E.I. merger involved no I.R.C. finance, whereas in the B.M.C.-Leyland merger £25 m. was committed.

It has been clear that the I.R.C. is not merely a merger broker with funds of 'soft' money.[13] Rather, it sees its financial assistance as being available at a time when the company might not be successful in the capital market. It is also prepared to be flexible in the form of the assistance.[14]

Secondly, the I.R.C. may provide financial assistance to an individual firm. The first case of this was the £1·5 m. loan to Reed Paper for the building of de-inking waste paper plants. The import-saving potential of this development provided the reason for the loan.

Thirdly, the I.R.C. has carried out various assignments, often confidential, commissioned by government or private industry. In the former category have been reports on G.P.O. purchasing, and the financial position, and nature of, assistance to Cunard. The British Paper and Board Makers Association has asked it to report on the structural problems of the industry.

By the end of 1969, the I.R.C. had spent, or been committed to spending, about one-third of its initial borrowing powers of £150 m. This does not mean that it has exhausted one-third of its resources, since the typical financial commitment is for 5–7 years. After some initial fears by businessmen that it represented 'back-door nationalisation' it has become generally accepted, despite opposition (and surprise) to its readiness to hold a view about the outcome of contested bids. Perhaps this is greatly due to its claim to be 'created by government but directed by businessmen'.[15]

This readiness to form an opinion regarding the national interest and to act upon it has various complications. It could lead to conflct with the Monopolies Commission. Bids supported by the I.R.C. are first 'cleared' with the relevant government department.

This difference of attitude is shown by the talks held by the I.R.C. resulting in the merger between Ross Group and Associated Fisheries—such a merger was the first to be turned down by the Monopolies Commission under the 1965 Act. We are not suggesting that the I.R.C. is a 'lone wolf', it receives views and information from many sources.[16] Nor are we suggesting that in this example either body is 'wrong' in terms of its objectives. That we now have a policy committed to increasing the size of the firm and another seeking to control size is consistent with economic theory, which predicts that concentration and increasing size may or may not be in the public interest according to circumstance. The problems are likely to be practical ones arising from differences in emphasis.

Certainly there may be advantages in intervening to re-allocate resources in favour of a small company[17] in a way which market forces are unlikely to bring about. Nevertheless in view of the lack of force behind arguments for widespread mergers mentioned at the beginning of this section, additions to the pace of such activity may be viewed with some scepticism.

Perhaps a more coherent policy regarding mergers would flow from links between the I.R.C. and the Monopolies Commission to enable the former to block mergers which its information shows to be probably against the public interest. This would be the reciprocal to its present powers of supporting mergers without necessarily ever publishing the reasoning behind its opinion. Until this happens its published statements still lend credence to the comment[18] that it tries to 'find the most efficient firm in Britain and merge the rest of them into it'. There have recently been signs that the government attitude to 'merger mania' has become more critical; this change of emphasis is the result of greater realisation that the motives to merge may be financial rather than economic and that the results of some large recent mergers have not been encouraging in terms of improved performance. Pre-merger profit forecasts have not usually been met.

SECTION 2

INTERVENTION IN THE CAPITAL MARKET All firms require money capital in order to function; this may be supplied internally, initially by the entrepreneur and later by retained earnings. In most cases, however, at least part of the finance required for expansion or for reacting to technical change is obtained externally.

The relative proportions of the whole, obtained internally and externally, may be affected by government intervention, e.g. compared to Germany our company tax system favours the retention of profits rather than their distribution in dividends. Governments may also affect the size of the capital market by monetary policy. A whole panoply of institutions has been developed in the capital market, from commercial banks to the mechanism of issuing and dealing in shares on the Stock Exchange, to offer a very differentiated product. This differentiation is based on the risk and length of time of the loan.[19] Given a perfect market mechanism we would expect the relationship shown in Diagram 1.

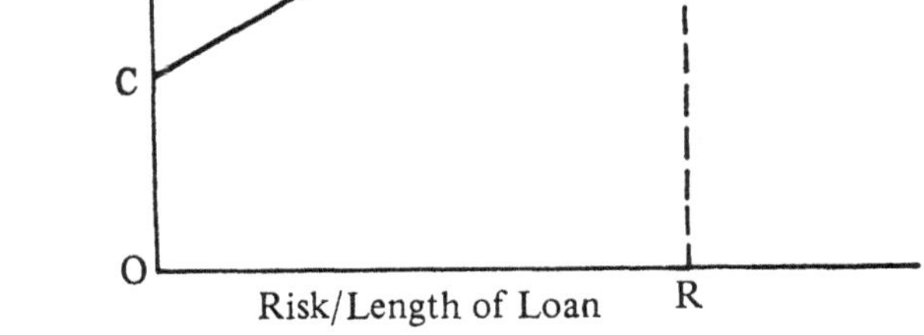

Diagram 1

The line CL is a function of the rate of interest and Risk/Length of loan. No significance should be attached to the fact that it is drawn as a straight line. We would expect it to slope in the direction shown and to intercept the vertical axis with a positive value (*OC*)—the opportunity cost of capital for no risk and a very short time period. As a result a change in bank rate would cause *OC*, and thus the whole function, to shift.

In practice, there has been evidence that (a) there may be gaps in CL indicating that funds are not freely available for certain time periods and (b) certain high-risk or long-period finance (*r*) may only be available at rates of interest (*i*) which, compared to the *m.e.c.*, make borrowing unprofitable. U.K. governments have intervened in the capital market by encouraging the creation of institutions to fill gaps or provide facilities not supplied by a freely operating market. We will consider three such institutions and their subsidiaries; the Agricultural Mortgage Corporation, the Industrial and Commercial Finance Corporation and the Finance Corporation for Industry. We are not suggesting that these organisations are directly financed or controlled by government; all were, however, created as the result of impetus from the government and have finance provided by public bodies.

The Agricultural Mortgage Corporation Ltd.

The A.M.C. was set up as a limited liability company in 1928, shares being held by the Bank of England and nine commercial banks. The object of the company is to make long-term loans, up to forty years, on first mortgages of agricultural property. Such loans may not exceed two-thirds of a valuation of the property. No restriction is made on the use to which the loan may be put (e.g. capital improvements, increases in working capital, buying a farm) but since the intention is to allow expansion or purchase of a farming enterprise, loans are not usually given when the main value of the farm is the house or buildings. Loans are repayable in fixed instalments at a rate of interest fixed for the period of the loan.[20] By 1970 the A.M.C. had made total loans of £225 m., of which £153 m. were outstanding.

The A.M.C.'s major source of finance has been the issue of Debenture Stock,[21] the cost of which is related to other capital market interest rates, but it has received direct assistance in the form of grants[22] and loans.[23]

Here we have an organisation providing loans at current market rates to an industry which receives considerable government assistance in other ways. The objectives of this policy may be 'economic' (Balance of Payments) and social (to encourage a property-owning small farming community). These objectives may, of course, clash with others, e.g. recent attempts to merge small farm holdings. The A.M.C. provides capital in a form not otherwise available on the market and receives only a small, but important, proportion of its funds from public sources.

The Industrial and Commercial Finance Corporation Ltd.

Both the I.C.F.C. and the Finance Corporation for Industry (see below, p. 212) were created in the immediate post-Second-World-War climate when the emphasis was on expanding output by re-establishing the economy on a peace-time footing. This was the era of 'Cheap Money Policy'[24] and the Capital Issues Committee.[25]

The I.C.F.C. was set up in 1945 with a capital of £15 m. in shares and £30 m. in loans. Shares were held by the commercial banks with a Bank of England holding of £½ m. in shares and £1 m. in loans.[26] The creation of the I.C.F.C. was the result of a suggestion by the government to the commercial banks, via the Bank of England, who recognised that the existing capital market did not cater for the long-term requirements of smaller companies[27] and that peripheral regions could be helped by access to finance on a regional basis.[28] Presumably it was felt that the benefits of finance used this way would outweigh the costs in terms of commercial bank lending forgone. The creation of an institution such as the I.C.F.C. may affect the demand for capital but does not (except insignificantly by Bank of England assistance) increase the overall size of the market measured by supply.

The objects of the I.C.F.C. were 'to provide credit and finance by means of loans or the subscription of loan or share capital or otherwise for industrial and commercial businesses or enterprises in Great Britain'.[29] As we shall see below the I.C.F.C. has diversified its activities in a number of ways; at 31/3/70 'this 'original' business outstanding was in the following proportions:

	£
Debentures and secured loans	69 m.
Unsecured loans	6 m.
Redeemable Preference shares	9 m.
Non-redeemable Preference shares	2 m.
Preferred Ordinary shares	6 m.
Ordinary shares	20 m.
TOTAL	£112 m.

Total finance outstanding at that date of £127 m. to over 2,000 companies. As can be seen, the normal form of assistance is a loan repayable with fixed interest over 10–20 years. Loans may be granted on original application within the limits of £5,000–£300,000. Existing customers have a final limit of £500,000. Where the risk element is high the I.C.F.C. is prepared to consider an equity interest. The I.C.F.C. claims never to interfere in company management but may seek the right to appoint a third-party director.

What we have described so far is a 'conventional' financial institution designed to offer a service not provided by the free market. This would be a very inadequate description of the present I.C.F.C., which is remarkable both for the way in which it identifies itself with all problems of smaller firms[30] and for the range of services now provided.

The I.C.F.C. is now involved in the following activities:

1 Providing advice, free or on a fee basis, to customers on management problems. It also operates an Export Department to help with overseas marketing problems. Customers may use the New Issue Department to make a public issue. Management Conferences are organised in various regional centres and explanatory booklets on new techniques published.
2 Offering leasing (over £6 m. at 31/3/70) and hire-purchase facilities on plant and equipment. Such activity falls within the ambit of monetary policy by requests and directives from the Bank of England and is subject to such limitations.
3 Providing assistance to the ship-building and shipping industry via the Ship Mortgage Finance Co. Ltd. Together with other I.C.F.C. subsidiaries, its main business is providing loans of up to 50% of the cost of new construction. It acts as government agent for two recent attempts to encourage the domestic shipbuilding industry, viz. 1963 Shipbuilding Credit Scheme (£75 m. assistance) and 1967 Shipbuilding Industry Act (£200 m. guarantees to British owners building in British yards).
4 Since 1962 the I.C.F.C. has managed EDITH (Estate Duties Investment Trust Ltd.). Since 1952 this organisation has invested over £7 m. in private or small public companies seeking to provide for, or pay, estate duty without damaging the capital structure of the company, e.g. by preventing the loss of family control.
5 Since 1966 I.C.F.C. has controlled Technical Development Capital Ltd., set up in 1962 by insurance companies and others to supply a need recognised by the Radcliffe Committee. T.D.C. aims

to fill a gap between N.R.D.C. before an invention reaches the production stage and existing I.C.F.C. help in financing expansion following from an innovation. T.D.C. seeks mainly to provide finance for the important step of putting a development into production. About £2·5 m. has so far been committed to 50 companies with a maximum £400,000 at first application.

6 Since 1964 I.C.F.C. has owned and managed Scottish Industrial Finance Ltd., a regionally orientated issuing house.

7 Industrial Mergers Ltd. is a wholly-owned subsidiary, operating since 1967, in the field of merger brokerage. It is prepared to give technical advice and put potential buyers and sellers in touch with one another. Since its particular interest is in private companies it is particularly active in certain industries where such firms are numerous, e.g. textile spinning. Another facet of its work is that £2 m. has recently been put into mergers.

This list gives some idea of the scope and nature of the I.C.F.C.'s work. What can be said about the effectiveness of such intervention? As is often the case, there has been little work done in this direction.

There has been a survey comparing growth and profitability of I.C.F.C. assisted companies[31] from 1955–64. This compared the results of 113 companies, 1955–64, and 187 companies, 1960–4, with Board of Trade statistics for *all* companies. It showed increases in profits and net assets for I.C.F.C.-assisted companies 1955–64 of 100% and 50%, compared to all companies results of 60% and 29%. Such results are,[32] of course, subject to a variety of statistical shortcomings (e.g. the industrial composition of the two groups). They have been used by the I.C.F.C. to emphasise the importance in the economy of smaller firms as being a fast-growing sector whose rate of return on capital is above average.[33] What this survey did not seek to do is to answer two questions necessary to evaluate I.C.F.C.'s work. What was the growth rate or profit rate of non-I.C.F.C.-aided smaller firms, and what effect did I.C.F.C. assistance have on firms which it helped—since it could be argued that successful companies would have, ultimately, obtained finance for expansion anyway.

The nature of the I.C.F.C.'s development has perhaps resulted in the nearest British equivalent to that arm of U.S. competition policy aimed at helping smaller firms, the Small Business Administration. Unlike the S.B.A., however, the I.C.F.C. is not directly government-subsidised (to which it has been opposed, see Davies, G., op. cit.) and does not have powers such as giving preferential treatment to small firms tendering for government contracts.

The Finance Corporation for Industry Ltd.

The F.C.I. was set up in 1945 to fill a gap in the capital market defined not, as in the case of the I.C.F.C., in terms of size of potential borrower, but in terms of the time period of the loan. Its purpose was to provide 'temporary or longer period finance for industrial businesses of the country with a view to their quick rehabilitation and development in the national interest, thereby assisting in the maintenance and increase of employment'.[34]

The gap which the F.C.I. has sought to fill has been between short-period finance provided by banks and permanent capital. In addition, the F.C.I. may help where 'because of political or economic circumstances, it is difficult to attract (permanent) capital at reasonable rates'.[35] Three conditions must always be satisfied; the project is important for the national economic interest, the funds cannot be obtained on reasonable terms elsewhere and over £200,000 is required.

The rate of interest varies with Bank Rate since the F.C.I. relies on short-term borrowing from banks. Rather more frequently than is the case with the I.C.F.C., the F.C.I. acquires an equity interest. Although this can be used to protect its commitment in a form of lending which is, of necessity, 'high risk', the usual policy is not to interfere in management.

The F.C.I. contrasts with the I.C.F.C. in that, not only does its business comprise a comparatively small number of large borrowers (so that no new loan agreements were called for in the year ending 31/3/60), but its expansion has been much slower. Thus not until 1966 did it reach the limit of its borrowing powers (£100 m.). Total loans to date have been about £300 m.

This slow rate of growth seems to be the result of three factors. Firstly, the smaller volume of transactions and the more limited type of service given have not offered opportunities for diversification such as those taken by the I.C.F.C. Secondly, an attitude towards the role of the F.C.I.

> 'The Corporation has no new projects under negotiation at the present time. It is not our function to canvass for new business. The Banks, Financial Institutions and industry generally know of our existence and a booklet describing our *modus operandi* and the conditions under which we are able to give assistance was widely distributed two years ago and further copies are available as required.'[36]

Thirdly, the results of its lending in the late 1950's resulted in some years of loss. In 1959 the Bank of England lent £5 m. at a nominal rate of interest for the first five years in order to allow the F.C.I. to build up reserves by establishing a wider margin between average interest paid on borrowing and received from customers.

The F.C.I. has published little which enables the nature and value of its services to be evaluated. It appears to have been heavily engaged in the steel industry. A large proportion of the £42 m. loan agreements made in 1966 was to steel companies who, by virtue of approaching re-nationalisation, were unable to obtain finance from usual sources. 'The alternative would have been to risk seeing the industry falling behind its overseas competitors for reasons not arising from its technical competence'.[37] As a result, in 1967 £56 m. of the £99 m. total loans outstanding were in the steel industry—which were repaid on re-nationalisation.

Two comments on the F.C.I. are relevant. Firstly, that the nature of its terms of reference (involving national interest) and the way that it has interpreted its role (not actively seeking new business, heavy involvement with the steel industry) point up the fact that this type of intervention involves many value-judgements. This is unexceptionable; it does, however, make scientific appraisal of the economic result of such policy difficult.

Secondly, that one could argue strongly in favour of finance to an industry (e.g. steel) being provided as a result of application to a government department such as the Board of Trade rather than by a general source of subsidised finance such as the F.C.I. Such a proposal would have the advantages of identifying the size of the assistance, ensuring public knowledge of any special pleading and enabling costs and benefits to be compared for the industry.

SECTION 3

INTERVENING IN THE PROVISION OF FINANCE

The National Research Development Corporation

The importance of technical change in affecting living standards is widely recognised. Some of the problems of considering it as a factor affecting public policy are dealt with in Chapter 10, its association with a particular form of market structure is treated on p. 231. The literature[38] is full of similar terms with differing meanings, e.g. technical progress, innovation, technological innovation. We will use *invention* as being a new combination of existing knowledge to satisfy human wants.[39]

One problem here is that there is no accepted view of the extent to which economic forces affect the rate of invention. Thus the relationship with R. and D. expenditure, which may or may not be aimed at invention, is unclear. We use *innovation* to mean the commercial exploitation of invention.

Both invention and innovation are considered desirable by the government; there has been a continuing belief that we lag behind other countries in this field.[40] Various techniques have been applied by the governments such as: the establishment of Research Associations immediately after the Second World War; the large number of research grants at universities and specific help to industries associated with rapid innovation such as aircraft manufacture, nuclear energy and computers.[41]

Our example of intervention in this context is the N.R.D.C. and we now narrow the field of vision to consider this institution only. The N.R.D.C. was created by the *Development of Inventions Act 1948*. Its powers have been varied by subsequent legislation, but at present it

> 'promotes the adoption by industry of new products and processes invented in government laboratories, universities and elsewhere, advancing money where necessary to bring them to a commercially viable stage. N.R.D.C. speeds up technological advance by investing money with industrial firms for the development of their own inventions and projects.'[42]

It obtains its finance by Treasury borrowing via the Ministry of Technology. In 1968[43] the ceiling was raised to £50 m.[44] The N.R.D.C. is a non-trading organisation and does not operate R. and D. laboratories. It uses its financial resources to support innovation by means of grants and investments (see below)[45] and obtains its revenue by levies on investment projects and licence fees on patents.[46] Its operations may be categorised as: firstly holding and seeking the exploitation of inventions for which it holds patent rights. Two-thirds of these inventions were the result of research wholly sponsored by government grants, the patents of which, since 1950, have been automatically transferred to the Corporation. Roughly one-third of patents have come from universities, where it has no automatic rights but is generally successful in offering to patent the invention and divide any royalties.

The remaining patents result from private inventors, whose encouragement is the second field of activity. Great importance was attached to this in 1948, there being a belief that important inventions never resulted in innovation due to institutional barriers to their acceptance. Experience has been disappointing and private inventions provide only a very small proportion of all inventions held by the Corporation. Only one of 10,000 private inventions submitted so far to the N.R.D.C. has resulted in royalties of over £1 m. (Cephorin). Three have brought royalties exceeding £100,000 and thirty over £10,000.[47] Three reasons may be put forward to explain this result viz. the N.R.D.C. can only help 'where the public interest so requires' which means that it is not interested in gadgets; most non-gadget inventors either work in an institutional framework or, alternatively, if the commercial applicability of their work is simple, do not need the N.R.D.C.'s powers;[48] and lastly that inventors may be poorly treated by the Corporation's insistence that patents are vested in itself and royalties shared with the inventor.[49]

The Corporation seeks to obtain licence agreements for patents which it holds either through industrial contacts which it has built up over time or by publicity—largely through a booklet *Inventions available under licence*. Its licencing policy involves a conflct between 'commercial' and 'public' interest. Thus it tends to prefer British firms and to forego exclusive licensing (which by creating a monopoly could lead to maximised royalties) in favour of licences available to two or three firms.[50]

The third operation of the N.R.D.C. is to finance the development of an invention,[51] not to the stage of innovation but until firms are prepared to take over. Such development projects have been small in number but have required heavy allocations of finance, e.g. hovercraft[52] dracones and fuel cells. The Corporation recognises that such projects may be 'uneconomic' in the commercial sense, indeed it is likely to be asked to help only those cases which are unattractive to industry.[53] It also recognises that there will be wider social benefits, and costs, to which it must pay attention.[54]

The fourth operation of the N.R.D.C., which is of increasing importance, is to develop inventions by a joint venture with industry. Thus in 1968 it became a 24% shareholder in a company, Whatman Biochemicals, formed to develop and exploit the commercial production of enzymes. It has committed £250,000 in this venture. Where the N.R.D.C. has put its financial resources at risk in some combination with private industry it levies charges designed, if the project is successful, to earn commerical rates of return.

Lastly, it assists particular industries, thus in 1966 it agreed with Elliott Automation to provide up to £2·4 m. finance to encourage firms to use computers.

The N.R.D.C. is an institution which quite clearly recognises that its responsibilities are public rather than private. Examples are: its refusal to develop gadgets, its sponsorship of very long-term research such as fuel cells and its refusal to allow patent-protected monopolies to result from licences. It also recognises that successful licences, by providing a flow of income, 'subsidise' the five-sixths of its inventions which earn no income.[55] Apart from those of disappointed inventors, there seems little general criticism of its operations. The economist must now seek to evaluate, or perhaps merely to ask the right questions, concerning the Corporation as an effective technique.

Clearly it has never been considered as the sole technique—as is made clear if we compare its financial resources to a national annual R. and D. expenditure of about £1,000 m. and realise that there are other government bodies at work e.g. MinTech. In several ways its value may be similar to the I.C.F.C. in that it provides a concentration of specialised financial resources and available expertise. It has been suggested[56] that university research grants be reduced and the resources given to the Corporation. The same Report indicates that probably not more than 20% of the total costs of innovation are in the area of the N.R.D.C.'s operations and emphasises that general increases in investment may be more important than assistance with innovation in promoting technical change. The Industrial Expansion Act, 1968, in setting up an Advisory Committee comprising N.R.D.C. and I.R.C. representatives to consider proposals for government-assisted investment schemes seems to be a result of this view.

Notes

1 See Chapter 10, Section I for theoretical considerations of monopoly and Section III for a treatment of the 1965 Act.

2 'First Report and Accounts, December 1966–March 1968', H.M.S.O. Quotation from Section 2 (1) of the Act.

3 *The National Plan*, Cmnd. 2764, H.M.S.O., p. 8 (1965).

4 p. 232.

5 While real economies are widespread in industry there is little evidence for *large* cost reductions resulting from a merger. See Sutherland A., *op. cit.*, p. 65.

6 Hamberg, D., 'Invention in the Industrial Research Laboratory', *Journal of Political Economy*, Vol. LXXI, No. 2 (April 1963).

7 Adams, W. and Dirlam, J. B., ' "Big Steel", Invention and Innovation', *Quarterly Journal of Economics*, Vol. 80, No. 2 (1966).

8 Speech by Minister of State, Board of Trade (Press release) (14 February 1968).

9 Pratten, C. F., 'The Merger Boom in Manufacturing Industry', *Lloyds Bank Review* (October 1968).

10 1st Report and Accounts, 1968, p. 7.

11 White Paper 'Industrial Reorganisation Corporation', Cmnd. 2889, 1966, para. 5. Note that public opinion appears to be satisfied that efficiency has been improved when the least efficient of two plants is closed after a merger. This may fall far short of maximising resource-use which may dictate the closure of both plants and the setting up and relocation of a new plant somewhere else. If resources are used in merging which would otherwise have been devoted to a new plant, resource-use suffers.

12 A separate case is that of the partiality of the I.R.C. in a contested bid. Thus the I.R.C.'s support of G.E.C. in the takeover of A.E.I. caused one of its members to resign. The I.R.C. helped Kent in its successful contest with the Rank Organisation to take over Cambridge Instruments.

13 1st Report, 1968.

14 Thus interest payments may be deferred for some years to allow profits from the merger to appear, the borrower may be able to

repay early if so desired; the I.R.C. is prepared to hold an equity interest.

15 1st Annual Report and Accounts, 1968.

16 Economic Development Committees, the National Board for Prices and Incomes, The Monopolies Commission, the Department of Economic Affairs, the Ministry of Technology and the Board of Trade in the case of the G.E.C.–E.E.C. merger.

17 Nuclear Enterprises. See p. 205.

18 Caves, R. E., *Britain's Economic Prospects*, p. 321, Allen and Unwin (1968).

19 We are not concerned with the form of capital which may be appropriate for a particular purpose.

20 9¾% mid-1970.

21 £152 m. at 31/3/70.

22 £1·8 m. under 1939 and 1944 Acts. It was agreed in 1961 that no repayment need be made until 1974 unless reserves were built up to £1·25 m. and a dividend declared. This reserve was created and the maximum dividend allowed by the Memorandum of Association, 3½%, was declared for the year ending 31/3/68. As a result £15,000 was repaid to the Treasury.

23 Under 1928, 1944, 1956 and 1958 Acts £6·5 m. has been lent at no interest for the first 60 years in order to provide a guarantee fund which forms part of the base on which debenture borrowing is limited. These loans must be invested in government securities.

24 Low interest rates to stimulate industrial investment.

25 A rationing device to allocate scarce capital resources in the direction of the national interest.

26 In 1959 the share capital was increased to £40 m. and further finance was obtained by debentures, totalling £81 m. at 31/3/70.

27 The 'Macmillan Gap'.

28 Davies, G., 'The regional significance of I.C.F.C.', *Journal of Industrial Economics*, April (1968).

29 See I.C.F.C. 'Background Notes' and 'News-Report'. It is a commercial undertaking, receiving no special financial facilities from the government, which may declare a dividend (7% year ending 31/3/70).

30 In this context, almost certainly an unquoted company with total net assets below £¼ m. In 1970, ⅔ of customers had outstanding advances of £50,000 or less, representing 16% of the total amount outstanding.

31 Boswell, J. S., *Small Firm Survey*, I.C.F.C.

32 In any case, for reasons which by now should be familiar to the

reader, profits may be an imperfect test to apply to discover the national interest in the matter.

33 The survey also showed that small firms were more sensitive to cyclical fluctuations. This could mean that a continuation of the Survey up to the end of 1968 might show a different result.

34 Chancellor of the Exchequer 23/1/45. Quoted in 'F.C.I. LTD'. The final phrase is a nice comment on the anxiety felt at the time concerning the prospects of maintaining full employment.

35 'F.C.I. LTD.'

36 Extract from Chairman's Speech 4/7/63.

37 Chairman's Statement. Accounts for year 31/3/66.

38 Johnson, R. E., 'Technical Progress and Innovation', p. 159, *Oxford Economic Papers* (1966).

39 This is similar to the concept used in Schmookler, J., *Invention and Economic Growth*, Oxford University Press (1966).

40 We cannot go into an examination of the nature and extent of the 'technological gap'. For a critical examination of the concept see 'The Technological Gap', *The Economist* (16 March 1968). Two detailed surveys of U.K. performance with policy suggestions for improvement are: Peck, M. J., 'Science and Technology' in Caves, op. cit., *Technological Innovation in Britain*, Report of the Central Advisory Council for Science and Technology, H.M.S.O., 1968.

41 But not motor car manufacturing. Although R. and D. expenditure is heavy in this industry governments have clearly distinguished between innovation in general and innovation aimed at product differentiation by styling changes.

42 N.R.D.C. *Inventions for Industry*, No. 32, July (1968).

43 Industrial Expansion Act.

44 The limit was raised from £10 m. to £25 m. in 1965. At the same time the Ministry of Technology, with Treasury consent, was given the authority to allow the N.R.D.C. to write off unsuccessful development expenditure. This was necessary to stop a possible situation in which the N.R.D.C. could no longer operate as a result of gradually having built up 'bad debts' equalling its borrowing powers. The Treasury may also exempt an advance from interest for the first eight years.

45 £22 m. by March 1968.

46 £7 m. by March 1968. The annual rate of return from both sources is now in excess of £1 m.

47 *The Observer*, p. 12 (9 February 1969).

48 cf. Technical Development Capital Ltd., p. 210.

49 Thus Sir Christopher Cockerell, inventor of the hovercraft, has

recently been critical of the division of returns between the two parties.

50 Grossfield, K., 'Inventions as Business', *Economic Journal* (March 1962).

51 For a good account of how the N.R.D.C. operates in a particular field see Bayliss, C. R., *N.R.D.C. and metal working machines, Inventions for Industry*, No. 31, N.R.D.C. (1968).

52 Here the total N.R.D.C. committment is about £5 m. All patents in the principle are held by the Corporation which in 1966 set up the British Hovercraft Corporation (shares held: 65% Westland Aircraft, 25% Vickers, 10% N.R.D.C.). Licences have been granted to other companies, e.g. Vosper Thorneycroft, and the N.R.D.C. is still directly financing research into hovertrains.

53 Grossfield, K., op. cit.

54 For a study of the results of support for a potato harvester, pointing out that its most valuable contribution may be not so much developing inventions which would not otherwise have been taken up, but in reducing the delay between invention and innovation, see Grossfield, K. and Heath, J. B., 'The Benefit and Cost of Government support for Research and Development: a Case Study', *Economic Journal*, LXXVI (September 1966).

55 Grossfield, K., op. cit.

56 'Technical Innovation in Britain', op. cit.

Bibliography

Section 1

See references in Chapter 10

Section 2

The institutions mentioned will supply literature on request

Section 3

PARSONS, S. A. J., *The Framework of Technical Innovation*, Macmillan, 1968

JEWKES, J., SAWYERS, D. and STILLERMAN, R., *The Sources of Invention*, Macmillan, 2nd Edition, 1969

MANSFIELD, E., *The Economics of Technical Change*, Longmans, 1969

Chapter 10

GOVERNMENT INTERVENTION BY LEGISLATION: MONOPOLIES AND RESTRICTIVE PRACTICES

SECTION I

This chapter deals with government intervention in the trading policies of firms who are held to be monopolists or who agree with other firms to carry out 'restrictive practices'.[1] The economist's models of monopoly, monopolistic competition and oligopoly will be examined to consider their predictive powers as far as 'the public interest' is concerned. We are concerned only with the welfare aspects of these models and will try to determine whether public policy could be safely based upon them. We shall also examine some of the more common layman's attitudes to monopoly, which he regards as 'economics' even if the economist would regard them as superstition, as government policy is sometimes based on such attitudes.

This very fact that monopoly legislation uses the 'public interest'[2] as its criterion draws attention to the inadequacy of economic theory as a basis for monopoly policy; it is an imprecise, immeasurable concept to which legislators must resort because economists have not produced a precise and measurable criterion.

The existence of any type of monopoly power or restrictive practice is, of course, incompatible with the model of perfect competition examined in Chapter 3. There are various ways in the theory of describing market situations which are not perfect competition. In our categorisation they are collectively termed imperfect competition. This in turn is sub-divided into monopoly (the sole producer of a good which has no close substitutes), monopolistic competition (a large number of firms producing goods which are differentiated,[3] and oligopoly (a small number of firms producing goods which may, or may not, be differentiated). We shall consider the conclusions drawn from the theory for each of the three in turn.

Diagram 1 shows the equilibrium positions of two firms with identical costs (MC and AC),[4] one producing under conditions of perfect competition and the other a monopolist. The monopolist is faced with a downward sloping demand curve ($=AR_m$) and a marginal revenue curve (MR_m). The firm producing under conditions of perfect competition faces an infinitely elastic demand curve ($=AR=MR$).

From this diagram it can be seen that

(i) competitive output is (OQ_c) greater than monopolist's output (OQ_m) and
(ii) competitive price (OP_c) less than monopolist's price (OP_m).
(iii) the monopolist is producing at less than the nadir of his AC curve (leading to the excess capacity discussed below).
(iv) he is receiving supernormal profits ($CP_m \times OQ_m$).
(v) under conditions of monopoly, price is greater than marginal cost, and thus misleads consumers about opportunity costs.

The only necessary condition resulting from a comparison of the two market forms is (v) above.

Diagram 2 illustrates, firstly, that monopoly price may be absolutely lower and monopoly output greater than their competitive equivalents, when costs change as a result of a change in market structure. It is, of course, plausible that the monopolisation of an industry will lead, for example, to greater economies of scale.

Diagram 2, secondly, illustrates that a monopolist may be earning no supernormal profits (in the case where, at equilibrium, output OQ_m, $AC_m=AR_m$).

Our last monopoly model considers the case of discriminating monopoly. Diagram 3 shows this for a monopolist who sells in two distinct markets '*A*' and '*B*' between which purchasers are unable to transfer the product and where different demand situations obtain. Assuming that costs of supplying both markets are the same, then he will produce that output where $MC=MRab$, allocating this output between markets in shares OQa and OQb and selling at the relevant price. Thus a policy of profit maximisation leads to different prices for the same article in different markets. The monopolist is acting rationally; on the other hand the consumer has different price marginal cost relationships in the two markets and may feel unfairly treated if he is aware that marginal cost is the same in both cases. The Monopolies Commission[5] has objected to this practice.

We cannot say on *a priori* grounds whether it is likely that monopoly will lead to a higher price and smaller quantity sold, since we do

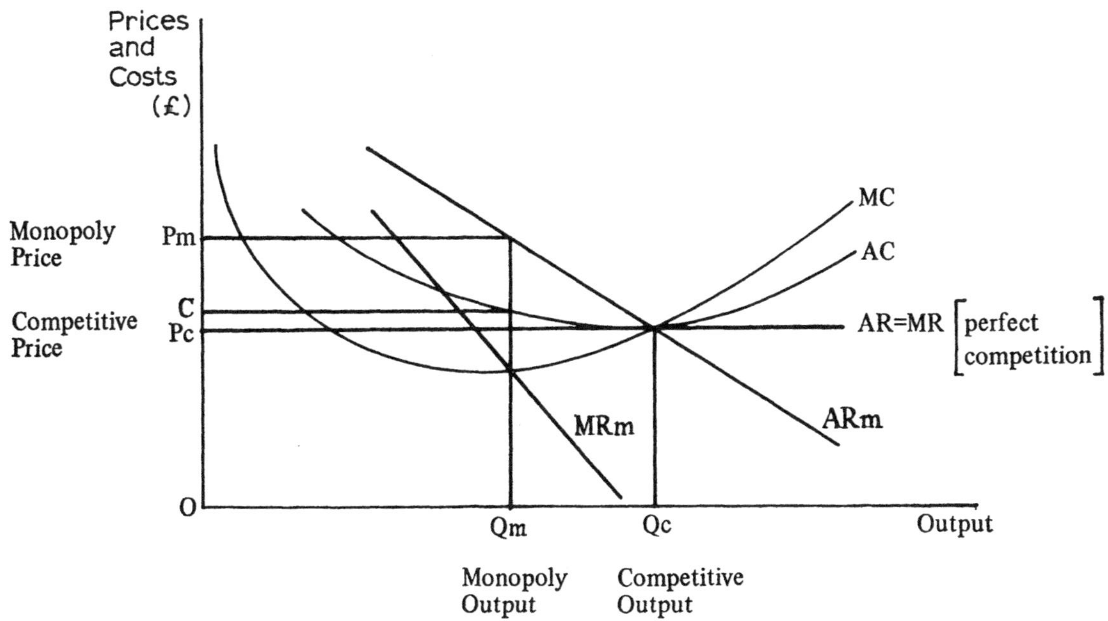

Prices
and
Costs
(£)
Monopoly
Price
Pm
C
Competitive
Price
Pc
O
MC
AC
AR=MR [perfect competition]
ARm
MRm
Qm
Qc
Output
Monopoly
Output
Competitive
Output

Diagram 1

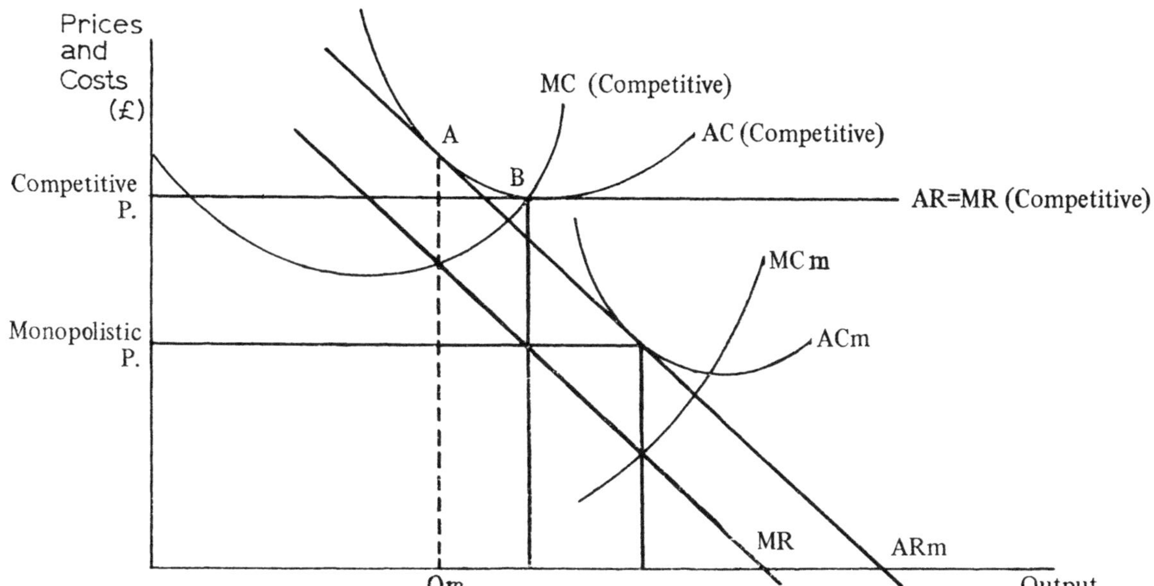
Prices
and
Costs
(£)
Competitive
P.
Monopolistic
P.
MC (Competitive)
AC (Competitive)
A
B
AR=MR (Competitive)
MC m
ACm
MR
ARm
Qm
Output

Diagram 2

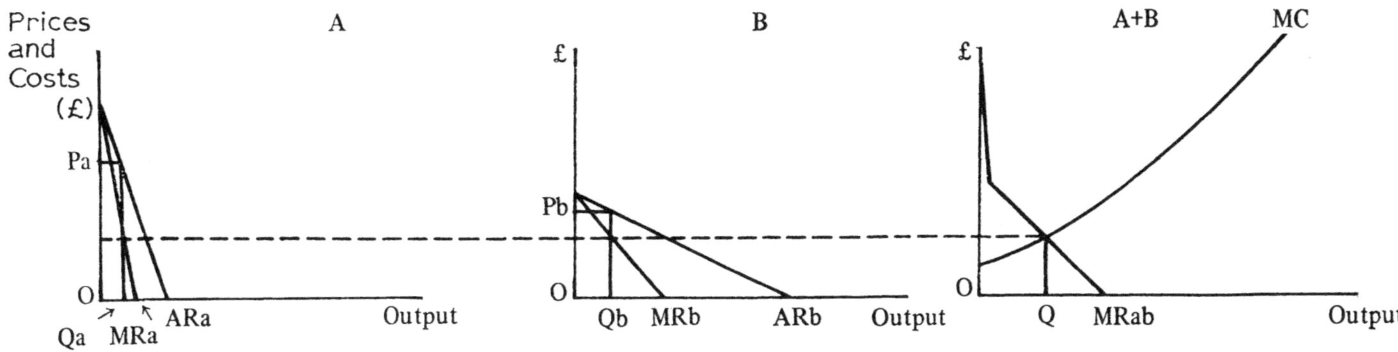

Prices
and
Costs
(£)
Pa
O
Qa
MRa
ARa
A
Output
£
Pb
O
Qb
MRb
ARb
B
Output
£
O
Q
MRab
A+B
MC
Output

Diagram 3

not know how likely a consequence will be cost changes. Similarly, we do not know how likely will be the case of price discrimination. This emphasises the inadequacy of general models—of which we have taken three examples—as a basis for policy making. The only consistent result is the welfare objection that consumers will, in all cases, be misled by the $P > MC$ result.

The second market situation distinguished in the theory is monopolistic competition.[6] This was conceived to provide a framework for markets lying between the single-firm or small-group situation and the large number of firms producing an undifferentiated produce under conditions of perfect competition. The two major predictions of this theory are: firstly, that output will be where P is greater than MC,[7] secondly, that such an industry will suffer from instability associated with excess capacity.

By 'excess capacity' is meant a situation where firms in an industry are producing at an output smaller than the lowest point of an average cost curve. This must mean that they have enough capacity to produce at a lower unit cost. This is important because while the entrepreneur is concerned with the lowest costs for a given output, society is concerned with the cheapest output from a given plant,[8] as this is the most efficient use of that plant.

We agree with those theorists[9] who challenge the value of the concept of monopolistic competition. These criticisms are of the two main kinds. Firstly, it is said that if there is a large number of firms in the industry and if the product differentiation is small then perfect competition is the appropriate type of analysis. On the other hand, strong product differentiation leads to a situation where monopoly or oligopoly is the appropriate model. The second line of criticism is that in terms of the theory itself monopolistic competition is likely to be self-destructive since either firms will recognise market links between their differentiated products (and thus act as monopolists or oligopolists) or competition between them is likely to cause such a reduction in the number of firms that oligopoly will be the result.

The theory of oligopoly is a field to which great attention has been paid in the last thirty years. Oligopoly is a market situation which exists in many types of industry. The difficulty here is that we are dealing with a small-group situation where in order to get a determinate solution it is important to be able to predict (in an industry with three firms, *A*, *B* and *C*) not only how *B* and *C* will react to a change in output or price by *A*, but how *A* will evaluate *B* and *C*'s reactions. Most models of oligopoly[10] predict a higher price and smaller output than would be the case under conditions of perfect competition. Price levels are likely to remain fixed for comparatively long periods of time[11] with the result that changes in demand affect not price and output (as in perfect competition), but output only.[12] Where firms produce differentiated products one likely type of competition will be to extend market shares, not by price changes, but by promoting the 'brand image' and changing the performance or physical appearance of the product. It must be emphasised that these are general predictions; they can be changed by the structure of the industry,[13] the differentiation of products, the existence of price leadership, the level of inter-firm knowledge and the extent of collusion between firms.

Although it may by no means be clear which, if any, of the oligopoly models has empirical content they all illustrate the small room for manœuvre open to the oligopolist. He is constrained in his pricing policy by the substitutability of his rivals' products and—although he will characteristically resort to a range of non-price competitive techniques—he finds it difficult to expand profits.[14] A presumption arises that he will turn either to collusive restrictive practices, or to amalgamation into a monopolistic market structure, to resolve his problems. An ironic sequence arises that the oligopolist solves his own problems by techniques that raise problems for society as a whole—those of restrictive practices and monopolies.

So far we have summarised the welfare predictions of economic theory in the case of monopoly, monopolistic competition and oligopoly together with criticisms and limitations of the theory inherent in the structure of the theory itself. We now turn to a consideration of the relevance and usefulness of these analyses to government policy.

Firstly, the point was made in Chapter 3[15] that comparisons of price and output are made between imperfect competition and perfect competition, rather than between forms of imperfect competition, because such different forms cannot be ranked in welfare terms while a clear welfare comparison can be made between imperfect and perfect competition. This is important in welfare theory but it is a non-operational distinction in public policy matters. The economist's models are based on assumptions so general that they lead to general presumptions about imperfect competition rather than a factual basis for government policy. Furthermore, perfect competition is hardly a workable market structure to which we might try to transform imperfect competition. It meets only the necessary conditions for optimality and there is no identifiable welfare advantage in changing only one industry to a perfectly competitive state while others remain monopolistic. There may be other advantages e.g. lower costs.

Comparisons of other market states with perfect competition run into difficulty over the realism of the assumption that costs will be the same whether, for example, the industry consists of one firm or a large number of firms. There is evidence of economies of scale in several industries.[16] These lead to average costs per unit of output declining as the scale of operation in a plant or firm increases. We will consider later the problem which exists in any particular case in comparing this lowered cost of output with the 'higher price, smaller output' prediction associated with monopoly.

Another problem of micro-economics is that the theory describes single-product firms. Those executing policy are frequently faced with firms producing more than one product, who are price-takers in some markets and monopolists in others. There has been an attempt, in the U.S.A., to connect sheer size with monopoly power; this remains unconvincing to the theorist.[17]

A fundamental disadvantage of the classical Theory of the Firm is that it is a 'comparative static' approach which cannot deal in a satisfactory way with the dynamism of real world situations. Thus price theory takes technical change as an exogeneously determined variable.[18] It is obvious that much of our higher real standard of living gained in the last hundred years is the result of technological change. These changes have involved opportunity costs in the form of investment in research and development. If it could be shown that, for example, oligopoly leads to a greater innovation and technological advance[19] then there would be a prima facie case for supporting oligopolistic as opposed to other market situations, provided the opportunity costs of the oligopolists are not greater than that of the same research and development sponsored by some alternative firm or body. Furthermore, the innovation must not be one more apparent than real to consumers. This is a difficult distinction to draw, particularly since consumers may obtain greater satisfaction from the wider variety of goods produced by an oligopolistic market structure. This extra choice would be obtained at a cost, since $P > MC$.

Before considering how the results of economic analysis can be used by those responsible for government policy, we will consider some of the 'folklore' arguments advanced for, and against, monopoly and restrictive practices. These arguments are rarely framed in terms of comparison between the market situations distinguished in the theory. However, where they compare large firms against small firms, or dominant firms against firms that face fierce competition, they are dealing with the layman's appreciations of monopoly and competition. Where they consider the problems of firms who band together to agree on trading policies, the theoretical equivalent is one of the possible results of monopolistic competition or the oligopoly situation.

A widely held opinion against monopoly is that competition leads to efficiency. If by an increase in efficiency we mean a firm incurring lower costs for any given output,[20] it can be shown that this stimulus exists, in theory, for a monopolist as well as a perfect competitor. In both cases increased profits will result from lower costs in this sense. The belief probably stems from the feeling that lower costs are the only way in which a firm meeting fierce competition can increase its profits whereas the monopolist has the cushion of profits, resulting from price exceeding AC, on which to rest. We know of no empirical evidence which can be adduced to support or reject this belief *in general.* On the other hand a case-study approach to an industry might[21] give evidence one way or another. Another probable basis for the belief is that monopolists do not have to fear new competition. There is no real evidence for this *simpliste* view of a functional relationship between market structure and efficiency.

The second folklore criticism of monopoly (or the dominant firm) is the effect on consumers and other firms of the methods adopted to establish or maintain monopoly power. A firm may establish a dominant position in an industry by being more efficient than its rivals, who may ultimately be forced to close down, or be bought out by the successful firm. This is unexceptionable, but the public interest may not be served by those firms who use coercion or engage in 'unfair' practices. Examples of such practices in American industry are well documented as a result of the prohibition of monopoly and restrictive practices which has existed since the nineteenth century. For example 'price-cutting gas station operators have been blockaded by 40 to 58 motor vehicles lining up to purchase a gallon or less of gas to be paid for with a \$20, \$50, or \$100 bill, the purchase to be completed by the complete run of free services'.[22] The National Cash Register Company in America 'hired their employees, bribed competitors' employees and employees of railroad, telephone and telegraph companies to spy on competitors, spread false rumours concerning their competitors' solvency, unjustly downgraded their products, publicly displayed their cash registers under labels which read "junk" and engaged in other such practices that gave National Cash Register, over a period of 20 years, control of 95% of the Nation's product of Cash Registers'.[23] In this country we have the case of the expert bribed by the British Match Corporation, at a salary of \$600 per month, to 'tactfully and earnestly work to discourage'[24] a potential competitor.

Another public belief concerning monopoly is that firms may preserve profitable markets by suppressing superior products. Examples are the folk legends of 'the match that would light 100 times' and 'unladderable nylon stockings'. No evidence exists to support these particular beliefs. However, electric lamp manufacture (also a highly concentrated industry) provides examples of just this point. Thus in the U.S.A. fluorescent tubes could have been produced by General Electric for 10 years before their introduction was pioneered by a small firm.[25]

In the U.K. (Monopolies Commission, 'Second Report on the Supply of Electric Lamps', December, 1968) the Commission's recommendation that manufacturers should make long-life bulbs (2,000 hours instead of 1,000 for a price increase of 4d.) available to domestic consumers was followed within a month by a small producer (7% of market share). Such bulbs had been made since 1962 for industrial users. The claim of the Electric Lamp Industry Council that such bulbs would increase distribution costs by increasing the product range while not, on balance, benefiting consumers because of a 7½% reduction in light output, contrasts with the industry's promotion of mushroom lamps whose light output is 8% less than that of the conventional shape.

A further point, relevant to the claim that large firms and oligopolists promote innovation, is the speed with which they react to technical changes in others. This may obviously be connected with the point made above. A major study concerning the time lag before the U.S. Steel industry invested in the L.D. steelmaking process shows a nine-year lag before the largest firm used the process, by which time the industry had put in 40 m. tons of outdated capacity.[26]

It must not, of course, be thought that efficiency or coercion are the only sources of monopoly. Many monopolies originate in the various 'barriers to entry'[27] to an industry. It is not suggested that all barriers are deliberately engineered or exploited by all firms, nor that firms should ignore circumstances that act in their favour, but it is likely that these factors work against wider competition in British as in American industry.

We now consider six popular arguments in favour of monopoly (or the dominant firm). The first three arguments do not detail advantages of monopoly. They are defences claiming that it is not a serious problem.

The first is that, although monopolists may possess the power to earn higher profits by restricting output and charging a higher price, the extent to which they use this power depends on the extent of potential, as well as actual, competition. Thus a monopolist may discourage new entrants by not charging the highest possible price. This may well happen. It would be a shortsighted monopolist who was not prepared to sacrifice some level of short-run profits for a lower but acceptable level of profit in the long run. On the other hand, it is an anomalous position for a monopolist to charge lower prices simply in order to avoid greater competition—which would itself produce these low prices.

The second argument is that a monopolist may have his power over price and output limited by the existence of a monopoly buyer. This concept of 'countervailing power' has been developed by Galbraith, although it is not conventionally assumed that the results of bilateral monopoly are necessarily the same as perfect competition.[28] A British example is the relationship between drug manufacturers and the Ministry of Health.

Thirdly, it is claimed that, in so far as those controlling modern public companies are motivated by desires other than those of obtaining maximum profits[29] from the company's operations they may not extract all possible advantages from their position.[30]

At best these three arguments may describe the realities of a market situation At worst they may explain why consumer interest is not as damaged as it might have been. They give grounds for suspecting that the costs of monopoly may not be *too* great, without really providing measurement and they do not deny the evidence of such costs.

The fourth argument claims that monopoly, or an industry containing large firms, has an advantage over a more competitive industry where small firms are typical, in that large firms devote a larger proportion of their resources to research and development. To prove this contention it would have to be shown that research and development would not be carried out at a smaller real cost by government sponsorship or specialist research organisations. Various attempts to obtain empirical evidence have been made[31] which have not resulted in a general prediction. At least one economist[32] has come to the conclusion that

> 'though a positive association between research and development intensity as a percentage of sales and industrial concentration apparently exists, it must be described as weak, as must also the case for industrial concentration as a stimulus for research and development both in absolute and relative terms.'

Where research is carried out, the welfare problem remains that resources have been used in improving the product when the community might have preferred the original product with the resources used in some other way.

The fifth argument in favour of monopolies is that they are better equipped to withstand bad trading conditions than small firms. Their greater resources mean that they can maintain employment and output. Their dominant market position enables them to maintain prices and thus diminish the impact of a depression. There would seem some validity in this latter claim if there were evidence that monopolists actually acted in this way; even if such evidence did exist the importance of this claim would be small since it is unlikely that the aggregate effect on total national levels of consumption would be large.

A sixth argument is sometimes advanced that monopolists, because they are big firms, have access to economies of scale quite beyond the hopes of small firms. This can be true in those industries where such economies are available. In such circumstances, the real resource-cost of a unit of production decreases—whatever happens to the money price. But even this advantage can be illusionary in the short-run situation where an amalgamation of two firms now produces in one 'existing' factory instead of two.

It is tempting to argue from Fig. 4 that, if each existing factory was producing OM_2, it is preferable to produce the same total OM ($OM = 2XOM_2$) from one factory, as average costs have fallen from OC to OC''.

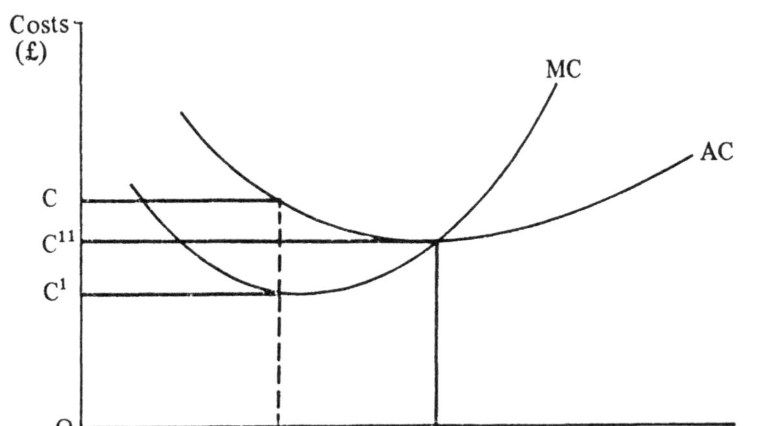

Diagram 4

This is erroneous. The factories already exist so the real opportunity costs are marginal costs and the cheapest way to produce *OM* is in two separate batches of OM_2 because OC' is less than OC''. This argument could not hold in the long run with the building of a new factory but it does illustrate the difficulties in what can look like simple clear arguments.[33]

In a section of a chapter it is not possible to review either all the various subtleties of economic theory[34] or all the various opinions of laymen. We have not examined the variety of theoretical models of oligopoly. In particular the treatment of the arguments surrounding restrictive practices is deferred to Section III. However, it should by now be clear that though, at first glance, the theoretical case against monopoly seems overwhelming it is, in fact, a poor basis for an anti-monopoly policy; firstly, because removing one, or all, monopolies does not necessarily improve welfare if monopolies, or other constraints, remain. Secondly, there is no scientific method for evaluating the costs and benefits of different market structures. Such advantages, such as research, that may be claimed for monopolies are not necessary characteristics of monopoly nor can they be shown to always outweigh the costs of monopolistic market structures. Finally, theoretical models are so generally framed as to have little application to any given real-world problem except as so far as it helps to formulate appropriate questions.

We have outlined the shortcomings of welfare analysis and positive economics as a basis for policy-making in this field. We would not have reflected all the work of economists in this field without mentioning the normative[35] concept of 'Workable Competition'.[36] This has been an attempt to look at competition not in terms of market states but of performance. Thus Clark outlines Workable Competition as a

> 'rivalry in selling goods in which each selling unit normally seeks maximum net revenue, under conditions such that the price or prices each seller can charge are effectively limited by the free option of the buyer to buy from a rival seller or sellers of what we think of as the "same" product, necessitating an effort by each seller to equal or exceed the attractiveness of the other's offerings to a sufficient number of buyers to accomplish the end in view.'

This statement was criticised as being too imprecise to enable measurements of the effectiveness of competition policy to be made. Nevertheless, the imprecision may provide a framework for normative judgements to be made in particular cases (e.g. a Monopolies

Commission investigation) so that G. C. Allen has called Workable Competition a 'handy tool of policy'.[37]

The situation remains, however, that economic analysis leads us to adopt an agnostic attitude to monopolies in general in our non-optimal world but it does provide us with an armoury of concepts to apply to any monopoly in particular.

SECTION II

This section concerns itself in some detail with the operation of legislation in the fields of single firm monopoly and restrictive practices. After briefly reviewing government policy up to 1948 it deals with legislation concerning the existing single firm monopoly and with the control of mergers (the latter being viewed as an attempt to inhibit the establishment of monopoly power). The fourth part of the section deals with restrictive practices. Collective and individual resale price maintenance are considered separately in the last part of this section, since although we consider them to be a type of restrictive practice, we also recognise that public discussion (and legislation) has tended to consider resale price maintenance as a separate issue.

1 HISTORICAL SUMMARY 1900–48 The most noticeable ways in which monopoly and restrictive practices increased during the period 1900–48 were in the fields of mergers and trade associations. Both had been developing since about 1880, largely as a result of overcapacity in some trades coupled with the growth of overseas competition.[38]

Both World Wars provided national emergencies where government intervention encouraged mergers and trade associations. The depression years of the inter-war period also encouraged industrial grouping in the face of falling sales and profits.

Over this period, in contrast to the years after 1945, more government action was taken to promote mergers and trade associations than to control them. There appear to have been two reasons for this permissive attitude. During both World Wars government policy actively encouraged mergers and trade associations on the grounds that national interest required that the government should directly allocate raw materials (particularly imports) made scarce by war-time conditions and that production should be concentrated[39] in particular firms in a trade to make resources available for the war effort. This policy resulted in greater links between government departments and industry. In particular it encouraged the growth of trade associations who could speak on behalf of their members and who could carry out the concentration, quota and production schemes. At the end of each war many of these trade associations were disbanded[40] but others remained to form the basis for price and output fixing bodies.

Government encouragement of mergers was also based on the view that 'Combinations' had brought advantages to German and American industry that put British industry at a disadvantage.[41] Thus the merger that produced Imperial Chemical Industries in 1926 was advocated as a way of improving technical and commercial efficiency and also claimed to make it possible for the British Chemical Industry to compete more easily with large continental groups. Identical arguments were used in 1967 at the time of the B.M.C.-Leyland merger (see Chapter 9, p. 205). Apart from promoting reconstruction schemes in industries such as cotton and steel, the government encouraged mergers by giving the Board of Trade powers to underwrite loans for promoting employment.[42]

Although no legislation was passed that sought to restrict monopoly powers[43] various committees did recognise that some mergers and trade associations might act against the public interest[44] and made suggestions about government action. None of these recommendations were followed.

The explanation for the lack of government intervention lies in strong acceptance of *laissez faire* doctrines, combined with an ambivalent feeling about the advantages and disadvantages of imperfect competition.[45]

This former feeling that the government should not interfere in the area of businessmen's decisions[46] rested on beliefs which have been discussed in Chapter 2. The results of this policy of non-intervention, except at times of national emergency (such as wars or deep depression), were to allow mergers and trade associations to grow unchecked[47] or to actively encourage them. Not until 1944[48] did the coalition government propose to find out 'the extent and effect of restrictive agreements and of combines' and to 'take appropriate action to check practices which may bring advantages to sectional producing interests but work to the detriment of the public as a whole'. This marks a turning point in government attitudes to intervention. Subsequent committees were more critical of the activities of trade associations.[49]

In 1948 an Act[50] was passed setting up a Monopolies Commission which, among other things, reported on various industries where trade associations operated. In 1955 its report on Restrictive Trade

Practices[51] provided the basis for the 1956 Restrictive Trade Practices Act. In our view the only consistent thread running through government action 1900–48 is a gradually increasing willingness to intervene. Much of the public discussion surrounding the 1948 Act seems to have been based on the 'folk-lore' arguments mentioned in Section I of this chapter.[52] There does not seem to have been an attempt to apply the results of economic analysis as a basis for policy,[53] although we have, in Section I of this chapter, given grounds for believing that the general predictive powers of this analysis are small. The 1948 Act was designed to continue the work of the war-time enquiries into the particular industries on a permanent basis. Great importance was attached to the Commission as a method of obtaining evidence which would then be widely publicised.

2 SINGLE FIRM MONOPOLY The *1948 Monopolies and Restrictive Practices (Inquiry and Control) Act* set up a Monopolies Commission[54] to report on cases submitted to it by the Board of Trade. These cases are those where 'one third or more of the goods in question were supplied in the United Kingdom by one person or a group of persons acting to restrict competition'.

On a reference from the Board of Trade, the Committee has to investigate, firstly, whether the 'one third rule'[55] applies, and, secondly, whether the structure of the industry operates 'against the public interest'. The Committee was empowered to make recommendations about what ought to be done to remedy a situation in an industry, but the Board of Trade was not compelled to take any action. Section 14 of the Act guided the Commission as to the interpretation of 'public interest'. Thus

> 'all matters which appear in the particular circumstances to be relevant shall be taken into account and, amongst other things, regard shall be had to the need, consistent with the general economic position of the United Kingdom, to achieve:
> (a) the production, treatment and distribution by the most efficient and economical means of goods of such types and qualities, in such volume and at such prices as will best meet the requirements of the home and overseas markets;
> (b) the organisation of industry and trade in such a way that their efficiency is progressively increased and new enterprises encouraged:
> (c) the fullest use and best distribution of men, materials and industrial capacity in the United Kingdom and:

(d) the development of technical improvements and the expansion of existing markets and the opening up of new markets.'

The *Monopolies and Mergers Act 1965* affected the size and scope of the Commission and also the powers of action given to the Board of Trade. Part I of the Act repealed the provisions of the 1956 Act[56] so that the 1953 Act[57] at present determines the size of the Commission. The scope of the Commission was extended to cover the provision of services and not merely goods. Part II of the Act gives the Board of Trade various powers where the Monopolies Commission reports that a monopoly of scale, or monopolistic practice, operates against the public interest. These powers may be exercised irrespective of the recommendations of the Commission and include powers (a), (b) and (c) given originally in the 1948 Act. These powers are:

(a) To declare it to be unlawful to carry out the agreement (unless the 1956 Act applies).
(b) To require the parties to give up all or part of an agreement.
(c) To declare it to be unlawful to withhold supplies or services or to make the supply of one good or service conditional upon the purchase of another.
(d) To declare price discrimination, preferential dealing and price notification schemes illegal.
(e) To regulate prices if the Commission's report finds that prices charged have been against the public interest.
(f) To prohibit or restrict take-overs.
(g) To break up a trade or business by the Board selling any part of the undertaking.

We now turn to an evaluation of the operation of the Monopolies Commission.[58] Excluding, for the moment, the basic question of whether or not the problem of single firm monopoly is best dealt with by a Commission, the arguments concerning the scope and effectiveness of monopoly legislation in the United Kingdom are

(a) whether or not the definition of monopoly is useful,
(b) what is meant by 'public interest',
(c) whether the Board of Trade should have discretionary powers of reference and action,
(d) whether a Commission's reports provide a suitable basis for action and
(e) whether the Board of Trade's powers are sufficient.

An initial reaction to the '$\frac{1}{3}$' definition might well be that what we are considering here as monopoly is a far cry from the theoretical concept of a monopolist. Those advocating control of monopoly recognised the considerable power over the price and output policy of a trade[59] which producing one-third of the output of a commodity brings. In practice, single firm references made to the Commission have all been concerning firms who have been generally recognised as having considerable power in their fields.[60] In fact, one criticism of legislation has been on the grounds that the '$\frac{1}{3}$' rule is too high, i.e. it does not permit the investigation of oligopolistic industries where production below one-third still gives considerable power over trading conditions in the industry.

The criteria on which an investigatory committee decides whether to report in favour or against a question referred to it is obviously of crucial importance. In the case of the 1948 Act it is quite clear that the criterion is the 'public interest'. The problem here is that the circumstances in Section 14 of the Act which are to be taken into account are expressed in such a general way as to involve the Commission in problems of weighing alternatives that cannot be quantified.[61] It would be unrealistic to expect from the Commission the consistency which an American court (concerned solely with the question of whether or not competition exists in an industry) can give.

The discretionary nature of the powers of the Board of Trade concerning whether it refers a case to the Commission are inherent in the approach to monopoly control shown by the 1948 Act. The Act does not condemn all monopoly but proceeds on the assumption that monopoly may not act in the public interest and this pragmatic approach accords with the results of economic analysis. Thus the Board of Trade selects industries in which it feels that there may be practices worth investigation, often based on a complaint which it has received about the trading methods of a firm. A more serious 'weakness' in the system is that there is no compulsion on the Board of Trade to act at all on the Monopolies Commission Report.[62]

Until the 1965 Act, the Board of Trade, assuming it decided to act, merely had a choice between prohibiting by Statutory Order,[63] all or some of the practices found to be against the public interest or seeking a voluntary undertaking from the industry that the practices would be given up. Few Statutory Orders have yet been used in respect of single firm monopoly and firms themselves have always preferred the voluntary undertaking which has been the result of negotiation with the Board of Trade. A voluntary undertaking has the advantage of removing firms from the public eye without the hindrance of legal sanctions. It has been suggested that arrangements should be made for formal reconsideration of the undertaking given by firms along the lines of U.S. legislation.[64] That the usual method of exercising its powers has been for the Board of Trade to negotiate with firms has led writers[65] to question the suitability of the Board of Trade as a 'trust-busting' agency on the grounds that the Board is hampered by the necessity of keeping on good terms with industry for many other discussions which may take place.

A more widespread criticism has been that in only one case[66] have all the Commission's recommendations been implemented.[67] In some cases no doubt the Board of Trade has decided to reduce monopoly power in other ways outside the scope of action suggested in the Commission's report. Thus in the case of matches and match-making machinery the report of the Commission was quickly followed by an agreement by the Board of Trade to import £500,000 of matches from Russia, which, while increasing competition faced by the British Match Corporation, nevertheless fell short of the price control which was one of the recommendations of the Commission. In other cases the Commission would have liked to recommend action which was not then *intra vires* the Board of Trade.[68] In many cases, however, the Commission made proposals, which it felt would make entry into the industry easier, and allow the growth of competition, only to be met with a refusal by the Board of Trade to implement them.[69] Lack of action by the Board of Trade should not be assumed to mean that the Board did not agree with the Commission's findings since, particularly in the early years of this legislation, great importance was given to the value of publicity of their practices as a sanction against firms. On the other hand, there may have been a belief that the Commission was a better critic of existing market structures than creator, via its recommendations, of superior structures.

Turning to the question of the suitability of the Commission's reports as a basis for action, we must consider whether or not the criteria used by members of the Commission have been sufficient and whether the depth of the information they have obtained from firms in industries they have examined has been enough.

In most cases, the Commission has attempted to evaluate price levels in the industry, often by making international comparisons. Furthermore, the Commission has considered the effect that the pricing policy of firms in the industry has had on profits earned. High profit rates (roughly above 20% on capital employed) have been condemned, although in the case of Molins Machine Co. Ltd. (Report on Tobacco, 1961), profit rates averaging 36% over 8 years were allowed since this firm was an acknowledged technical leader in an industry where risk was high as a result of overseas competition. That firms in more secure industries might expect to earn lower profit margins was demonstrated by Imperial Tobacco's lower profit rate in the same reference.

Price discrimination has been condemned by the Commission. In several references concerning industries supplying items sold both as a component part and in the replacement market, examples of the prediction of the discriminating monopoly model[70] have been discovered. Thus a 6½ in. DL clutch was sold as initial equipment for £1 12s. 11d.; as a spare £6 1s. 1d.[71] Discrimination between the price charged a subsidiary and a customer has also been disliked. From the viewpoint of economic theory two points should be noted. Firstly, profits related to historical cost aggregates such as 'capital employed' differ from the measurements of profit in price theory. Secondly, from the aspect of efficient resource allocation it is not merely the profit proportion of total revenue which is in question but the level of costs on which the profits are based. We are concerned not only with different profit percentages based on revenue (or costs) but with the fact that a profit margin of 20% on costs of 100 gives a worse result from the aspect of public interest than a profit margin of 30% on costs of 80. The whole concept of determining public interest, even partially, by comparing profit margins earned with 'average' margins is highly subjective; it could be argued that a monopolist (or any firm) seeking to maintain sales in a declining industry should do so only at *below* average profits.

Whereas the Commission has always condemned 'unfair competition', e.g. by British Match Corporation (quoted on p. 229), it has not objected to mere market domination. In addition to profits earned, it has attached great importance to the rate of technical progress in an industry and in the view of one writer[72] has accepted the view that 'high concentration . . . is conducive to technical progress'.

Details of the membership and procedures followed may be found in Rowley, where he concludes that the Commission's reports have been painstaking but they suffered from the lack of use of sophisticated techniques and, in particular, have not been able to measure efficiency.[73] Reports on a single firm monopoly have always been more difficult to frame than those dealing with restrictive trade practices since, in the latter case, if the agreement was felt to be against the public interest the Commission could recommend the abandonment of the agreement whereas in the former case the Commission has to suggest an alternative industrial structure.

Earlier criticism of the system of controlling single firm monopoly on the ground that the powers of the Board of Trade were too limited has been met by the increase in the Board's range of powers given by the 1965 Act. In particular the power to break up a firm, paralleling the American courts' 'divesting decrees', is providing a powerful final sanction. One valuable course not yet opened to the Board of Trade is that of reducing tariffs. The American dictum 'tariffs are the mothers of trusts' still applies and these have helped to create barriers to entry in such industries as fertilisers, wallpapers and cellulosic man-made fibres.

Any lack of impact made by the Monopolies Commission in the field of single firm monopoly reflects three factors. First, from 1948 until the 1956 Act, the Commission was largely concerned with reporting on restrictive agreements. Second, the restricted number of references that it could handle and the slowness of its progress were, until 1953, the result of its being too small, run on too limited a budget and unable to work in Committee but only as a single Commission. Thirdly, there was a general switching of attention from the Commission after 1956 when it dealt with cases which did not bring it into the limelight.[74]

In the last five years there has been a resurgence of interest in the efficiency of British Industry and the methods by which this could be improved—much of this interest resulting from arguments by proponents of the United Kingdom joining the European Economic Community, who suggest that Britain's entry may bring about by market forces results which legislation has tried to bring about. Others have seen in the restructuring of industries a possible solution to the problem of increasing growth.[75] Perhaps, as a result of this recent renewed interest, reports of the Monopolies Commission have once again been widely publicised.

One example is the reference on the distribution of petrol. The scope of the reference precluded the Commission from examining the petroleum industry as a whole—which would have been particularly interesting since it is a unique world-wide industry dominated by vertically integrated oligopolists and—much of the debate suffered from narrowing the reference merely to distribution. The report sought to make new entry easier by firstly limiting agreements between tied garage ('solus site') proprietors and petrol companies to not more than five years. Secondly, the practice of 'full line forcing' whereby tied outlets were allowed to sell only certain brands of ancillary products was stopped. Lastly, firms supplying more than 50 m. gallons p.a. were stopped from increasing the number of company-owned stations. Such firms were not allowed to make more than 15% of their sales through such stations.

All three recommendations were accepted by the Board of Trade which sought to make voluntary agreements with the firms. Total Oil refused to agree (and as a result received a Statutory Order). The considerable opposition by all firms resulted in the third restriction being temporary—it was removed in August 1968. Although the first two agreements are still operated it is difficult to identify changes in petrol distribution brought about by the intervention as opposed to increased competition (e.g. trading stamps and cut-price petrol) resulting from the growth of smaller companies and changes in the world supply/demand situation.

This generally disappointing case resulted in a dispute between two economists, H. Townsend[76] and T. Barna[77]. Barna felt that there were too many retail outlets and pointed out that retail margins were anyway higher than in continental distribution systems where throughput tended to be lower, rather than higher, than in the U.K. He also felt that restrictions on entry had been partly responsible for the chronic post-war shortage of refining capacity, leading to the import of refined petrol. Townsend argued that there was no evidence of a surplus of outlets and felt that the solus site system had improved standards of service at petrol stations.

We can summarise the differences in viewpoint regarding the industry as follows. Barna believes that vertically integrated oil companies with the degree of control over their retail outlets which they had had in the U.K. have been over-secure from outside competition. Townsend believes that planning regulations have caused existing petrol sites to have a monopoly site value, that this value has been capitalised in the price of stations and has resulted in any high costs of distribution which may exist.

Since 1965 the Commission has also received references in a wider field than that of monopolies of scale. In February 1967, under the powers in the 1965 Act to consider the supply of services, it was asked to investigate the professions. In October 1968 it received a general reference on the refusal of certain manufacturers and wholesalers to supply some retailers. This is believed to be a method of imposing sanctions against price-cutters subsequent to the 1964 Resale Price Maintenance Act (see page 252).

3 MERGERS AND TAKEOVERS Several different types of operation, with very different objectives and effects on industrial structure are included under the blanket description of a 'merger'. The essen-

tial characteristic which they all have in common is a change in the control of at least one firm. A merger may take the form of one company acquiring (either by purchase or an exchange of shares) a controlling interest in a second (usually smaller) firm—often called the takeover bid. Such an operation may have as its motive the control over the flow of revenues and profits of the firm now acquired or, alternatively, the purchase of 'excess' manufacturing capacity which could then be closed down. A further motive may be that the assets of the taken-over firm may have become undervalued.

The desire to close down excess capacity may be the result of a decline in demand for the industry's output or perhaps the result of an 'overgrowth' and the consequent need for rationalisation in an industry. Similarly, a merger of two or more firms into a new legal entity may be the result of bad trading conditions, extremely rigorous competition, or technological changes favouring larger scale operation.

Both the takeover and the merger described above have similar objectives to those of the single firm monopolist or the collective restrictive trade practice. However, it cannot be said that every linking of a number of firms in a new legal unit, or every takeover by one firm of another, has as its objective some purpose incompatible with the public interest. To grow by taking over, rather than by internal expansion, is to choose one of two ways or progressing and which of the two methods the firm decides to use will presumably be based on a consideration on the relative merits of each.[78] It should be noted that, although an individual firm can grow by merger, the output of the industry as a whole will remain unaffected, in contrast to the situation where firms grow internally.

The *Monopolies and Mergers Act 1965* states in Part III that where it appears to the Board of Trade that arrangements are in progress for a merger (or that one has taken place within the last 6 months) so that, either:

1 ⅓ of the supply of goods or services in the United Kingdom will be controlled by one company or
2 assets taken over by the merger exceed £5 m.
then the merger can be referred to the Monopolies Commission.

The Commission must report within six months as to whether the merger is against public interest—and if so it may recommend what action should be taken.

Part IV of the Act makes the transfer of a daily, Sunday or local newspaper to a proprietor so that the circulation, per issue, of the new group is over 500,000, unlawful (and thus automatically referred to the Monopolies Commission)—unless the Board of Trade gives its consent after a Monopolies Commission report. However, if the Board of Trade is satisfied that the newspaper being taken over is not economic as a going concern, it may give its consent without a Monopolies Commission report if a newspaper is not intended to continue as a separate newspaper and if its circulation is not over 25,000.

The British approach to the control of mergers has been that the State is concerned here with one way in which monopoly may come into being. Since the attitude of the legislature to monopoly has been that each case must be considered on its merits in the light of public interest, the Act follows the 1948 pattern in having cases referred by the Board of Trade, when it thinks fit, to the Monopolies Commission for a report. A difference between the two Acts is that in the case of mergers, conditions are laid down in which a merger *must* be referred to the Board of Trade, whereas the initiative comes from the Board in the case of monopolies of scale. Furthermore, proposed and existing mergers (within a six months time limit) are included. So far out of a total of about 3,000 mergers some 365 have been presented to the Board of Trade, which has referred 12 of them to the Monopolies Commission.

Four mergers have been turned down, viz. Ross Group–Associated Fisheries, United Drapery Stores–Burton and Barclays, Lloyds–Martins banks, Rank–De La Rue. In other cases proposed mergers have continued after assurances have been given on such matters as redundancies and undertakings to continue to supply. This has happened both at the 'vetting stage' and before the Monopolies Commission.

An attempted merger between United Drapery Stores and the Burton Group was the second to receive an adverse Monopolies Commission report. U.D.S. claimed that the merged group would obtain increased profits, partly as a result of further economies of scale. Burtons denied that the profitability of their men's shops could be increased although they did admit that certain parts of the group (e.g. Peter Robinson) were not very profitable. Their major reason for agreeing to the bid seemed to be a desire to obtain younger directors. The Commission, in opposing the bid, saw no technical advantages flowing from the merger and were sceptical that any further economies of scale could be obtained. While giving little weight to the complaints of wool textile manufacturers that they would suffer by having to sell their output to a monopolised tailoring industry, they did place great importance on the U.D.S.–Burton

Group controlling over one-third of the market in men's suits, particularly since each firm was, at present, the other's main competitor. They felt that Burtons should be able to obtain the younger directorate they required through the labour market. This Monopolies Commission report was not unanimous; those who saw the merger as not against the public interest stressed that this was a retailing industry where local competition was important and that entry into the industry at the retailing level was comparatively easy as the minimum optimum size of firm is small.

Although only four out of 3,000 mergers coming within the scope of the Act have been blocked by Monopolies Commission reports, the overall effect of the Act can reasonably be said to have been much wider than this. Firstly, an unknown number of mergers will presumably not have taken place because it was felt that they would fall foul of this legislation, secondly, in at least one case[79] the Board of Trade insistence that the proposed bid would be referred to the Commission was enough to cause the bidder to withdraw.

Despite its youth this Act seems to have already made its mark. The newness of the procedure has caused problems,[80] such as the fact that potential bidders and their advisers are discouraged by not having a body of 'Case Law' on which to judge whether or not the Commission is likely to allow their bid. This is inevitable when an investigatory, rather than judicial, process is used.

All bids coming within the scope of the Act are, of course, made more difficult because of the delays involved in discussing the proposed bid with the Board of Trade—even if it is unlikely that the scheme would be referred to the Commission.

Two further criticisms of the legislation have been made. Firstly, that the 'one-third rule' allows oligopolistic situations to go unchecked where no single firm has a high enough proportion of output to qualify. Secondly, that bids for part of the shareholding of a company, rather than a controlling interest, escape the Act completely.

We have already considered in Chapter 9[81] the paradox of the appearance of the Industrial Re-organisation Corporation—a government-sponsored body to encourage mergers—within a year of the Act to control them.

4 RESTRICTIVE TRADE PRACTICES In addition to resale price maintenance (r.p.m.), the Monopolies Commission report in 1955[82] considered various types of collective discrimination by sellers against buyers and aggregated rebate schemes. In general such agreements concerned themselves with prices, market shares and trading

arrangements. A wide variety of agreements existed, extended by a still wider variety of names; those mentioned in footnote [84] below seem self-explanatory.

It concluded that, in general, they acted against the public interest. A distinction between the arguments for restrictive practices and those for monopoly is that they cannot claim lowered costs by economies of scale, in comparison with perfect competition, since the number of business units is not reduced. Furthermore, an advantage sometimes claimed that they promote the progress and dispersal of technical knowledge (e.g. the Electric Lamp Manufacturers Association) ignores the argument that such co-operation need not be associated with trade restrictions. Even when the agreement is solely concerned with technical matters, it may serve as a barrier to new entrants who are denied the knowledge.

Restrictive agreements may also be disliked by the economist on the grounds of resource-use. Thus 'the Administrative Office set up to deal with the returns of the electric lamp manufacturers . . . had to analyse about 200,000 invoices a month. This . . . was equivalent to two-fifths of the number of Customs documents handled monthly for producing the Trade and Navigation Returns of the United Kingdom'.[83] Parties to agreements have claimed that the public interest is served by lowered costs, resulting from reduced risks, due to the maintenance of a stable price structure. See page 249 for a case where this was accepted by the Restrictive Practices Court. This report, and the 1956 Act which followed it, were not the first to deal with restrictive practices. The Monopolies Commission had been concerned with them since 1948 and many of the references made up to 1956 involved this type of situation in an industry.[84] In general, the Commission seemed to be most critical of those practices which restricted competition by making it difficult for existing low-cost producers to expand and which created barriers to the entry of new competition; it also attached great weight to the effect of agreements on research and development and the spread of technical knowledge in industry. A mere agreement on prices may not stop competition in an industry, since low-cost producers may devote their super-normal profits to innovation and thus, in time, drive out less efficient firms.

Part I of the *1965 Restrictive Trade Practices Act* set up a Registrar, a Register of Agreements, a Restrictive Practices Court and defined the system of judicial investigation.

Any agreement where producers or suppliers or their associations have mutual restrictions concerning prices and/or terms of trading must be registered, although any agreements relating exclusively to export or overseas production and trading are not registerable.[85] If the Registrar suspects the existence of a non-registered agreement he may bring persons before the High Court for examination on oath.

Subject to the 1968 Act, the Registrar must bring registered agreements before the Restrictive Practices Court, in an order which he decides. This Court makes final decisions on fact but there is a right of appeal to the Court of Appeal on decisions of law. The Restrictive Practices Court declares whether a restriction is contrary to the public interest. It may then declare an agreement void and make an Order restraining the parties where repetition of the offence is likely.

The Court works on the presumption that all registerable agreements are against the public interest. It is up to the parties to the agreement to 'prove their innocence', which they attempt to do, firstly, by showing a benefit to the public resulting from the agreement under one or more of the seven 'gateways' scheduled in the Act.

These gateways are:

1 That the agreement is necessary for the protection of the public from physical injury.
2 That a specific or substantial benefit or advantage results to the public as purchasers, consumers or users.
3 That the agreement is necessary as a counter measure to another's restrictions.
4 That the agreement is necessary to protect the parties against large buyers and sellers.
5 That removal of the agreement would be likely to have a serious and persistent effect on unemployment in an area.
6 That the abolition of the agreement would result in a reduction in the export business of the country or of the industry.
7 That the agreement is a necessary adjunct to another agreement approved by the Court.

The Registrar then attempts to prove the existence of detriments to the public which result from the agreement. Finally, the Court then 'balances' the detriments to the public proved by the Registrar with the advantages resulting from any successfully pleaded gateway(s). For an agreement to succeed under the Act the Court must decide:

> 'that the restriction is not unreasonable having regard to the balance between those circumstances[86] and any detriment to the public or to persons not parties to the agreement (being purchasers, consumers or users of goods produced or sold by such parties,

or persons engaged or seeking to become engaged in the trade or business of selling such goods or of producing or selling similar goods resulting or likely to result from the operation of the restrictions.'[87]

Criticisms of the 1956 legislation resulted in the:—

1968 Restrictive Trade Practices Act

This Act

1 Exempted from registration

(a) Agreements of importance to the national economy, which are, on balance, in the national interest, may be exempted by the Board of Trade.[88]

(b) A government department can, for 2 years, exempt an agreement relating only to prices and designed to obtain lower prices or restrict price increases.

(c) Agreements seeking only to enforce standards are exempted.

2 Required the registration of information agreements concerned with prices, terms of trading, sales, costs, processes, classes of customer and areas.

3 New agreements must normally be registered before their restrictions can be applied. Unregistered agreements are void and their implementation unlawful.[89]

4 The Registrar need not put before the Court, with Board of Trade approval, insignificant agreements.

5 Created an extra gateway: 'that the restriction does not directly or indirectly restrict or discourage competition to any substantial degree'.

6 The Board of Trade may annul an agreement, unless already approved by the Court, if it conflicts with E.F.T.A. rules.

While a detailed consideration of the success or failure of pleadings under the various gateways is outside our scope[90] we will mention some of the cases where the agreement was approved on grounds on which the economist might comment.

So far, the great majority of cases which have come before the Court have resulted in an adverse judgement. Amongst successful applicants the second gateway (benefit to the public) has been most popular. Most of these cases have aroused comment and the Court's judgement has been attacked, usually on the ground of inconsistency.[91] We will consider five of these 'successful' cases.

In the Black Bolt and Nut Association Case[92] the agreement was approved, on the grounds that the slightly higher prices resulting from the agreement were 'outbalanced' by the savings in administration of users who did not have to shop around to get the best price. This argument seems to accept one of the points made by those who approved of r.p.m. and implies that buyers are unable to evaluate the costs of enquiry as measured against the benefits received. Certainly the benefits and costs were not measured.

In the case of the Cement Makers Federation[93] the Court found that the agreement and the basing point price system[94] that formed part of it kept down the price of cement below the competitive level. This happened because the decrease in risk lowered the return on capital required by firms in a capital intensive industry.[95] This supposes a relationship between costs and prices in a collusive oligopolistic market not recognised in most economic models.

That part of the agreement relating to aggregated rebates[96] was held to be against the public interest as it encouraged small orders and favoured only buyers large in terms of total annual orders. In contrast, special rebates to merchants were upheld (on the grounds that they provided a service in distribution and stockholding) and rebates to asbestos manufacturers were approved as it was shown that the costs of meeting this business were less.

In the case of the National Sulphuric Acid Association's Agreement the Court upheld the agreement on the grounds that the Association (which was a purchasing pool of the U.K. importers of sulphur for making sulphuric acid) was able to withstand the dominant position of its largest supplier (Sulexco, an American cartel) and thus to obtain lower prices.

Our next case is that of the Standard Metal Windows Group.[97] The Court found effective competition in this industry between members of three groups, viz. the Association, Crittalls (who shared four-fifths of the metal windows trade equally with the Association) and metal windows in general with wooden windows. The agreement promoted the exchange of technical knowledge and cost data between members in a way that helped to keep down members' costs and (because of the competitive nature of the trade, on which this decision was founded) helped lower prices for metal and wooden windows generally.

Our last case is the agreement concerning the price of scrap between the British Iron and Steel Federation[98] and the National Federation of Scrap Iron, Steel and Metal Merchants. The Court favoured this agreement on the grounds that the public (as users of steel) benefited as a result of lower steel prices resulting from the lower scrap price stemming from the agreement. Presumably these prices were lower than would have been the case under a free market system; here we have an example of the Court being prepared to allow an interference with free market resource allocation.

These five cases have been selected to illustrate reasoning by the Court to which the economist may bring some special expertise. To summarise from the economist's point of view: firstly, there was a patronising attitude to consumer's ability to determine their own interest (Black Bolt and Nut Agreement)[99] despite the ability of firms to cost different buying policies. Secondly, there was a particular view of the relationship between risk, cost and price in an oligopolistic situation (Cement Manufacturers Agreement) which differed from the economist's view that cost fluctuations and price stability are often compatible in oligopoly. Thirdly, it accepted a form of agreement because of benefits resulting from cheaper raw materials (National Sulphuric Acid Association) without considering whether a similar benefit could have been obtained without the price rigidity inherent in a pool. Fourthly, the Court accepted that the public interest was safeguarded by an agreement in which small firms pooled their technical knowledge in order to remain competitive with the market leader (Metal Windows). Finally, there was a willingness to allow a distortion from a free market resource allocation in the interests of the public, even to the detriment of some members of the public, namely the members of the Association (Scrap Iron).

We now turn to the effectiveness of this legislation in the control of restrictive practices.[100] There is evidence[101] of over 2,000 agreements being registered by 1959, together with a growing number of abandoned agreements. The abandonment of agreements both before and after the Court started to operate reflected associations' views about their chances of success. The Registrar's choice of order of appearance before the Court was designed to obtain judgements on as wide a range of agreements as possible.[102] This fact, coupled with the very small number of agreements which were proved, quickly reduced the number of overt agreements operating in this country. We say 'overt' because the very small chance of success has stimulated firms to attempt evasion. The Act may also have had an effect on the structure of some industries. An argument supporting the *Monopolies and Mergers Act 1965* (see page 243) was that firms who were unable to combine by agreement had consolidated by merger. Information agreements and open price agreements were not caught by the 1956 Act, resulting in a belief that this type of agreement was increasing, with the clandestine object of allowing restrictive practices to continue. The basis of an open price agreement is that parties supply price information to all the other members either prior to the change in price, or after the price change has been made. In addition, in some agreements, information regarding costs may be made available. It has been suggested[103] that even where such agreements are not collusive in nature the increased level of information at the disposal of each firm may effectively result in an oligopolistic situation. At the present time, information agreements coming before the Court as a result of the 1968 Act are not being defended. A series of bilateral agreements in an industry falls outside the Act but may have a restrictive effect. The Registrar[104] has complained that parties may react to unfavourable judgements by setting up a new agreement, sufficiently different to be operable until it comes before the Court.[105]

It is unlikely that firms are prepared to continue to operate agreements that have been declared illegal. Heavy fines, in addition to adverse publicity, have been involved in the two such cases dealt with so far[106]—although the Court has yet to impose jail sentences.

If we try to *measure* the changes brought about in British industry by this legislation we find, as usual, little evidence[107] and the inevitable problem of what should be the basis of comparison. The Registrar[108] has stated that in some industries there is clearly now keen competition between the former parties in price and the various aspects of service

> 'I would suggest that the stimulant to competition after long periods of uniformity of price is most likely to come from buyers whose orders are big enough for the retention or loss of them to make a substantial impact on the manufacturers.'

He also recognised that rigidities, due to an oligopolistic situation, or inertia, due to long-established practices may also cause change to be slow. We believe that a real factor in the situation is time and that it may take years for the personal links established between firms in an old agreement to become eroded by changes in staff until they at last snap under the strain of competition.[109]

5 RESALE PRICE MAINTENANCE By resale price maintenance (r.p.m.), we mean the attempt to force on retailers the price at which they can resell a commodity. This price is normally a minimum price, but may be a fixed price or a maximum price. The enforcement may be by the individual firm or by a group of firms all of whom agree to take action against a retailer who does not follow the r.p.m. policy of the group. Resale price maintenance was the subject of three official investigations this century[110] before the 1948 Monopolies Act brought examples of r.p.m. before the Monopolies Commission. A report of

the Commission in 1955[111] resulted in the 1956 Restrictive Trade Practices Act which made *collective* r.p.m. illegal.

Part II of this Act, however, strengthened the operation of *individual* resale price maintenance by providing a basis for action on the part of a manufacturer against a retailer even where no direct contractual relationship existed. Prior to the act the manufacturer could only sue for breach of contract. This would only be possible where he had sold direct to the retailer (i.e. with no wholesaler intervening), unless the goods were protected by patent, in which case he could take actions against the third parties. The difficulties faced by individual manufacturers in maintaining resale prices in these conditions had been an important factor in the development of collective resale price maintenance.

Between the 1956 Act and 1964, r.p.m. broke down widely in the retail grocery trade.[112] In other fields, however, price maintenance continued to be effective, sometimes as a result of the trade association financing and co-ordinating the enforcement of individual members' r.p.m. Public criticism of all forms of r.p.m. increased. Ammunition was provided by the well-publicised examples of supermarkets forced, by manufacturer's action, to maintain high profit margins on items on which they wanted to cut prices, together with complaints by price-cutting retailers of the arbitrary way in which r.p.m. was being enforced. Various committees[113] reported against individual r.p.m. prior to the 1964 Act. While it is difficult to obtain satisfactory evidence it would seem that the 1956 Act had only a small effect on the proportion of consumers' expenditure on price-maintained items.[114] It must be remembered, however, that collective r.p.m. was only one form of collective action which the 1956 Act was designed to control.

The *Resale Price Act 1964* repealed the powers of enforcement given to the individual firm under Section II of the 1956 Act. Any agreement between a supplier and a dealer which imposes on a dealer a restriction not to resell at less than a specified or ascertainable price in the United Kingdom was made void. It is illegal for a supplier to publish a minimum price list. The enforcement of maximum prices was unaffected.

Exemption from the Act may be sought by suppliers who, firstly, register the class of goods[115] with the Registrar of Restrictive Practices and, secondly, successfully plead for their exemption before the Restrictive Practices Court. While awaiting the Court's consideration the goods are exempted from the Act.

Procedure before the Restrictive Practices Court is similar to that under the 1956 Act. The Court may grant exemption in a case where the public interest suffers more by a system of maintained minimum resale prices than it benefits under any of five gateways.

The five gateways are:

1 That in the absence of the agreement the quality of goods would be substantially reduced.
2 That the removal of the agreement would substantially reduce the number of retail establishments.
3 That higher retail prices would result from the abolition of the agreement.
4 That the removal of the agreement would be likely to cause danger to health.
5 That necessary services would be reduced as a result of the removal of the agreement.

Manufacturers may still take action against a firm selling one of its products as a loss-leader without agreement, although their response is limited to withholding supplies for twelve months.

Before examining further the scope and effects of these Acts, we will consider the arguments for and against the collective and individual forms of this restrictive practice. Few pieces of government economic intervention have been so extensively debated.[116]

Because, as we shall see, overt r.p.m. has virtually disappeared from the U.K., we will merely list the arguments against and for this practice:

Against:

1 It results in new entrants into a trade being unable to demonstrate their efficiency by lowered prices. It is significant that from 1880 onwards, collective r.p.m. was developed in trades where retailers were meeting competition from new types of retailing.
2 Recommended margins may allow inefficient outlets to stay in business.
3 Rigid price structures reduce pressure on manufacturers to lower prices.

In favour:

1 R.P.M. allows a built-in level of service which consumers might not get otherwise. On the other hand, consumers' choice regarding the level of service they require is limited.
2 R.P.M. allows less popular parts of a range to be sold at a lower

price. But this involves consumers of, e.g. baked beans subsidising consumers of, e.g. mushroom ketchup. Economists cannot say this is undesirable; they should point out that the amount of such cross-subsidies should be known.
3 Price-cutting resulting from the abolition of r.p.m. would cause instability by changing prices and uncertain sales in the industry, which could lead to higher costs associated with shorter production runs. In particular the manufacturers of brand leaders would suffer.
4 Without r.p.m. the number of outlets would be reduced. In practice, this becomes the emotive 'small street corner shop v. supermarket' argument—emotive because of the number and political importance of shop keepers.

This list of arguments for and against resale price maintenance has been, necessarily, selective. The controversy was a good example of a situation where some discussion was really based on social or political values and where economists were able to point out the consequences of departure from the perfect competition model and to predict the results of government intervention.

It would seem that retailers had most to gain from r.p.m. and that it might not act in favour of any one manufacturer. Why were manufacturers generally not in favour of its abolition? Three factors may have applied here. Firstly, manufacturers in a trade may have become unused to,[117] or may have deliberately decided to forgo, price competition. Secondly, there would have been a considerable disadvantage in being the first to break r.p.m. in a trade where the loss of goodwill from organised retailers was important. Thirdly, manufacturers may have believed that the abolition of r.p.m. would reduce the number of retailers and that this would have reduced sales and profits.

Two questions concerning r.p.m. remain to be answered: How did government intervention operate and what effects did the legislation have on trades where r.p.m. was widespread?

The Monopolies Commission was concerned with examples of both individual and collective r.p.m. during the period 1948 up to the 1956 Act. Between 1957 and the 1964 Act it was concerned solely with individual r.p.m. In the earlier period it was invariably hostile to the collective arrangement and enforcement of r.p.m., but usually favoured individual enforcement. The one exception to this general tolerance was in the case of tyre manufacturers (in 1955) where the Commission recommended[118] not only the scrapping of the existing collective r.p.m. agreement but the prohibition of the individual r.p.m. which it felt was likely to follow in such an oligopolistic industry. Between 1957 and 1964 the Commission dealt with three cases involving individual r.p.m. In the report of cigarettes and tobacco they favoured its continuation so long as the industry remained at the same level of competition. In both the electrical equipment for cars and the wallpaper reports, they found against individual r.p.m. largely on the basis of the monopolistic situation which existed in these trades.

The 1956 Act caused a large number of agreements (some of which concerned r.p.m.) to be abandoned and a great number of agreements which were registered and ultimately came before the Restrictive Practices Court. Almost without exception, the Court found the agreement to be against the public interest.

The exception was the Net Book Agreement (1957) which came before the Court in 1962.[119] Publishers who were party to the agreement (drafted after the 1956 Act) did not have to 'net' every book and could fix the resale price themselves.[120] The purpose of the net book system was to ensure that purchasers of such books undertook to resell at the net price, less a standard discount in certain cases, e.g. public libraries. It was agreed that individual r.p.m. was impracticable without the agreement. The Court held that the agreement was in the public interest as without it stock-holding booksellers would be driven out of the trade as a result of losing sales on popular books to price-cutting outlets and specialist library suppliers. Thus the public would lose the advantages of bookshops holding wide stocks. The reduction in pre-publication orders and stocks from stock-holding booksellers would increase the price of books by reducing publishers' printing runs. Publishers would be reluctant to print such a wide range of titles. The accepted view of this case is that the Court seemed to have a special attitude to book publication and was willing to overlook the likely economic advantages to the public resulting from the cessation of the agreement (i.e. cheaper popular books) in favour of 'cultural' advantages.[121]

The 1964 Act[122] was greeted with expressions of defiance by manufacturers involved in individual r.p.m. It was alleged that the Court would be swamped by the number of registered and defended schemes. In the event, the vast majority of cases were withdrawn or undefended as, in industry after industry, the major firms decided that r.p.m. was not in their interest, or could not be shown to be in the public interest.[123]

So far only two examples of registrable r.p.m. have been approved: in 1968 the Registrar offered no evidence against r.p.m. for books and maps on the grounds that collective r.p.m. had been approved in 1962. The Chemists' Federation's agreement is the only case to have been fought and won. Two cases[124] have been condemned by the Court. Their failure, and the heavy costs[125] of defending them, have meant that there are, at present, no agreements left to be considered.

The confectionery case hinged on the extent to which the Court accepted the manufacturer's view that abolition would involve extensive price-cutting by supermarkets and that the resulting switch of buying would involve the closure of 30% of large, 19% of medium sized and 14% of small sweetshops. This could result in higher prices, following higher profit margins being required by those shops remaining, coupled with higher manufacturing costs resulting from a smaller volume of sale through the smaller number of outlets.

The Court decided that a 10% reduction in shops was a more likely figure as it did not see supermarkets becoming major outlets.[126] This detriment was more than outweighed by the public advantage of a more flexible price structure in confectionery, where popular items might be frequently reduced in price,[127] even though a general decrease in prices was not envisaged.

We now turn to the consideration of the effectiveness of this legislation in terms of public interest. Three major predictions were made in the argument surrounding the abolition of r.p.m.; firstly, that prices would rise/fall, secondly, that there would be fewer retailers (and more scope for other forms of consumer trading) and, thirdly, that manufacturers' costs would be increased. It may be felt that here is a clear-cut case where

1 economists and others have predicted what would happen as the result of government intervention;
2 that intervention has taken place, and
3 that all three of these predictions are capable of being tested by an appeal to the facts.

We know of no empirical evidence of this kind[128] however, nor do we feel that such evidence would 'prove' or 'disprove' any of the arguments discussed. Firstly, there have been so many changes in other factors which affect consumers' demand, as well as falls in the value of money, that a crude comparison of 1956–66 prices and costs would be inconclusive. Secondly, the useful comparison is not 1956–66 but 1966 *with* and *without* r.p.m.[129] This involves unmeasurable considerations regarding the 'with r.p.m.' growth of supermarkets, mail-order firms, etc.

What can be said is general. A large number of items are now being sold at below 'recommended price'.[130] Price-cutting has been most widespread for goods where well-known brand names offering good retail margins have attracted supermarkets to stock them. In some cases (e.g. paint) supermarkets have moved into fields which they had hitherto left alone. This development has been curtailed by the refusal of some manufacturers to supply. In some cases (e.g. shoes) such manufacturers are prepared to make 'own brand' lines. It is noticeable that price cuts, although widely practised, have not been as large as was anticipated in spirits, despite the 1961 change in the law which allowed licensed outlets to sell during normal shopping hours. The great difficulty which supermarkets have found in getting a licence has hindered new competition here, as has the small percentage reduction possible, due to high taxation. The widespread price cuts in consumer durables have not had an extensive effect on the structure of retailing since 'trade-in' prices have always provided a method of concealed price reductions. In addition the growth of discount clubs (obtaining goods at wholesale or near wholesale prices) which were unaffected by the abolition of r.p.m. has probably been a distinct and important influence on trading in this field.

Despite some growth in retailers' own branding, major brands still appear to have a dominant place in the market. The predicted slaughter of the small man does not appear to have occurred, partly because they have reacted by improving marketing techniques.

SECTION III

CONCLUSION The Monopolies Commission was set up in 1948; the Restrictive Practices Court was formed in 1956. After at least ten years' experience of the operation of the Commission and the Court, what are current opinions about the effectiveness of these two approaches, each quite different from the other? What can the economist contribute to this discussion?

Monopoly and restrictive practices policy cannot have a basis in the rules of welfare economics as the latter do not identify optimality as the position where there is less, rather than more, monopoly. So the policy must be regarded not as an exercise in welfare economics, but as a technique for achieving some particular goal, such as the reduction of economic power possessed by producers.[131] Thus the economist can say nothing on the qualitative impact of monopoly policy but might be able to comment on its quantitative results.

The Monopolies Commission has continually been under fire for its slowness and lack of consistency in reporting. Its supporters claim that this has been the result of inadequate resources being used to enforce the legislation[132] and claim that a process of enquiry is the only one which can reflect the attitude that, *a priori*, a monopoly cannot be condemned. This case-study approach has a basis in economic theory, which does not lead to any general laws about the practical advantages or disadvantages of monopoly.

Detractors point out that, in at least one case,[133] the Restrictive Practices Court has approved practices disapproved of by the Commission. In the case of detergents[134] the Commission recommended price reductions within a year of the National Board for Prices and Incomes finding price increases of up to 20% justified on the grounds of higher costs. What is disturbing in this, is that there is a tendency for the Board of Trade and government to ignore so many of the Commission's more drastic recommendations.[135] Another indication of lack of confidence in the Commission's reports as a basis for policy can be found in the way in which large mergers and reorganisations involving foreign control (such as Philips-Pye and Chrysler-Rootes) have been inspected by the Ministry of Technology and not dealt with through the Board of Trade and Monopolies Commission machinery of the 1965 Act. These difficulties arise both from the piecemeal approach and from the fact that the public interest cannot be quantified.

Not all criticisms of restrictive practices intervention have been met by the 1968 Act. The C.B.I. has favoured a Commission rather than a Court. A further comment has been that the danger in allowing 'agreements in the national interest' to be exempted is that not only may this provide a 'back-door' method of approval but it may result in an undermining of the absolute authority of the Court. This might result in the situation which faces the Commission, which has no certainty that all monopolies will be referred to it, and where there is no compulsion on the Board of Trade to act on its recommendations.

It is generally felt that the legislation concerning r.p.m. has been so effective that, with the exceptions mentioned in the text, the practice will soon become extinct. Nevertheless the system of continued 'recommended prices' has been held to be 'concealed r.p.m.'.[136] Some price-cutting supermarkets have found that manufacturers have reacted (quite legally) by withholding supplies on the grounds that they are not authorised or qualified dealers.

The enforcement of legislation controlling monopoly and restrictive practices in this country has suffered from three handicaps. Firstly, there are two quite different approaches (either Court or Commission) with the result that one may contradict the other as in the case of Metal Windows quoted above. Secondly, only the Court has final legal authority, whereas other government departments may ignore, reject or not act on the Commission's report. This has become more important with the development of government interest in other forms of intervention (e.g. Prices and Incomes[137] Economic Development Committees). Lastly, both Court and Commission are asked to evaluate basing their decision on 'public interest'. Economists have something to say on this last point—and that is that they cannot yet measure the public interest.

In contrast, in the U.S.A. the courts are concerned simply with the structure of industry, in determining whether or not it provides a competitive environment and with deciding whether or not there has been any collusion between firms. Such a decision is based on facts proved to the satisfaction of the Court. It implies a belief in the virtues of competition from the consumer's point of view.

> 'We are clear, however, that a merger the effect of which "may be to substantially lessen competition" is not saved because, on some ultimate reckoning of social, or economic, debits, and credits, it may be deemed beneficial. A value choice of such magnitude is beyond the ordinary limits of judicial competence and in any event has been made for us already, by Congress when it enacted the amended Section 7. Congress determined to preserve our traditionally competitive economy. It therefore proscribed anti-competitive mergers, the benign and the malignant alike, fully aware, we must assume, that some price might have to be paid.'[138]

In contrast, in the United Kingdom any decision involves the weighing of advantages and disadvantages which may not be subject to accurate measurement,[139] against a criterion of public interest which is not always clear.[140] In addition the factual information presented to the Court of the Commission has to be used to provide a basis for predictions[141] about what could happen if the agreement or monopoly were removed. How can predictions be made when an unrestricted industry has not operated for many years?[142] The alternative is to try the perilous business of making international comparisons. In addition the views of expert witnesses are called —whose views presumably also are based on comparison and predictions.

It is not claimed that the approach in the U.S.A. is better (there is no way of measuring for comparative purposes) but it is clear that the British solution involves inconsistencies over time as the variables are weighed in a different way. Some of this confusion stems from the inability of economic theory to provide models which give specific answers to the problems facing policy-makers. Writers are driven to analysing decisions and cases with the object of constructing models on which the Court is thought to have acted;[143] models based on theory which is not universally accepted by theorists.

To some extent any anti-monopoly and restrictive practice policy attempts an impossible task. Its success cannot be measured by the failure rate before the Court[144] or Commission; even after more than seventy years the United States is still involved in active legal action. In the same way that direct taxation results in a profession of tax-avoiders so legislation such as ours involves avoidance which has to be stopped by further legislation. In the last analysis, as U.S. experience shows, it is very difficult to get evidence to convict[145] those who operate unwritten 'gentlemen's agreements', or to act against oligopolists who are determined to act defensively.

Monopoly policy may appear to be an economic problem, but in fact it is largely a political problem: it is concerned with political goals such as reducing economic power in private hands. The economist's function is to predict and observe the consequences of the policy but he has an insufficient basis for qualitative judgements on welfare aspects[146] and for quantitative judgement in the sense both of measuring concepts like 'efficiency' and the 'public interest'.

Notes

1 See footnote 84, for a list of restrictive practices.

2 See p. 236 for a quotation from the 1948 Monopolies and Restrictive Practices Act defining 'public interest'.

3 The differentiation is from the point of view of the consumer, who distinguishes between various brands or qualities sold in a market.

4 The realism of such an assumption is considered on p. 232.

5 See p. 240.

6 Chamberlin, E. H., *The Theory of Monopolistic Competition*, Harvard University Press, 8th Ed. (1962).

7 See Chapter 3, page 57 for the significance of this inequality.

8 Compare *A* and *B* on Diagram 2.

9 e.g. Cohen, K. J. and Cyert, R. M., *The Theory of the Firm*, Chapter 11, Prentice-Hall (1963).

10 See Cohen, K. J. and Cyert, R. M., *op. cit.*, Chapter 12.

11 Although occasional 'price wars' are also a feature of oligopoly.

12 An example is the fluctuating sales and employment in the motor car industry.

13 Thus the following three oligopolistic market structures are likely to lead to different results: (a) a very small number of firms of equal size, (b) a small number of firms varying from large to small, (c) a dominant firm with a large number of smaller firms. Concerning oligopoly models Cohen, K. G. and Cyert, R. M. (p. 260) say: 'Unfortunately there is no empirical evidence available to indicate the extent to which any of these models is particularly applicable to real-world behaviour.'

14 The reader is advised to accept this as received doctrine on oligopoly. Examples and proof of models demonstrating this may be found in Cohen, K. G. and Cyert, R. M., *op. cit.*

15 Page 59.

16 Theoretically, economies of scale are divided into those which relate to the individual firm (internal) and those shared by all firms in the industry as it grows (external). For the theoretical distinction

between the two see Lipsey, R. G., *An Introduction to Positive Economics*, Second Edition, Weidenfeld and Nicolson (1966).

For a descriptive approach see Edwards, R. S. and Townsend, H., *Business Enterprise: its growth and organisation*, Macmillan (1964).

For examples in British Industry see Pratten, C. and Dean, R. H., *The Economics of Large Scale Production in British Industry*, Cambridge University Press (1965).

17 Edwards, O. C. D., 'Conglomerate bigness as a source of power', in N.B.E.R. *Business Concentration and Price Policy*, Princeton (1955).

18 For a forthright discussion see Schmookler, J., 'Technical Change and Economic Theory', *American Economic Review* (1965).

19 A view advanced by Schumpeter, J. A., *Capitalism, Socialism and Democracy*, Allen and Unwin, 4th Edition (1961). A similar view is taken by Wiseman, J., in 'Monopoly, Technical Progress and Public Policy', *Yorkshire Bulletin of Economic and Social Research*, Vol. 8, No. 1 (1956).

20 i.e. a new lower average cost curve, not a movement along an existing cost curve.

21 Such as a Monopolies Commission investigation.

22 Keiser, N. F., *Economics: Analysis and Policy*, Wiley, p. 606, 1st ed., (1965).

23 Purdy, H. L., Lindahl, M. A. and Carter, W. A., *Corporate Concentration and Public Policy*, quoted in Keiser, op. cit.

24 Monopolies Commission, *Report on the Supply and Exports of Matches and the Supply of Matchmaking Machinery*, para. 145 (1953).

25 Hamberg, D., 'Invention in the Industrial Research Laboratory', *Journal of Political Economy*, Vol. LXXI, No. 2.

26 Adams, W. and Dirlam, J. B., 'Big Steel, Invention and Innovation', *Quarterly Journal of Economics*, Vol. 80, No. 2 (1966). McAdams, A. K., 'Big Steel, Invention & Innovation reconsidered', *Quarterly Journal of Economics* (August 1967). Adams, W. and Dirlam, J. B., 'Big Steel, Invention and Innovation, a reply', *Quarterly Journal of Economics* (August 1967).

27 See Bain, J. S. *Barriers to New Competition: their Character and Consequences in Manufacturing Industry*, Harvard U.P. (1965).

28 Galbraith, J. K., *American Capitalism: the Concept of Countervailing Power*, Houghton Mifflin, Boston (1958).

29 Other possible motives not connected with profit maximisation are: the desire for good public relations, a wish to serve the public, status with fellow industrialists, moral and religious beliefs in a 'fair market price' or the 'satisficing' goal of the Behavioural Theory of the Firm.

30 This view has been accepted at times by the Monopolies Commission, thus in the *Report on the Supply of Flat Glass*, February 1968: 'We believe that Pilkington has acted with a full sense of responsibility to the public interest in the past and that it is likely to continue to do so unless there should be some unforeseen change in the character of the management.' 'This sense of responsibility may be associated to some extent with the long-established dominance of the Pilkington family within the business.'

Pilkington control 90% of flat glass sold in the U.K.

31 e.g. Mansfield, F., 'Size of Firm, Market-structure and Innovation', *Journal of Political Economy* (December 1963). Markham, J. W., 'Market Structure, Business Conduct and Innovation', *American Economic Review* (1965).

32 Hamberg, D., quoted in Cohen, K. J. and Cyert R. M., op. cit., Chapter 18, p. 388. See also, Johnson, P. S., Size and Technological Change', *Moorgate and Wall Street Review*, Spring 1970.

33 See Stigler, G. J., *The Theory of Price*, p. 126, 2nd Edition, Macmillan (1962).

34 The theory of monopoly or imperfect competition in the market for productive resources (i.e. inputs as opposed to outputs) has been ignored, except in the theory of 'Countervailing Power' referred to on p. 231.

35 For this and other normative approaches see De G. Fortman, B., *Theory of Competition Policy*, North Holland Publishing Co., Chapter 3 (1966).

36 Clark, J. H., 'Towards a Concept of Workable Competition', *A.E.R.*, (June 1940), Mason, E. S., 'The Current Status of the Monopoly Problem in the U.S.', *Harvard Law Review* (June 1949).

37 Allen, G. C., *Monopoly and Restrictive Practices*, Chapter II, pp. 23–4, Allen and Unwin Ltd (1966). He produces no evidence that the concept has actually been used by the Commission. See also O'Brien, D. P. and Swann, D., *Information Agreements, Competition and Efficiency*, Chapter 3, Macmillan (1968).

38 For examples of mergers in this (and later) periods see Evely, R. and Little, I. M. D., *Concentration in British Industry*, Cambridge University Press 1960, especially parts (VIII) and (IX). For a discussion on the beginning of restrictive practices see Yamey, B. S., *The Economics of Resale Price Maintenance*, Part II, Pitman (1954).

39 The economic basis for a concentration policy is to get 'economies of scale' by producing at capacity in a smaller number of firms and/or plants which had hitherto not been fully utilised. The freed resources would then be available for other uses. See page 232 for an analysis showing that, in the short run, this reasoning may be wrong.

40 In some cases, where an association had already existed, firms who had remained outside the association joined it for the war period in order to safeguard their share of raw materials, and left at the end of the war.

41 *Final Report of Committee on Commercial and Industrail Policy after the War, Cd.* 9025 (1918).

42 1921 *Trade Facilities Act.*

43 *The* 1919 *Profiteering Acts* could be cited as the sole exception. They were, however, almost completely ineffectual.

44 The 1918 *Committee on Commercial and Industrial Policy* after the War suggested that agreements should be made public. It also recommended that international combines of which British firms were a part should be registered with the Board of Trade. The 1919 Committee on Trusts suggested research into the size and scope of trade associations. It also recommended a tribunal, rather along the lines of the Monopolies Commission, to investigate combinations.

45 c.f. the apparent inconsistency between the present policy of control of mergers and monopoly by legislation together with the establishment of the I.R.C. to promote mergers (Chapter 9, p. 201).

46 e.g. 1918 *The Economist.* 'The first requisite of industry is the restoration of freedom'. Quoted in Rowley, C. K., 1931 Committee on Restraint of Trade, the 'Ordinary right of freedom to contract ought not to be withdrawn without some compelling reason.'

47 For statistical evidence concerning the growth of trade associations see P.E.P. *Industrial Trade Associations*, Chapter 1, London (1957).

48 White Paper, *Employment Policy*, Cmd. 6527 (1944).

49 e.g. 1948 Committee on the Distribution of Building Materials and Components (The Simon Committee).

50 *The Monopolies and Restrictive Practices (Inquiry and Control) Act.*

51 'Collective Discrimination'; a Report on Exclusive Dealing, Collective Boycotts, Aggregated Rebates and other Discriminatory Trade Practices, Cmd. 9504.

52 Hunter, A., *Competition and the Law*, p. 78, George Allen and Unwin (1966), emphasises the role played by Civil Servants who, as a result of links between ministries and industry during the war, knew of and were concerned about the scope and nature of trade association's restrictive practices.

53 Brock, C., *The Control of Restrictive Practices from* 1956, McGraw-Hill, 1966, p. 33, gives no evidence for her view that the models of imperfect competition developed by Chamberlain, E. H. and Robinson, J. had been fully absorbed by 1948 in the field of government reports.

54 4/10 members.

Since this chapter was written the Department of Employment and Productivity has taken over from the Board of Trade.

55 Thus in June 1968 the Commission found that a reference on men's haircutting failed as the National Hairdressers Federation had a membership of only 1/5 of U.K. barbers.

56 In 1953 the *Monopolies and Restrictive Practices Commission Act* increased the size of the commission to 25 and allowed it to deal with up to three references at any one time by working on a group basis.

57 In 1956 the *Restrictive Trade Practices Act* Section III reduced the commission in size to the level of the 1948 Act. The scope of its operations was restricted to single firm monopolistic practices or to practices involving the export trade whether by a single firm or by an agreement between firms.

58 It must be remembered that the operation of the Commission during its history has been greatly affected by legal variations in its size and scope. In addition, the policy of the Board of Trade regarding cases to be submitted to it, and the powers, and the willingness to exercise them, of the Board have varied considerably during the period. The importance of this discretionary power, which means that the policy is now centred around a government department, rather than the Commission, is shown in 'Mergers: a Guide to Board of Trade Practice', H.M.S.O. (1969).

59 We do not discuss the problems of definition of a trade, or of a commodity in this sense. For an exhaustive analysis, see Evely, R., and Little, I. M. D., *Concentration in British Industry*, N.I.E.S.R., Cambridge University Press (1960).

60 In 1966 the Commission abandoned an inquiry into the aluminium industry when its investigations brought to light an agreement between firms which they agreed should go before the Restrictive Practices Court.

61 We return to this point in Section III.

62 Although, on the other hand, the Board of Trade may in fact appeal against a Monopolies Commission Report (to the House of Lords) should it wish to take action when the Commission has not reported the practices as being against the public interest.

63 Statutory Orders have the advantages of providing a legal remedy to an individual (or the Board of Trade) in the event of their being broken. On the other hand they suffer from the disadvantages of written legislation, e.g. their wording must be drafted without ambiguity; they have a rigid approach.

64 e.g. British Oxygen withdrew in 1963 voluntary undertakings which it had given as a result of the 1956 Report.

65 McLachlan, D. L. and Swann, D., 'Next Steps in Monopoly Policy', *Scottish Journal of Political Economy* (June 1964).

66 Report on the Supply of Dental Goods (1950).

67 Thus in the Report on the Supply of Household Detergents (August 1966) the Commission recommended that selling expenses should be reduced by 40%, prices by 20% and that both should be subject to continued review. After 8 months' negotiation the Board of Trade and the duopolists agreed that there should be a continuation of the standstill on prices, resulting from a 1965 Prices and Incomes Board Report, together with a trial period of selling unadvertised brands of powder.

68 e.g. breaking up the British Oxygen Corporation. Such powers were given to the Board of Trade by the 1965 Act.

69 e.g. 1961, Report on Tobacco. The Commission recommended that the Imperial Tobacco Company's 42·5% shareholding in Gallahers should be relinquished. The Board of Trade merely obtained an agreement from the Imperial Tobacco Co. not to interfere in the management of Gallahers. Probably the basis of this view was that competition in cigarettes had already intensified and that I.T.C.'s holding had been reduced to 37% by a share exchange between Gallahers and the American Tobacco Company.

70 Section I, page 222.

71 *Clutch Mechanism for Road Vehicles Report* (1968).

72 Hunter, A., op. cit., p. 248.

73 Rowley, C. K., 'The British Monopolies Commission, Part V, Statistical Measure of Economic Performance'. This examines the data presented to the Commission and discusses various alternative forms of measurements of efficiency possible. This section has been subject to criticism. Thus Cohen, R., reviewing the book in the *Economic Journal*, December, 1966, quotes from p. 300 'audit costs clearly attributable to sloth and inefficiency should be added back to profits for rate or return on capital measurement. The Commission has never attempted this in practice'. Her subsequent comment is 'How could they?'.

74 Since publicity has been felt to be an important sanction on firms involved in a reference, it is perhaps a criticism of the Board of Trade that cases were not selected which would have caught the public eye.

75 Caves, R., op. cit.

76 Who represented an oil company before the Commission. See Townsend, H., 'Exclusive Dealing in Petrol: Some Comments', *Economica* (November 1965).

77 Who sat on the Commission and dissented from the majority report,

believing that there were no virtues in the system. See Barna, T., 'Exclusive Dealing in Petrol: A Reply', *Economica* (May 1966).

78 Penrose, E. T., *The Theory of the Growth of the Firm*, Chapter VIII, Blackwell (1959).

79 The Imperial Tobacco Co's bid for Smiths Crisps Ltd. The Imperial Tobacco Company controls Golden Wonder Crisps.

80 See *Financial Times*, 28.2.66.

81 p. 202.

82 See footnote p. 84.

83 Quoted in Allen, G. C., *Monopoly and Restrictive Practices*, p. 38 footnote, Allen and Unwin (1968).

84 *Common price agreements* were condemned by the Commission in the case of the Cable Makers' Association and the Federation of Calico Printers. The British Insulin Manufacturers' agreement was accepted subject to Board of Trade supervision. The *collective tendering agreement* of the London Builders Conference was condemned. The *market sharing agreements* of the Electric Lamp Manufacturers' Association, the Cable Makers' Association and the Federation of Calico Printers were condemned.

Exclusive dealing and *collective boycotts* were condemned in Cast Iron Rainwater Goods reference, the Electric Lamp Manufacturers' Association, the Cable Makers' Association and the Timber Trades Federation.

The *aggregated rebate scheme* operated by the Electric Lamp Manufacturers' Association was condemned by the Commission but the recommendation was not accepted by the Board of Trade.

For details on this aspect of the Monopolies Commission's work see Rowley, *op. cit.*, especially Part III.

85 The Register is open for public inspection, with the exception of agreements disclosing trade secrets.

86 i.e. gateways 1–7.

87 Restrictive Trade Practices Act 1956. Section 21 (i).

88 This clause resulted from criticism by the N.E.D.C., C.B.I. and D.E.A. that agreements, such as reorganisation in the chemical industry so that one firm only should produce a commodity now being imported, had been held to be registerable under the 1956 Act. In our view, the economist must remain sceptical of the long-term national advantages from reductions in international trade commenced in this way.

89 So far only one case, traffic light equipment manufacturers in 1967, had been brought under the 1956 Act. Each firm was fined £500 for not disclosing an agreement. The Registrar's problem has been the difficulty of detection.

90 For an account up to 1964 see Brock, C., Yamey, B. S. and Stevens, R. B., op. cit., also deal with individual cases.

91 The Water-Tube Boilermakers Case is a good example. See Brock, C., *op. cit.*, pp. 75–8, Stevens, R. B. and Yamey, B. S., *op. cit.*, pp. 194–200.

92 July, 1960.

93 March, 1961.

94 A price structure in which the price paid by a consumer depended on the basic price of the basing point of the particular geographical zone in which he happened to be, plus an extra depending on the customer's distance from the basing point.

95 Beacham, A., in 'Some Thoughts on the Cement Judgement', *Economic Journal* (June, 1962) is critical of the Court's findings in this case, largely on the ground that if the agreement did bring about lower prices (and therefore profits) it was not in the interest of the parties. It is unlikely that firms would make, and adhere to, an agreement not in their own best interests. A possible explanation for a profit lowering agreement would be fear of new entry. This did not appear important in this case. Beacham also points out that the risk in a competitive situation may effect minimum rates of profit to attract new capital into the industry but should not affect average rates of return to capital already employed. Thus a price system which gives a 10% rate of return on new investment may cause firms to accept such a low return because they can be certain that it will be achieved. Such a price system also guarantees a commensurate rate on capital already employed.

96 Under an aggregated rebate scheme a buyer receives a rebate calculated (in this case on a progressive scale) on the total of his purchases from members of the association per annum, irrespective of the size of the individual orders and their allocation between members.

97 July, 1962.

98 A body which has statutory control over prices and costs in the industry. January, 1964.

99 Allen, G. C. (op. cit.), p. 93, says that this judgement has been regarded by economists as an 'aberration of judgement similar to that which occasionally causes weary examiners to award high marks to a mediocre script'.

100 For the effects of the 1956 Act on r.p.m., see page 254.

101 Brock, C. (op. cit.), pp. 67–8. See also Hunter, A. (op. cit), Chapter 8, Section A.

102 Since the Court, like other British Courts, could rely on the rule of precedent to apply a judgement to similar agreements.

103 O'Brien, D. P. and Swann, D., 'Information Agreements—a problem in Search of a Policy', Manchester School (September, 1966). For a very full treatment pointing out the pros and cons for public interest see O'Brien, D. P. and Swann, D., *Information Agreeements, Competition and Efficiency*, Macmillan (1968). In a postscript dealing with the 1958 Act they feel that the relevant clause 'could' enable effective proceedings to be taken. In general they object to the gains, in new classes of registration, under the 1968 Act being offset by the larger category of exceptions.

104 Registrar's Report, 1/7/63–30/6/66.

105 They may have no intention of defending the new agreement but use it as a method of gaining time.

106 Galvanised Tank Manufacturers 1965. Eight firms were fined a total of £102,000. Tyre Manufacturers 1966. Eight firms were fined £10,000 each. See O'Brien, D. P. and Swann, D., op. cit., Chapter 5.

107 Heath, J. B., 'Restrictive Practices and After', *Manchester School* (May, 1961) found some evidence of increased competition and reduced prices.

108 Report 1/7/61–30/6/63.

109 For a discussion of criticism about the suitability of the type of legislation involved in the 1956 Act see Section III of this Chapter, page 258.

110 1920 Sub-Committee on Fixed Retail Prices, 1930 Committee on Restraint of Trade, 1949 Committee on Resale Price Maintenance Cmd. 7696 (The Lloyd-Jacob Committee). This influential Committee supported individual r.p.m. (largely on the grounds that it protected branded goods from being used as loss-leaders) but recommended the abolition of collective r.p.m.

111 1955 Cmd. 9504 'Collective Discrimination'; a report on exclusive dealing, collective boycotts, aggregated rebates and other discriminatory trade practices.

112 See Pickering, J. F., *Resale Price Maintenance in Practice*, Allen and Unwin (1966). Chapters VII–X.

113 The Council on Prices, Productivity and Incomes 1958 (Cohen Council) advocated the abolition of r.p.m. The Committee on Consumer Protection (Cmnd. 1781), 1962 (The Maloney Committee) reported that the abolition of individual r.p.m. 'might greatly benefit consumers'. The N.E.D.C. Report *The Growth of the Economy* (1964) was also in favour of abolition.

114 Pickering, J. F. in Chapters III and XI gives the various measurements which have been made of the extent of r.p.m.

115 Since the Register is one of classes of goods and not agreements

any manufacturer of a class of good can continue to impose r.p.m. where any other manufacturer has registered the class.

116 Yamey, B. S., *Economics of Resale Price Maintenance*, Pitman (1954). Yamey, B. S., *Resale Price Maintenance*, Hobart Paper No. 1. The Institute of Economic Affairs, 4th Edition, 1964 (1st Edition 1960). Andrews, P. W. S. and Friday, F., *Fair Trade, Resale Price Maintenance re-examined*, Macmillan (1960).

117 e.g. evidence given to the Court in the confectionery case by McClelland, Professor W. G., commenting on reactions to freed competition, 'I found myself in the same situation in respect of our own stores [he is Chairman of a group of stores] when bacon was derationed. I had no experience of dealing with bacon in conditions of free supply; one does in fact, very quickly learn' (*Financial Times* Report, 8/6/67).

118 No action was taken—partly in view of the 1956 Act.

119 For a summary of this case see Register of Restrictive Trading Agreements *Report for the period 1/7/61 to 30/6/63*, Cmnd. 2246, (1964). For a comment on the case see Brock, C., op. cit., pp. 88–9. For a full account, including a verbatim report of the proceedings, see Barker, R. E. and Davis, G. B., *Books are Different*, Macmillan (1966).

120 Thus the Association could have fought the case on the grounds that it was not a collective agreement and was not registrable.

121 L.R.3 R.P.246,320 (quoted in Brock, L., op. cit.) 'The new author with something important to say, the scholar with new knowledge to communicate, the poet or the artist seeking to bring more beauty into the world, the philosopher desiring to increase understanding and illumining the minds of those who will read what he writes; these, we think, are the writers who will find it harder to get their work accepted for publication. . . . We cannot doubt that this would deny to the reading public specific and substantial benefits.'

122 See p. 252.

123 e.g. Distillers Company Ltd. abandoned r.p.m. in February 1965 with the result that the wine and spirits trade decided in March 1966 to abandon r.p.m. The decision of Hoovers Limited to abandon r.p.m. caused a similar result among other manufacturers of household equipment. Motor car manufacturers decided not to seek exemption in October 1964.

124 Manufacturers of Sweets and Confectionery, 1967. They pleaded gateways (a), (b), (c) and (e). Branded Shoe manufacturers, 1968. They pleaded gateways (a), (c), (d) and (e).

125 Both occupied the Court for over 40 days, defendants' legal costs exceeded £100,000 on each occasion.

126 Messrs. Bassetts, Cadbury Bros., J. & S. Fry & Sons, John Mackintosh & Sons and Rowntree Ltd., July, 1967. Perhaps the manufacturer's insistence on arguing that sales would be reduced by fewer outlets, as confectionery was often bought on impulse, backfired by supporting the Registrar's view, accepted by the Court, that price cutting by supermarkets would not cause much diversion of buying.

127 See page 253.

128 For a brief discussion of some of the problems of measurement see 'Resale Price Maintenance' Studies edited by Yamey, B. S., Weidenfeld and Nicolson (1966), pp. 5–7 inclusive. The section on U.S.A. by Hollander, S. C., in this book gives a summary of the empirical evidence regarding retail failure rates and prices (pp. 94–8). Comparisons between r.p.m. and non-r.p.m. states give inconclusive evidence on the second question because of 'little evidence that r.p.m. reduces failure rates'. More evidence can be found in Reddaway, W. R., 'Effects of Selective Employment Tax, First Report on the Distributive Trades', H.M.S.O. (1970).

129 It must be remembered that the full effects of the 1964 Act will not yet have been felt. Many major classes of goods were not freed until 1968.

130 Pickering, J. F., *op. cit.* (p. 152), estimates that in 1964 the saving to the consumer as a result of price cutting on brand leaders in the grocery and allied fields is in the region of 1s. 6d. in the £. This cannot, of course, be treated as a measurement of benefits gained by consumers as a result of the abolition of r.p.m. Firstly, we have no way of knowing what the recommended prices, on which the cuts were based, would have been if r.p.m. had been continued. Secondly, money is a subjective measure of benefits.

131 Or, for example, a narrow objective such as improvement in the balance of payments by import substitution, approved in the 1968 Act.

132 Thus from 1956 to 1965 the Commission met, on average, less than once a week. Its budget for the year 1966/7 was £155,000.

133 Standard Metal Windows Group's Agreement, 1962.

134 A Report on the supply of Household Detergents (August, 1966).

135 See Rowley, C. K., *op. cit.*, Chapter 19. None of the recommendations that the government should fix selling prices (e.g. in the reports on oxygen and matches) have been implemented. Sometimes because at that stage the Board of Trade did not have the necessary powers, and sometimes because publicity was relied upon to bring about the desired results.

136 This has been the subject of a general reference to the Monopolies Commission.

137 Which, in its first report, on road haulage rates, criticised the system of recommended rates.

138 Mr. Justice Brennan, Supreme Court, United States v. Philadelphia National Bank, 374 U.S. 321,371 (1963). Quoted in Stevens, R. B. and Yamey, B. S., *op. cit.*, p. 139. For a good, brief, description of policies promoting competition and controlling monopoly in the U.S.A. see Caves, R., *American Industry: Structure, Conduct, Performance*, Chapter 4, Prentice Hall (1964).

139 e.g. Net Book Agreement (1957), 1962.

140 e.g. Yarn Spinners Agreement, 1959. Here the '*public*' detriment of a substantial local increase in unemployment was held to be outweighed by the benefit of lower yarn (and therefore fabric) prices to the '*public*' as consumers.

141 Thus Q.C. for the Registrar in the confectionery case said, in his final submission to the Court, 'apart from basic facts on which there was a large measure of agreements between the parties it would not be truth that would assist the Court but rather the gift of prophecy' (*Financial Times* report, 13/6/67).

142 e.g. Net Book Agreement which had been operating since 1899. The Newspaper Proprietors' Association Ltd.'s and National Federation of Retail Newsagents, Booksellers and Stationers' Agreement had operated since 1919.

143 Brock, C., op. cit., Chapter 7.

144 Less than 1% of all agreements registered have been accepted by the Court.

145 Smith, R. A., 'The Incredible Electrical Conspiracy', *Fortune*, April and May (1961).

146 Hunter, A., *The Monopolies Commission and Economic Welfare*, Manchester School (1955). See also Allen, G. C., *Monopoly and Restrictive Practices*, op. cit., p. 80: '. . . the economist members of the Commission . . . had realised that welfare economics had little relevance to the practical questions before them'.

Bibliography

GENERAL

BAIN, J. S., *Industrial Organisation*, John Wiley & Sons, 2nd edit., 1965, chs 11–16

ALLEN, G. C., *Monopoly and Restrictive Practices*, Allen and Unwin, 1968

HUNTER, A., *Competition and the Law*, Allen and Unwin, 1966

HUNTER, A. (Ed.), *Monopoly and Competition*, Penguin Modern Economics, 1969

UTTON, M. A., *Industrial Concentration*, Penguin Modern Economics, 1970

MONOPOLIES

ROWLEY, C. K., *The British Monopolies Commission*, Allen and Unwin, 1966

SUTHERLAND, A., *Monopolies Commission in Action*, University of Cambridge, Department of Applied Economics, Occasional Paper 21, C.U.P., 1969

MERGERS

COOK, P. L. and COHEN, R., *Effects of Mergers*, Allen and Unwin, 1958

Mergers: A Guide to Board of Trade Practice, H.M.S.O., 1969

RESTRICTIVE PRACTICES

BROCK, C., *The Control of Restrictive Practices from 1956*, McGraw-Hill, 1966

STEVENS, R. B. and YAMEY, B. S., *The Restrictive Practices Court; A Study of the Judicial Process and Economic Policy*, Weidenfeld and Nicolson, 1965

RESALE PRICE MAINTENANCE

YAMEY, B. S., *The Economics of Resale Price Maintenance*, Pitman, 1964

YAMEY, B. S. (Ed.), *Resale Price Maintenance*, Weidenfeld and Nicolson, 1966

PICKERING, J. F., *Resale Price Maintenance in Practice*, Allen and Unwin, 1966

Chapter 11

LOCATIONAL AND REGIONAL POLICY

SECTION I

By Locational and Regional Policy we mean the body of legislation operated at various times by various government departments, which has concerned itself with some aspects of the migration of labour, intervention in the locational activity of firms and in the economic life of regions. This chapter is divided into four sections, in the first we deal with the aims of the policy and summarise the techniques which have been used. In the second we survey the economic theory relevant to regional questions. The third section outlines the development of legislation and deals with techniques in greater detail. Lastly, we seek to establish the degree of effectiveness of the intervention and consider some criticisms of the policy.

A regional policy may have as its objective any or all of those outlined below. As is usual in such cases, some would attach greater weight to one objective rather than the other. It is also believed that some of these aims are contradictory.

Historically the first aim in this country, and probably still the major one from the point of view of a political party's platform, is the reduction of the high levels of unemployment which for over forty years have characterised some regions. This objective may be expressed in two ways, either 'to reduce unemployment in a region' (in which case not only specifically regional policy but general macro-economic intervention on unemployment rates may be helpful) or 'to reduce the inequalities of unemployment between one region and another'. We may include attempts to increase low regional activity rates (see page 296) in this last objective.

The second objective may be to reduce regional inequalities in income per head and thus regional differences in the standard of living. Thirdly, the government may seek to reduce the size of cyclical fluctuations in a region. Fourthly, regional policy may seek to reduce population movements which are considered to be undesirable (e.g. the 'drift to the south') either because they increase congestion above socially desirable limits in the recipient area, or because depopulation in another area is not liked. Fifthly, regional policy may seek to preserve amenities such as areas of beauty or social structures which are considered by groups to be desirable. Some of those who seek to check the depopulation of highland Scotland have these motives in mind. Lastly, a regional policy may be undertaken on the grounds that by treating regions differently the overall rate of growth of national income may thereby be increased by using unemployed resources and enabling the economy to be operated at a higher rate without generating localised inflation.

Most techniques of government intervention in this field take as their unit of measurement a region[1] and then involve devoting resources to those which satisfy some criterion[2] as being in need of special assistance. For example, these resources may be in the form of expenditure by the central government on the retraining of workers. In addition, such a region may be made more attractive to firms who expand in it, or move into it, and who satisfy other criteria, such as being in the manufacturing sector of industry and making a substantial contribution towards employment in the region, who will then receive temporary assistance. A feature of government help to firms in this country has been that it is either on a 'once and for all' basis, as in the case of capital expenditure, or on a continuing but not permanent basis, as in the case of continued items of expense. Thus a contribution towards running costs is limited for the first few years and the Regional Employment Premium is guaranteed for seven years. Governments have not been prepared to subsidise activity in any region for an indefinite period of time, although, of course, one firm may qualify more than once and in more than one region for benefit. Expenses for which firms may receive assistance may be: increased costs of operation in a region or, for example, assistance with re-training labour.

Secondly, regions may be given a stronger form of assistance generally available, thus investment grants are available to certain firms anywhere in the country, but a higher rate is given in some regions. Thirdly, selected regions may benefit from a 'negative' policy whereby they are not subject to controls of economic activity which are applied elsewhere; the use of Industrial Development Certificates is an example of this. Lastly, the intervention may be quite general geographically in its nature but may be intended to help certain regional problems; thus grants and allowances to workers are very generally available but are rightly considered part of regional policy in that they are an attempt to encourage migration between regions.

It can be seen that, depending upon the aims which are selected as being important and the techniques used to implement them, the policy may or may not involve a total 'regional concept'. By this we mean that it would be possible to select particular geographical areas (e.g. the Durham Coalfield), identify the problem and seek to remedy it. Alternatively, one may divide the whole of the nation state into a series of regions, so that all regions in the total equal the geographical area of the country, identify regional differences in the light of an economic criterion such as unemployment or income per head and then take action which discriminates between one or all of these regions. These two approaches are significant for the following reasons. The first may appeal to those who are intellectually opposed to the idea of planning, who believe in 'a free play of market forces' but who may, nevertheless, be prepared to accept remedial policies for particular areas. The second approach, associated with the idea of regional planning and regional analysis, brings with it the problem of defining a region.[3]

SECTION II

This section deals firstly with 'traditional' economic theory which is applicable to regional policy and, secondly, it goes on to consider regional economics treated as a branch of economic theory.

Traditionally, intermediate economic textbooks, when they deal with regional policy, rely mainly on the micro-economic theory of location, together with the use of certain macro-economic concepts, such as the multiplier applied to a region and regional inflationary pressure. Location theory of this kind seeks to explain why firms and industries are located in a particular geographical pattern and why this pattern may change over time. The following is a typical comprehensive list.[4]

1 Manpower
2 Supplies of components, sub-contracting facilities and professional services
3 Power
4 Water
5 Raw materials
6 The main markets

7 Personal communications
8 Waste disposal
9 The ethos of the locality
10 Site facilities

Factors 1–9 above may be thought of as determining the area in which a firm may locate; perhaps the equivalent of a region of the U.K. They will not provide a unique answer; a firm must look for a suitable site within the area.

Such a list seeks to identify the variables with which a firm may have to deal in a decision regarding location. It is generally assumed that a firm acting on the precepts of rationality, assumed in the conventional Theory of the Firm, will select a location and site which produces the highest profit.[5] Location may affect both costs and revenues. Since knowledge has a cost, the firm will be restricted in the number of potential locations and sites which it considers.[6] The strength of the direction of such locational factors in certain industries is a matter of common observation—such as the Lancashire textile industry.[7] Studies are also available[8] of the effects on costs, profitability and growth of firms being forced to locate away from areas which they would, themselves, have selected.

A similar approach to the study of location is a survey of reasons for plant location conducted in American industry.[9] Ranked in order of importance to firms answering the questionnaire, locational factors were:

1 availability of labour
2 convenience of location to markets
3 the availability of buildings or other property
4 lower labour costs
5 the availability of raw materials
6 less unionisation
7 local co-operativeness
8 the home of management[10]
9 climate
10 transportation costs
11 adequate power
12 the centre of the particular industry
13 transportation facilities
14 decentralisation of operation
15 favourable tax structure
16 financial aid

Obviously a different ranking could be expected in the U.K.

The approach outlined above represents the economist's use of the location theory originally outlined by Weber,[11] greatly elaborated by Hoover,[12] which was then developed by Isard[13] in conjunction with some of the problems of international trade theory to produce one of the strands of regional economics (see below). As will be shown later,[14] empirical investigation does not always support the belief that firms do act rationally or as profit maximisers in applying the theoretical concepts outlined for them. Nevertheless, this approach provides the intellectual basis for those who believe that firms, free from any outside government intervention, will in accordance with market forces locate themselves in such a way as to maximise the benefits to the community. What follows is one example to show that free competition does not necessarily equal public interest.[15]

Consider a long beach which has people evenly distributed along its length, each person in a time period prepared to buy one ice cream and prepared to walk to purchase the ice cream. In the case of total supply being provided by one ice-cream seller, he will be indifferent as to where he locates himself, although each individual customer would prefer him to be located close by, and a public official with the authority to fix the vendor's location would maximise the public interest by locating him at the median point. In the case of two ice-cream sellers, competing with each other and each attempting to maximise sales, the only stable solution to their location would be if both were located at the centre point of the beach, each then selling to half the total number of customers. This quite clearly does not maximise the public interest in their location, and a public official who located one seller one quarter of the distance from one end of the beach, and the other three-quarters of the distance from the same end, would cut the total consumers' walking by half.

Here we have the case of a linear example used to demonstrate that a free market does not necessarily produce optimal resource use.

We now turn to a consideration of regional analysis, or more particularly regional economics.[16] Over the last twenty years regional analysis has developed as an applied science in its own right, incorporating into its theoretical structure not only economics but aspects of geography, sociology, and demography.

A knowledge of the 'factors affecting location' is no longer sufficient by itself to enable the student to appreciate the results of the type of analysis which is highly relevant to the regional problems of the United Kingdom. Our aim here is not to give a short course in regional analysis, which we are not qualified to give, but rather to outline some of the relevant concepts and tools which we feel the applied economist should understand.

One major strand of regional economics remains location theory. This has developed along two main lines, one the Weber-Hoover-Isard approach mentioned above and the other the highly theoretical and elegant analysis of Losch.[17] Losch explains how on a plain, where raw materials are distributed completely equally and where economic activity commences as self-sufficient production, firms may develop into an area which consists of a series of hexagons at the centre of each of which there will be a form of economic activity. The analysis is very similar to that of the Theory of the Firm in conventional economics, only here diagrams are rotated about their vertical axis to give, for example, cones of demand for the marketable output of a centre of economic activity. The area covered by each cone becomes a hexagon rather than a circle since Losch points out that a series of circles would leave gaps at their intersection and geometrically a hexagon affords the largest demand per square mile provided that the total area of the hexagon is the same as the circle. The results of this analysis give an elegant transport and settlement plan resulting from nets of hexagons of various areas.

Here we have a two-dimensional example which, as in the 'ice-cream' case above, shows non-optimal resource use resulting from a free market system. It can be seen that such a theory is as general in its predictions as is the Theory of the Firm. Like the pure generalised Theory of the Firm it has little to offer the policy-maker and has in fact had 'no empirical implementation'.[18]

The Weber-Hoover-Isard approach to location theory has been much more valuable in the insights which it has provided. An example of this is its emphasis on the way in which the spatial concentration of economic activity is often the result of the importance of transport costs and how such costs may not increase in a regular way as distance from the source of inputs or the market increases, due to discontinuities caused by transhipment points from one form of transport to another. Great importance is also attached to changes in weight loss or weight gain during the transformation process affecting the relative advantages of being near sources of raw material or the market.

The theory demonstrates how improved transport systems coupled with the use of less bulky raw materials and generally available power sources have led to the increasing importance of industries with no strong locational ties (footloose industries).

In the end, however, such an approach suffers from the fact that it is a completely micro-economic one which copes quite easily with the case of the single-product, single-establishment firm, which assumes that demand for the product is an exogenous variable (whereas demand may depend on location, e.g. near a large conurbation) and ignores competitive pressures in the market (which may, for example, induce a firm to locate elsewhere, away from competition).

Regional analysis proper, therefore, started to develop when it took as the unit with which it concerned itself the region rather than the firm.[19] Regional analysis largely developed as a response to two great questions to which economists could be expected to provide an answer: firstly, to explain the reason for differences between regions, i.e. patterns of land use, incomes per head, unemployment rates, secondly, what could be done about the less developed regions of under-developed countries.[20]

The first problem is that of the definition of a region. Three types of definition can be distinguished.[21]

1 Definitions based on the homogeneity of an area in terms of some common physical or economic factor, e.g. the 'mountain states' of the U.S.A. or the Lancashire cotton belt.

2 The nodality of a region, where the common feature is the centring of economic activity of the area around some nodal point (e.g. the London conurbation).

3 The region as an administrative unit. This definition of a region, which is frequently used in empirical work, and, for example, is the basis of virtually all the work done for the United Kingdom[22] referred to in this chapter, is relevant for two reasons. Firstly, the administrative region (which may have evolved as the result of the workings of the historical process) may be the only form in which disaggregated information is available to the economist. Secondly, the administrative region may be the only practical unit so far as the implementation of any policy is concerned.[23] It has been pointed out[24] that the analyst should separate firstly the representation of factual knowledge and secondly the search for the 'best' region. Thus different purposes should lead to different sub-divisions of the same geographical area.[25] Although the availability of the requisite information and possibility of implementing a policy through the existing machinery may be pressing reasons why the regional analyst accepts 'administrative regions', such a departure from the ideal does carry with it important dangers. Firstly, the disaggregation of information along these lines may conceal problems unique to a part of the administrative region and may also conceal similarities between geographical

areas which are, for administrative purposes, divided amongst several regions. Secondly, the subjective nature of the definition of the region may be forgotten, thus for some purposes the United Kingdom could be considered to be a 'region' of Europe, while for other purposes it may be useful to separate out a smaller area such as the Durham coalfields from the Northern region.

We will now deal with those parts of regional economic analysis which seem relevant to the scope of this chapter. The contributions of regional analysis to such questions as transportation policies and urban land use problems will be ignored as being outside our scope.

An important part of regional analysis can be demonstrated in considering the two major approaches to the development of regions; the centre-periphery and the concept of spatial equilibrium.[26]

Centre-periphery models involve the idea that economic activity is concentrated in certain areas (core regions) which act as focal points for surrounding geographical areas. London may be considered to be a core area for the United Kingdom, while a corridor running from northern Italy via the Rhine and continuing into South East and Midland U.K. might be considered the core region of Europe. That certain areas become concentrations of economic power at some stage in the development of a country is observably true; thus C. Clark[27] points out that with few exceptions the successful industrial areas in Europe now are the areas which already had the dense population 200 years ago, with the exceptions of Scandinavian countries, Lancashire and Scotland. Why this may occur and why the location pattern is perpetuated is not altogether clear. After all, it would seem that with the increasing importance of industries which are not materials orientated, with the more widespread availability of power, with the improvement in transport systems leading to greater mobility of labour (particularly over a short distance, e.g. the growth of the commuter) one would expect the industrial development in a region to become less, rather than more, geographically concentrated over time. Four reasons may be advanced why this does not happen.

1 Firstly, the persistence of internal and external economies of scale. Net external diseconomies just do not appear in the centre region. Thus, despite some social diseconomies, e.g. congestion concentrations of industries continue to act as a magnet 'the really significant geography thus becomes the latter concentration of man himself, his works, his institutions and his inventive momentum'.[28]

2 Entrepreneurs may be irrational in their choice of the centre rather than the periphery as an area for development.[29]

3 The centre region may be involved to a greater extent in manufacturing production, which forms part of the inter-regional trade pattern, as opposed to periphery regions which may concentrate, for example, on agricultural production for the regional centre.
4 The centre region probably has the most highly developed service sector in the country. To the extent to which this is associated with technological change, the centre region may continue to have a competitive advantage *vis-à-vis* its periphery.

It is possible to interpret 1 and 4 above as producing a distribution of resources which may hamper overall growth or, alternatively, that such concentrations of economic activity and the unequal rates of economic growth that follow from them may be essential to obtain overall growth in an economy.

The second approach may lead to a contradiction between two possible aims of regional policy, namely a growth objective, in which the fastest increase in national income within the production possibilities of the economy is the aim and a welfare criterion, where the aim will be to re-distribute the available national resources more equally between regions. The evidence for countries such as the U.S.A. and the U.K. seems to be that regional differences have been reduced[30] rather than increased over time, although divergence may occur in less developed economies. On the other hand this does not preclude the possibility that in the absence of government intervention 'The play of the forces in the market normally tends to increase, rather than decrease, the inequalities between regions',[31] or that the peripheral regions may lag behind in receiving the benefits of economic growth or may receive it intermittently. This last approach is associated with A. O. Hirschman,[32] who, using a model where a country is divided into the North which is economically advanced, and the South which is economically backward, distinguishes two contradictory affects of the North on the South called 'trickling down effects' and 'polarisation effects'. Trickling down effects will be favourable to the South for reasons such as that an increase in aggregate demand in the North will enable some Southern unemployment to be absorbed and will lead to an increase in investment in the South. On the other hand, polarisation effects, such as the contraction of less efficient Southern industry in competition with the North and the fact that the South may have to buy Northern manufactured goods which are being sheltered by a tariff wall rather than importing more cheaply from outside the country, will be unfavourable. In addition, the tendency will be for skilled and enterprising workers to migrate from the South to the North. Hirschman believes that in the end trickling down effects will be more important than polarisation effects and thus a policy of 'controlled disequilibrium' may be in the long-run interests of the country as a whole. He then compares a Northern region versus Southern region model with a Country North versus Country South model. Although he believes that 'on balance the forces making for inter-regional transmission of growth are likely to be more powerful than those making for international transmission', an underdeveloped region may be worse off than an under-developed country, since regions cannot determine their exchange rate, and are unable to impose tariffs with the result that inter-regional trade may be conducted on the basis of absolute advantage, whereas international trade is conducted on the basis of comparative advantage.

Whereas Hirschman sees disequilibrium as a virtue, as it speeds the pace of development and economic growth, an alternative view of the proper goal of development policy is that of spatial equilibrium. This is an extension of the welfare criterion which would exist when, given perfect knowledge and perfect factor mobility, any alteration of the distribution of factors of production between their use and their location would result in a reduction of national product. Analysis along these lines suffers from the limitation of all equilibrium analysis in that it is essentially static. Furthermore, the period of adjustment to the equilibrium position may be undesirably long from the point of view of the policy-maker. Spatial equilibrium (associated with the ideas of Losch) does not, of course, postulate an even spatial distribution of economic activity; it is, however, associated with those who believe that an objective of government policy should be a more widespread dispersal of economic activity, for example from 'prosperous' to 'depressed' areas.[33]

We have attempted to show above how the basic economic analysis of external economies of scale, sometimes called agglomeration economies, having their effect upon the geographical distribution of firms and industries, has been extended into regional economic analysis which concerns the spatial distribution of economic activity taking as its unit the region. The concepts used have varied in their abstraction and their capacity for empirical verification. It should now be obvious that neither of the two main approaches, spatial equilibrium or controlled disequilibrium, are of great value as criteria for the policy-maker. Firstly, this is a result of the essentially subjective nature of the region. Should regional definitions seek to emphasise the centre-periphery situations where they arise? Should one not expect to find unbalanced growth inside areas of regions which at the regional level appear to be balanced? The second problem is that of the essential generality of the models. What is optimal imbalance? Alternatively, what should be balanced growth, real income per head, or return on investment?

Regional economics makes use of certain techniques in analysing regional behaviour. In most cases, however, these are no more than particular applications of techniques available to economists in general. Firstly, in the analysis of region one may look for the 'economic base' of the region. Such an economic base consists of those industries which are, at present, successful in exporting from the region. It is then possible to measure how the change in the level of activity in industries in the base will affect total regional income and regional export performance.[34] The concept of the multiplier has three applications in this type of analysis: firstly, the one outlined above, secondly, the conventional investment multiplier[35] and thirdly the idea of a labour multiplier. By this is meant the change in employment brought about by the creation of an extra job in the region or the migration of one worker from the region. Thus D. Jay[36] points out that if such a multiplier has the value of one, and if Scottish unemployment stands at 100,000, and 10,000 workers move from Scotland per annum, the resulting unemployment will not be a reduction to 90,000 but will be the maintenance of the 100,000 figure (since 10,000 secondary jobs will be lost).[37]

In most cases, the object after having determined the economic base of the region is to find out whether or not the base can be extended. To do this, comparative cost analysis may be used (i.e. comparing the differing costs of supplying the standard product to a standard market from various regions)—a process akin to simple analysis in the theory of international trade. In cases where this may give unreliable results, resort may be made to industrial complex analysis, which in turn can only be done by using the techniques of input tables (see Chapter 7). Cost-benefit analysis is also used (see Chapter 8)—in fact the techniques of this process were first used in America in examinations of water conservation projects, reflecting some of the earlier emphasis of regional analysis. In this country, cost-benefit analysis has been used in transport surveys[38] and in considering whether or not government assistance in the provision of jobs in development areas has been worth while.[39]

It is hoped to show in the next two sections of this chapter how policy-makers and possibly, to a greater extent, their critics have made use of these concepts and techniques.

SECTION III

We now turn from the general to the particular, that is, from the consideration of regional analysis in abstract to an outline of the scope and extent of this type of government intervention in the United Kingdom[40]

Government intervention in this field started in the 1930's when the recognition that market forces could not be left by themselves to solve the pressing problem of that era, namely, the fact that not only were general levels of unemployment high but that these figures embraced great regional variations in unemployment. From the start, two distinct approaches were used; firstly, a system of grants and allowances to transferred workers introduced in 1928. This policy is popularly referred to as 'encouraging the mobility of labour'. Secondly, there has been a policy of providing inducements for firms to expand and locate themselves in areas which have satisfied various criteria over time for being 'problem areas'. This is popularly referred to as 'taking work to the workers'.

This technique was started in 1934 with the *Special Areas (Development and Improvement) Act*, strengthened and extended by the *1936 Special Areas Reconstruction Agreement Act*. These Acts nominated four Special Areas (Central Scotland, S. Wales, West Cumberland and the North East Coast). Commissioners were appointed to facilitate the economic and social improvement of such areas. By 1938, £21 million had been spent or committed in the form of help to firms setting up in such areas, not only with capital finance but also contributions towards rent, rates and income tax. The resources used were not large when compared with the problem and had little effect on regional variations in unemployment, probably because expanding firms could easily find spare capacity in parts of the country which appeared more congenial than the depressed areas. Probably the most enterprising form of intervention during this period was the establishment of government trading estates, which by 1939 had grown to ten in number and provided employment for 12,000 people. (See note 49.)

In 1937 a Royal Commission on the Distribution of the Industrial Population had been set up which reported (the *Barlow Commission Report*) in 1940. The three main recommendations of this influential commission were that: firstly, congested areas should be redeveloped, secondly, there should be a disperal of the population from such congested areas and thirdly, there should be the encouragement of a 'proper industrial balance' of industry in the various regions. No definition was submitted of this best pattern of industrial diversification. A minority reported in favour of the creation of a Cabinet Minister with powers to control overall industrial location.

The Second World War with its associated reductions in overall levels of unemployment[41] solved the problem. It was feared, however, that post-war, the post First World War pattern would assert itself, namely that of boom followed by depression.

The 1944 White Paper on Employment Policy committed governments to intervention in the location of industry 'in the case of a large industrial population the government is not prepared to either compel it to transfer to another area or to leave it to prolonged unemployment and demoralisation'.[42]

The immediate post-war legislation had two main objectives: firstly to do something about the urban rather than regional problems of congestion, housing shortage and poor social infrastructure which existed. Secondly, to help the problem areas by encouraging firms to locate in them.

The first objective was pursued in the *1946 New Town Act*.[43] Although we will not expand on the provisions of this Act or its subsequent progress, this does not mean that it was not an important pathbreaking technique of government intervention.

Although, originally, the majority of new towns were overspill developments from the London conurbation, the subsequent emphasis on locations in development regions (e.g. Cumbernauld in Scotland, Peterlee in the North East) has increased their importance as a technique of regional policy. 'The New Towns policy was a radical departure, in theory at least, because, for the first time in contemporary western history, the pattern of urban and regional development was explicitly considered variable subject to control or manipulation from the vantage of national policy.'[44] Rodwin points out that economists were not convinced about the relevance of a New Towns policy since they were preoccupied with the twin problems of helping depressed areas and increasing exports. On the other hand, planners who were less interested in inter-regional than intra-metropolitan development, and for whom the London conurbation was the great problem, were much more interested.

The second strand of intervention, aimed at relieving problems of congestion and improving social amenities, was begun by the *1947 Town and Country Planning Act*.[45] This was a non-permissive piece of legislation which placed on local authorities the obligation to draw up development plans for their areas and to regulate applications for development. The policy was co-ordinated by the Ministry of Housing and Local Government, but only in so far as it would avoid inconsistencies between neighbouring authorities. Again we do not intend to expand on the development of planning under this Act, which largely concerned itself with urban problems at the local authority level (for example 'green belts' around Greater London).

However, the Act did institute one piece of intervention vitally important at the regional level, namely giving the Board of Trade powers to grant or refuse Industrial Development Certificates for factories or factory extensions exceeding 5,000 square feet.[46] Although the Board of Trade could only withhold an I.D.C. on the grounds that it would contribute to industrial congestion, in practice this power has always been exercised as an arm of government policy, although intervention of this sort has been more active at some times than others.

The 1950 Distribution of Industry Act completed the pattern of legislation by setting up development areas[47] in which the Board of Trade had powers, subsequently amended, to acquire land on which buildings were to be built, to authorise Treasury grants towards running expenses and settling key workers, and in exceptional cases, making grants for losses incurred in setting up in such areas. In the period 1945–60 during which these Acts operated, Treasury expenditure by the Board of Trade reached £78 m.

These Acts completed the 'stick and carrot' policy which has been the main characteristic of post-war government intervention in this field; the stick being the possibility of an I.D.C. being withheld for a company wishing to expand or set up a new branch, the carrot being the incentives available if it will site the expansion in a development area.

In the immediate post-war period the 'stick' was augmented by physical controls on materials operated by Building Licences. An important part of the 'carrot' was the occupation of disused ordinance factories.[48]

The *1960 Local Employment Act* abolished the Development Areas and substituted for them Development Districts—which were Ministry of Labour unemployment exchange areas where 'high and persistent unemployment exists or is threatened'. A high level of unemployment was defined as an average 4½% for 1959. Subsequently these Development Districts were added to, or subtracted from, several times a year in accordance with changes in local unemployment figures. In 1960 Development Districts covered 18% of the insured population. The Board of Trade was given complete control over the allocation of financial assistance which now included making grants to firms building their own factories, grants towards the cost of machinery and help with working capital. The same legislation set up three Industrial Estates Management Corporations which in addition to running trading estates[49] were empowered to build factories and advance factories which could then be sold at cost price with payment over 15 years or rented for 21 years at rents which were lower than free market prices in the area, to firms who were prepared to move into Development Districts. I.D.C.s were now required for processing and repair trades as well as manufacturing industries. In addition an I.D.C. was required for modifying the use of existing buildings.

This Act which seemed, at the time, to have the great advantage of flexibility in terms of the areas which it covered, has subsequently been widely criticised on the grounds that the unit (the local employment exchange area) was far too small, so that some parts of a region with an obviously common problem would be inside the legislation and others excluded. Secondly, the unemployment criteria often meant that 'borderline areas' were not attractive to firms who could not be sure that a planned location would still be eligible for assistance by the time the plans came to fruition. The criteria meant that the emphasis had now swung to a consideration of employment, perhaps the result of the high unemployment levels in 1958, rather than the pursuance of a pattern of industrial distribution. It has also been argued that the scale of assistance was anyway too low.[50] Nevertheless, for the next six years Development Districts remained the physical units in which the policy was couched.

Developments in intervention continued along three main lines:

1 Tinkering with existing controls: for example the *1965 Town and Country Planning Act* and *Control of Office and Industrial Development Act* extended the I.D.C. system to cover industrial development down to 1,000 square feet in specified areas of the Midlands and South East where congestion was a problem and included office development exceeding 3,000 square feet in the Birmingham and London conurbations. Tinkering with incentives: thus in the 1963 budget 'free depreciation' provision allowed firms to write off buildings and equipment in development districts for tax purposes at a rate to be decided upon by the firms, in addition the Board of Trade was empowered to give standard grants towards the cost of plant and machinery.

2 Secondly, the scope of intervention was broadened. In 1963 the

Location of Offices Bureau was set up by the government as an official agency designed to function as an information service providing facts regarding the resiting of offices around the London area.[51] In 1965 new funds were made available to the Arts Council for promoting the Arts in the regions.

3 There was in addition a growing opinion that the best hope for a solution to the problem of development districts lay in treating it as a regional problem and therefore putting intervention on a regional basis. This point was made in the very influential 1963 National Economic Development Council Report.[52] which, in addition to recommending improved financial incentives and increased spending on the social infra-structure, supported the idea of policies directed towards larger regions, coupled with the encouragement of growth points within such regions. This was supported by reports on the South East, North East England, and Central Scotland.

In 1964, the newly created Department of Economic Affairs took over the Board of Trade's work in co-ordinating regional policy. England was divided into eight regions (the South West, West Midlands, North West, Northern, Yorkshire and Humberside, East Midlands, East Anglia and the South East) which together with Scotland and Wales each had a Regional Planning Council and a Regional Planning Board. R.P.C.s have approximately 24 members drawn from local authorities, industry and independent members in equal proportions, their powers are advisory and non-executive, their function is to concern themselves with the long-term strategy of the region. Regional Planning Boards are composed of senior civil servants drawn from various ministries. They also have a secretariat which, in addition, services the R.P.C. The original function was to prepare the regional plan, and they are responsible for co-ordinating the work of government departments in the region. The machinery, sitting as it does between central and local government, has important administrative implications which are outside our scope.

The culmination of these three strands of development was the *Industrial Development Act 1966* which replaced development districts by Development Areas[53] selected according to a much wider range of economic criteria. Thus population changes, migration, and employment trends are relevant in addition to the level of unemployment. Policy is aimed at encouraging the growth and proper distribution of industry. It is recognised that Development Areas will remain as such for a period of about ten years. At the same time, the existing initial and investment allowances were abolished in favour of a system of cash investment grants. These give a flat-rate repayment in cash to a firm in the manufacturing, construction and extractive industries of 20%[54] of expenditure on plant and machinery. Assistance is also given to firms buying computers, ships and hovercraft. Expenditure within Development Areas qualifies for a 40% grant.[55] The main advantage of this system compared with the investment allowances and free depreciation provisions which it replaced has been ease of comprehension. Flexibility is possible by varying the rates (e.g. the temporary increase up to the end of 1968) and by accelerating or retarding the lag between expenditure and reimbursement.

Government intervention in regional policy at the present time takes the form of aid in three main categories:

1 *To the Firm*

Some of these are shown on Table 1 which not only relates the type of project to the type of aid which may be received but attempts to show the probability of a firm receiving a particular form of assistance. It is hoped by this to remove any impression that firms qualify as of right for certain types of assistance. In particular, items B, C, and D in the table were instituted under Local Employment Acts and the increased employment is an important factor in deciding whether or not they are given:[56]

(i) investment grants—mentioned above.
(ii) the provision of factory accommodation.
(iii) building and operational grants; loans to companies.
(iv) The Board of Trade in co-operation with the Ministry of Employment and Productivity is prepared to give grants towards the costs of training and to provide instructors for in-company training. Such costs, and the possibility of training and re-training, are believed to have been serious disadvantages hindering expansion in Development Areas. The *Industrial Training Act 1964* and the emphasis in locating new Government Training Centres[57] are attempts to remedy this.
(v) Since September 1967 the Selective Employment Tax has been developed to give a regional bias. Thus an employer in the manufacturing sector in a Development Area at present pays 48s. S.E.T. contribution per man per week. He receives back his S.E.T. contribution plus a Regional Employment Premium of 37s. 6d. This subsidy on labour is discussed on page 301.

TABLE 1. REGIONAL POLICY: PRINCIPAL INCENTIVES RECEIVED BY FIRMS*

	A	B	C	D	E	F	G	
Incentive / Type of Project	Investment Grant	Building Grant (a)		Operational Grant (a)	Training Grants	Regional Employment Premium & SET	Board of Trade Loan	Remarks
		25%	35%					
Factory for coming manufacturer	✓	✓'	✓	✓'	✓	✓	✓	C and D almost certain if S.D.A. chosen
Expansion by existing manufacturer	✓	✓	✓'	✓'	✓	✓	✓	C and D possible if firms at present outside S.D.A. and expansion is in different products and uses different management
Factory for newly-formed company	✓	✓	✓'	✓'	✓	✓	✓	Quality of backing crucial
New or expanded service centre and warehouses		✓'	✓'		✓'		✓	B or C depends on employment factor
Incoming office employers		✓'	✓'		✓'		✓	No problem if employer building own offices
New hotel		✓					✓	Special Assistance available
Incoming Capital-Intensive Manufacturing Project	✓	✓'		✓'	✓	✓	✓'	Scaled-down B and D likely a ceiling on G

N.B. ✓ = probable eligibility ✓' = possible eligibility

S.D.A. – Special Development Area. Set up as a result of the White Paper on Fuel Policy (1967). Originally areas likely to be especially affected by mining closures, they have been extended so that Millom (Cumberland) is now included.

(a) Preference shown for developments where male jobs exceed 50% of total.

*Adapted from *A Guide to Government incentives for firms expanding in North East England*; North East Development Council (April 1969)

2 *To the individual worker*

Grants and allowances to transferred workers have continued, although at an unimportant level since 1928. Current annual expenditure is about £0·5 m., with perhaps about 6,000 individuals affected.

3 *To the development areas as a whole*[58]

In addition to public investment in motorways, roads, airports and port facilities, this includes increased levels of grants to local authorities for rehabilitating derelict sites, the location of government offices (Ealing P.A.Y.E. is dealt with in Middlesbrough) and particular notice being taken of regional requirements in the allocation of defence projects. Ministers frequently refer to the higher per capita expenditure on social capital in Development Areas. Whether this represents a grant or subsidy depends upon the results of comparison between such projects and others not in Development Areas.

In general we can say that the last thirty odd years have seen an increase in the scale of intervention together with development of new techniques. It must not be thought that there has been a positive correlation between legislation and action. Thus (on page 288) we have described the period 1960–6 in terms of 'tinkering' with *legislation.* In fact there was considerably greater attention and *resources* devoted to the policy in this period.

Up to 1964 the policy was one of (marginally) promoting the migration of the labour force, together with the techniques of 'taking work to the workers'. Since 1964 there has been considerable emphasis placed on the idea of regional development, exemplified by the creation of regional machinery and the emphasis on the development of the region as a whole.

The final section of this chapter attempts to evaluate intervention in this field, firstly by considering the various reasons for the existence of the regional problem which have been put forward. These determine the objectives which, it is considered, the policy should have had. Lastly we consider the effectiveness of the policy in the light of those objectives.

SECTION IV

All western countries appear to have regional problems,[59] although the nature of a problem may differ. On a general, intuitive basis, this may be seen as no more than a reflection of absolute declines in regions associated with reduced output (e.g. worked-out mines, home-produced textiles being replaced by imported goods)—together with inequalities in growth rates causing some regions to be relatively worse off than they were before. After all, countries have different growth rates and these rates differ over time; economic regions are subsets of nation states.

Before discussing the causes of the regional problem in the United Kingdom we should once more consider those effects which are considered to be the ends in themselves so far as government policy is concerned and thus are used as criteria for judging the success or failure of any intervention. Since they are the results of the operation of economic forces they should be viewed largely as symptoms and since all could be the result of one factor they may obviously not be causally independent.[60]

1 Variations in unemployment figures were, historically, the symptom which brought about intervention in the 1930's and are still the most politically significant symptom.

Table II shows recent unemployment percentages for Development Areas and compares them with the national result.

TABLE 2 *Percentages of unemployment 13/4/70*

Great Britain	2·5
Development Areas	
South-Western	5·3
Merseyside	4·1
Northern	5·2
Scottish	4·3
Welsh	4·6
TOTAL all Development Areas	4·6
Northern Ireland	6·9

SOURCE *Employment and Productivity Gazette*, May 1970, pages 431 and 434.

Table 3 shows how regional unemployment percentages have varied as a ratio of national unemployment percentages over time. Thus we are here concerned not with absolute but relative differences. Such comparisons are made very difficult by the fact that the regional boundaries have been changed in 1964 and 1965. Rendall shows that over the period 1954/1963, taking the arithmetic means of annual average unemployment figures for regions they may be ranked as in Column 1. Column 2 shows the standard deviation of each region from the mean. The important differences between two rankings are firstly, in the case of Midland and North Midland regions, where low levels of unemployment are associated with high fluctuations (this may be explained as a result of the importance of the motor vehicle industry in those regions; an industry highly susceptible to general

TABLE 3 *Average and Fluctuations of Regional Unemployment 1954–1963*

	Arithmetic Mean Col. 1	*Standard Deviation Col. 2*
North Midland	0·58 (1)	0·116 (6)
London and South-East	0·62 (2)	0·036 (1)
E. and W. Ridings	0·68 (3)	0·111 (5)
Midland	0·70 (4)	0·170 (8)
South-West	0·93 (5)	0·087 (2)
North-West	1·11 (6)	0·101 (4)
Northern	1·47 (7)	0·282 (9)
Wales	1·57 (8)	0·088 (3)
Scotland	1·88 (9)	0·147 (7)
Northern Ireland	4·20 (10)	0·728 (10)

(Calculated from the ratio of regional percentage unemployment to national percentage unemployment) *Ministry of Labour Gazette,* January 1965.

macro-economic intervention such as hire-purchase controls), and secondly, Wales and S.W. England where high average unemployment figures are associated with low fluctuations. This may again be explained in terms of the industrial composition of the regions. Coal and steel are important industries in Wales; they tend to be non-growth industries at least as measured by employment, and in the case of coal-mining have been protected by government policy during the period. The relative importance of agriculture and service industries in the South West may explain stability here. Nevertheless Rendall found a general tendency for high average unemployment figures to be associated with high fluctuations in employment. Over the ten years period the national unemployment rate had a rising trend; in four regions, however, the trend was a falling one, namely the South West, London and the South East, Wales and Northern

Ireland. The falling trend in the last two regions can be taken as some evidence as to the success of regional policy over this period.

2 The second symptom of regional problems concerns itself with demographic concepts of inter-regional migration and regional differences in employee activity rates. 'The drift to the South East' is part of everyday folklore; there are, however, considerable statistical problems in obtaining such information. For some purposes one may be concerned about the migration of employees into and out of a region—and perhaps, in particular, the net effect of such movement.[61] Such migration is only one aspect of labour mobility; it is estimated that 2–3 m. job changes occur per annum: the difference between this figure and the Ministry of Labour figure is partly the result of job changes inside a region and multiple changes during a year. Oliver,[62] has shown that high unemployment regions tend to lose workers whereas low unemployment regions tend to gain. More specifically, the best statistical explanation has been a correlation between the difference between the national unemployment rate and the regional unemployment rate. This can be taken to support the classical *laissez-faire* economic proposition that population will move so as to even out unemployment rates. That this tendency has existed is not denied, however the persistence of the regional differences mentioned in 1 above show it to have been weaker than the forces creating regional differences in unemployment. Two reasons for this immediately suggest themselves: firstly, the Hirschman theory of disequilibrium,[63] secondly, the action of the regional employment multiplier.[64]

If we conceive inter-regional migration as involving a change in domicile as well as a change in work place, then further regional problems arise. Firstly, the increase in regional aggregate demand resulting from the increased employment in the receiving region would lead to inflationary pressure; certainly the problems of the loser region will be made worse. This will be mitigated by the extent of money transfers to the home region by the workers who have moved and by any reduction in unemployment caused by the filling of his vacancies by the unemployed. The vacancy may be filled, of course, by an increase in the working population of the region. The effect of migration on the loser region may be deepened if the emigrants are amongst the best equipped, youngest part of its labour force—particularly since social costs of training such a worker in the form of education costs, etc., will have been borne by a region which does not receive benefits in the form of subsequent earnings.

To the extent to which it is the worker only who moves, and not his family, migration will obviously affect Employee Activity Rates—which may be defined as $A/B \times 100$ where

A = estimated number of employees in an area on a place of work basis.

B = estimated number of persons in the home population on a place of residence basis.[65]

A includes the unemployed together with irregular or part-time workers. B is basically defined as persons over 15 and therefore includes those not available for employment (e.g. students, married women), the armed forces, self-employed and unpaid family workers, persons residing in a region but working in another region. Such calculations show considerable regional differences. However, A. J. Brown asserts that if the servicemen, the self-employed and family workers are included in numerator *and* denominator regional differences are small for men—and largely due to the age structure of the population. For women the differences are much larger and seem due to an industrial structure which traditionally uses women and seems to have 'elicited a high propensity of women to go out to work' . . . 'there are large unused reserves of female labour, especially in Wales, the North, and the South West. They are unused not so much because of deficiencies in the total demand for female labour. That reserves can to a large extent be drawn on is shown by their gradual shrinkage over the last decade or more'.[66]

3 A third symptom of the regional problem is the existence of regional differences in income per head.[67]

For 1959/60 Coates and Rawstron show that even larger differences exist within sub-regions, thus average incomes per head ranging from £1,158 in the City of London to £512 in Fermanagh. It must be remembered that regional differences in incomes may not reflect parallel differences in standards of living—as would be obvious to anyone wanting to sell a house in Fermanagh and to buy one in the City of London. Pullen found that the best hypothesis to explain relative regional earning is that they are some function of relative regional unemployment.

4 A further sympton of a regional problem would be the existence of differing growth rates, for example in terms of gross regional income per head. Little direct evidence of this nature exists for the United Kingdom. The only relevant regional social accounting figures for the United Kingdom are by Brown[68] and these are not a time series. Growth has therefore been looked at via regional industrial growth or in terms of increases in employment.

TABLE 4 *Regional variations in per capita income, before tax*

	Index of average per capita incomes	*Index of average per capita incomes*	*Index of growth of per capita income*
Standard Regions	*1959/60*	*1964/5*	*1969/60–1964/5*
South-East England	115	115	121
East Anglia	82	86	124
West Midlands	108	108	101
East Midlands	97	95	95
York and Humberside	98	98	101
South-Western	86	89	111
North-Western	97	96	95
Northern	86	81	77
Wales	83	83	101
Scotland	87	87	100
Great Britain	100	100	100

SOURCE 106th and 109th Reports of the Commissioners of H.M. Inland Revenue.
Reproduced from F. J. B. Stillwell, Location of Industry and Business Efficiency, *Business Ratios*, Winter 1968.

Table 4 shows differences in average regional incomes per head at 1959/60, 1964/5 together with growth between the two dates.

Humphrys[69] examined the regional distribution of the six industries which grew fastest in absolute as well as relative terms measured by employment in the period 1951–60. These were professional scientific services, banking finance and insurance, distributive trades, engineering and electrical goods, vehicles, paper printing and publishing. The first three, which may be called service industries, were allocated approximately in accordance with the population of the region. Exceptionally, London and the South East had a high concentration in banking finance and insurance while Wales and North Midlands had a low share compared to their population figures. However, the three manufacturing industries were distributed in a very uneven fashion; as a result over 50% of employment in those three growth industries was located in only three regions—London and the South East, Midland, and the North West.

Before looking at some of the suggested causes of the regional problem and suggestions regarding the best techniques for solving it, we repeat that the symptoms listed 1–4 above, provide explanations for public concern about the regional problem and at the same time may provide criteria for judging the success of the policy. There is nothing wrong with treating symptoms; the treatment may be more successful, however, if the causes of the disease are understood.

Apart from a general contention that the regional problem is the result of the 'interplay of market forces' (examined in the conclusion to this chapter), three causes of a regional problem are generally suggested; composition i.e. problem regions are in that position because they have a high proportion of stagnant industries in their industrial structure; growth i.e. regions may grow slowly with the result that a growth industry in some region may not be a growth industry in a problem region; and thirdly, that the national trade cycle has a more severe impact in some regions than others.

Stilwell[70] has analysed regional employment growth 1959–67 into

1 The regional share. The increase in employment which would have occurred if growth had been at the national rate.
2 The composition component. The extra increase or decrease resulting from the industrial composition of the region.
3 The differential component, resulting from industry in the region growing at a different rate from the national rate. The results are shown in Table 5 below.

He found 2 to be positive for the South East and West Midlands, neutral for the South West and negative for all other regions (with Northern and East Midlands worst). On the other hand 3 was favourable for the South West with the North West and Scotland having the largest negative figures. The policy implications of this analysis are that the North West and Scotland need resources devoted to their infrastructure to speed up growth while regions such as Wales, Yorkshire and Humberside and Northern require a redistribution of growth industries in their favour.

Another exercise on the relative importance of composition and growth[71] shows that 'the growing industries have grown less fast and the declining ones have declined faster in regions containing development areas than elsewhere. If industries in the areas grew in the relevant rates of 1952/63, the areas' total gain of employment would be less than three-fifths (two-fifths in manufacturing) of that which would result from industries growing at 1953/63 national rates.' This reinforces the view that there have been both regional and structural handicaps.

Thirlwall[72] emphasises that regional unemployment differences widen as the national unemployment rate increases. He finds that about half of this difference is a result of the composition of the region in terms of the importance of industries which are sensitive to cyclical fluctuations, e.g. capital goods and consumer durables. The other half he believes must be the result of the same industry being more sensitive in some regions than others. This latter phenomenon could be the result of the distribution of industry policy causing firms to locate new branches in the problem regions. Such branches could

TABLE 5 *Analysis of the regional pattern of employment growth 1959–1967*

Standard regions	(1) *Total increase in employment*	(2) *National growth*	(3) *Total shift*	(4) *Composition shift*	(5) *Differential shift*
	(as a percentage of regional employment in 1959)				
South-East East Anglia	8·9	5·9	+2·9	+3·2	−0·3
Southern Western	9·5	,,	+3·6	+0·2	+3·4
West Midlands	8·2	,,	+2·3	+1·4	=0·9
East Midlands	10·3	,,	+4·4	−4·7	+9·1
Yorks. & Humberside	3·2	,,	−2·6	−3·2	+0·6
North-Western	0·9	,,	−5·0	−0·8	−4·2
Northern	1·2	,,	−4·7	−5·0	+0·3
Scotland	1·3	,,	−4·6	−1·9	−2·7
Wales	3·0	,,	2·9	−3·5	+0·6
Great Britain	5·9	5·9	0	0	0

SOURCE Department of Employment and Productivity.
Note: Rounding up to one decimal place has resulted in minor anomalies in one or two figures.

well be the first to suffer as a result of cyclical fluctuations either because employment is maintained at head office rather than the branch when redundancies occur, or because branches produce newer products with higher price and income elasticities which could be more subject to cyclical fluctuation. Alternatively, where average unemployment figures have been high, there would be little incentive for firms to hoard labour through the cycle.

Lastly, we turn to criticisms of the recent policy. By 'recent' policy we mean since 1966. Although there has been a policy since the 1930's the weight given to it was stepped up in 1945 and again in

1964. Prior to 1934 the problems of depressed areas were viewed as resulting from depression in the staple industries of the area; thus action was taken to protect industries such as shipbuilding and cotton from overseas competition rather than to support the regions where employment was affected. These criticisms are of two main types, firstly those which suggest that the policy is wrong in its emphasis, secondly those which accept the emphasis as being correct but believe that the techniques used are wrong or the resources devoted to the intervention are insufficient.

The first type of criticism involves those who would like to see the emphasis on increased labour mobility and migration[73]. They point out there is already a considerable amount of labour mobility[74] but not all of this movement, as Kahn points out, is purposive and thus marginal changes could be extremely important. It has been pointed out[75] that between 1959 and 1962 annual net migration between the North and Wales to the Midlands and the South was equal to only about one-sixteenth of the unemployment. They emphasise that countries with high growth rates e.g. Italy, Germany and France have had these associated with considerable migration of labour. Sweden has found re-training and other policies associated with increased mobility of labour effective. It can be argued that the U.K.'s rate of growth in the nineteenth century may have been less had the North-West not been allowed to develop *vis à vis* other regions. Critics claim, that the argument for the 'Work to the Workers' policy that it helps to reduce congestion in the South-East, firstly, assumes that all parts of the South-East are congested in comparison to, for example, the North-West and secondly, the analysis of costs and benefits rests on highly subjective valuations of costs (e.g. 'Londoners like crowds'). Secondly, based on a Tyneside survey of 203 men, that mobility could be improved if better benefits were available.[76]

A second argument against the 'Work to the Workers' policy is that it would result in an unsatisfactory distribution of industry in the sense that, if successful, firms would be persuaded to locate in areas where costs would be higher than otherwise. At first sight this is a strong 'efficiency' argument—but one which we feel is not supported by the empirical evidence. Luttrell[77] shows that firms do not often act rationally in this matter either by selecting from a wide range of sites and, indeed, often do not devote large resources to the problem. Perhaps this is because 'for most firms, the question of looking for new locations at which to manufacture seldom arises'.[78] Considerable information about cost differences in different regions is not available but there is indirect evidence that these may not be very great, thus:

1 In the immediate post-war period, overseas companies were ready to locate in the new development areas.
2 The Toothill Committee[79] found that firms on Scottish industrial estates had transport costs of less than 2% of sales.
3 Luttrell found that in comparing differences in costs at branches and parent factories those within an industry were greater than those between head office and branch.
4 A survey[80] established that there were no differences between the average growth rates for the English and Scottish companies examined if compared in regional groups.

The second major criticism of the present policy comes from those who agree with the push/pull approach but quarrel with the way in which it has been implemented. Apart from those who agree with Holman[81] that I.D.C.s can never be a completely effective form of control, critics tend to be concerned with the scale and nature of the incentives.

Needleman[82] has shown that, based on 1960/63 figures, the costs incurred by the Board of Trade in creating a job, were £340 compared to benefits of £1,200. Such calculations support the case that the authorities have been too timid in applying available techniques and have attached too great a weight to the soundness and profitability of the applicant before the Board of Trade Advisory Committee.

The investment grants system has been criticised as being a benefit to both profitable and unprofitable companies. In addition, since it discriminates in favour of capital intensive industry, there is a danger that problem regions may find themselves with 'the modern equivalents of the heavy, cyclically-sensitive nineteenth century industries which, in their twentieth century decline, have been the sources of so many of the development areas' woes'.[83]

Thus, prior to the introduction of the Regional Employment Premium, little had been done to provide monetary incentives for the labour intensive firm, although such firms could obviously help in the short run, at least, to meet the unemployment problem. The R.E.P. has been criticised, in the purely micro-economic and not regional context, as being an incentive to labour hoarding, particularly of skilled labour where the incentive to avoid retraining costs is greatest.

Furthermore, the omission of service industries from benefit excludes a highly mobile sector which could contribute towards the proper distribution of industry which remains an objective of the 1966 Act.

After thirty years of locational and regional policy the problem regions still remain; this does not necessarily mean that the policy has been ineffective as without intervention the situation may have been worse.

To reiterate the points made in the opening paragraph of this section, all western countries appear to have such problems and that they continue to exist should not surprise us. Government intervention in this field has an uncertain basis in economic theory. In Section II we examined some general models, which by their nature are of little use to policy-makers. On the other hand theory may identify specific functional relationships which may be important. Thus it is a question of positive economics to show the relationships between policy and the attainment of objectives.[84] Howard's study is an example of a second problem of positive economics; that of isolating relationships and measuring the results.[85]

The biggest questions remain those of normative economics e.g. should we put national economic growth at risk in order to foster equality between regions. Economics, as such, can give no guidance but merely demonstrate the choices that have to be faced.[86]

Should we therefore have a regional policy? Governments apparently think so, as total expenditure in regional assistance reached £250 m.p.a. for 1968/69—which is much greater than the level of intervention for the year 1964/65. We are sceptical about intervention flowing from the consideration of regions as economic units.[87] Further problems arise when a Planning Board is constructed based on these 'artificial' units.[88] Sargent argues that regional authorities will be useless and perhaps harmful in regional policy which needs to be supra-regional. Thus a Midland local authority would want to relocate a mobile industry in an overspill area whereas the Board of Trade would try relocation in a Development Area. He emphasises the crucial importance of the secondary, inter-regional trade effects of relocation. For example a car assembly plant relocated in Wales might obtain its components from Birmingham while an identical plant relocated in Scotland might obtain components from northern England. In addition to this, more jobs may be created in Birmingham and the north than in Wales or Scotland.

A fundamental fault in regional strategy may have been to divide the U.K. into simply those areas requiring, and those not requiring, special assistance. Evidence of criticism along these lines has been pressure for assistance to 'Grey Areas', i.e. problem areas adjacent to Development Areas, reported on by the Hunt Commission.[89] A case could be made for varying differentials in investment grants and R.E.P. This view has some common ground with Robertson[90] that regional policy has a 'fatal wish for comprehensiveness' and that action should be confined to problems in particular regions, e.g. the shortage of labour and land in the South-East, the high unemployment in Northern Ireland, rather than construct the elaborate machinery covering the whole country which we now have.

We have more sympathy with the view that the disaggregation of national data may be valuable. Thus G.N.P. can be broken down into industries and also into regions. This is now being done as part of a N.I.E.S.R. research project.[91]

To conclude: There are those who see the problems of Development Areas as the result of deep economic forces—which does not mean that such forces are irresistible or that their causes should not be investigated. Thus C. Clark can say of the location of industry and population, 'I believe the free market does not give fully satisfactory results on this important matter'.[92] Perhaps a common attitude would be that in terms of equilibrium analysis the market is slow to reach the equilibrium.

It is, we believe, very easy to overemphasise the importance of intervention based on such an artificial and multi-definable concept as the region. Perhaps regional analysis has its greatest applicability in under-developed countries where the geographical areas are larger and intervention can shape the initial infrastructure and create locational advantages. This would leave the major contribution of regionally disaggregated information as being the insights which it brings into the operation of the economy. The fundamental impetus for some of regional policy is still socio-political. Whether economists are equipped to judge whether the techniques which have been used are consistent with the objectives is uncertain.

What economists can do is to make it clear that although a regional policy is part of our conventional wisdom, it is by no means clear that it is unreservedly worth while. There are always costs in the form of alternative resource-use and growth elsewhere foregone. The presumption arises that in some cases costs exceed benefits.

On the other hand, in the name of consistency an agnostic attitude is permissible to the reverse side of the coin. It does not follow that because a firm regards a particular location as second best that it is second best from the viewpoint of the welfare of society. To believe this would be to believe that resource-use in a free market is optimal; this is unquestionably not so.

Even if some such approach could be sustained it would be unquantifiable, for the costs are future economic growth foregone by the whole economy and the benefits present growth enjoyed by a particular region. We thus have the problem of discounting future costs to compare with present gains. However, the social rate of time discount is an unresolved problem (see page 177), furthermore we would need to compare the welfare gained by some with that lost by others, and interpersonal comparisons of utility cannot be made scientifically.

Notes

1 See page 289.
2 Usually unemployment, see p. 293.
3 See p. 289.
4 These headings are taken from Chapter Six of Edwards, R. S. and Townsend, H., *Business Enterprise. Its Growth and Organisation*, Macmillan (1958).
5 See p. 231.
6 But see footnote 77 for evidence that firms do not always devote many resources to this enquiry.
7 For an example of Weberian location theory applied to a particular industry see Chapter 5 of Oliver, J. L., *The Development and Structure of the Furniture Industry*, Pergamon Press (1966). Pergamon series of Monographs on Furniture and Timber, Volume 7.
8 See p. 300.
9 See a study by The International Information Centre for Local Credit, *Government Measures for the Promotion of Regional Economic Development*, p. 22, Martinus Nijhoff (1964).
10 Compare Luttrell, W. F., *Factory Location and Industrial Movement*, Volume I, Chapter 4, N.I.E.S.R. (1962). In the context of discussing the factors considered in the location of a branch 'the case we examined in which the visiting manager's mistress lived by the branch is, to the best of our knowledge, quite exceptional'.
11 Weber, A., *The Theory of the Location of Industries*, University of Chicago Press (1957).
12 Hoover, E. M., *The Location of Economic Activity*, McGraw-Hill (1948).
13 Isard, W., *Location and Space Economy*, Massachusetts Institute of Technology Press (1956).
14 See p. 300.
15 It is a paraphrase of the example in Friedmann, J. and Alonso, W., *Regional Development and Planning*. Chapter 4 by Alonso, W., 'Location Theory'. This essay is reprinted in Needleman, L. (Ed.), *Regional Analysis*, Penguin Modern Economics (1968).

16 A useful introduction to the concepts involved in regional analysis may be found in the books in the bibliography.

17 For a summary see Losch, A., *The Nature of Economic Regions*, referred to in bibliography.

18 Meyer, J. R., *Regional Economics: A Survey*, in Needleman, L., *op. cit.*

19 'Neither of the two traditional instruments of determining the geographical distribution of production can solve it, the theory of location cannot because it is applicable only to a single establishment, not to a whole industry; and the theory of comparative costs fails because it is applicable only to trade between men, not between countries', p. 113, Losch, A., 'The Nature of Economic Regions', Chapter 5, Friedmann, J. and Alonso, W., *op. cit.*

20 Some of the most important applications of regional analysis have been to the problems of under-developed countries. See Chapters 32-5 in Friedmann, J. and Alonso, W., *op. cit.*

21 See Meyer, J. R., *Regional Economics: A Survey*, Section 1, in Needleman, L., op. cit.

22 'What Sort of Regions?', *Economist* (22/6/68). Acton Society Trust, *Regionalism in England*, Vol. 2, 'Its nature and purpose'.

23 See p. 289.

24 Friedmann, J., *Regional Development Policy*, Chapter 3.

25 For an interesting account of how the criteria have changed for these reasons see Friedmann, J., 'The Concept of the Planning Region—The evolution of an Idea in the U.S.', Chapter 25 in Friedmann, J. and Alonso, W., op. cit. In his article he shows very clearly how in the 1930's regional planning in America meant largely the development of water resources and as a result the criterion for the planning area was the watershed (and thus a river basin, e.g. the Tennessee Valley Authority). In addition there developed the idea of the homogeneous 'folk region', e.g. The South. By 1945 the emphasis had swung to enquiries in the fields of transport, urban land use, metropolitan communications, and the metropolitan region then became a planning region.

26 See Friedmann, J., *Regional Development Policy*, Chapter 1, *op. cit.*

27 'The Location of Industries and Population', *Town Planning Review*, p. 195, October (1964).

28 Ullman, E. L., 'Regional Development and Concentration', Chapter 8, in Friedmann, J., and Alonso, W., *op. cit.*

29 Hirschman, A. O., 'Interregional and International Transmission of Economic Growth', Chapter XXXII in Friedmann and Alonso explains this in terms of social psychology, in which he suggests that a growth area is probably over impressed by success and pictures the

rest of the economy as being 'lazy, bungling, intriguing and hopeless'. As a result to move outside the centre area requires the quality of the innovator. See also measurements of cost differentials in the problem areas of the U.K., page 301.

30 See Note 41.

31 Myrdal, G., quoted in Ullman, E., 'Regional Development and Concentration', Chapter VIII in Friedmann, J. and Alonso, W., *op cit.*

32 'Interregional and International Transmission of Economic Growth', Chapter XXXII in Friedmann, J. and Alonso, W., *op. cit.*

33 See the Local Employment Act, 1960, p. 287.

34 See Meyer, Chapter 1 in Needleman, *Regional Economics.* See Isard and Cumberland, *Regional Economic Planning*, Chapter 1 for general surveys of regional analysis techniques.

35 See Brown, A. J., Lind, H. and Bowers, J., *The Green Paper on the Development Areas*, N.I.E.R. (May, 1967), Appendix 'A' for a calculation of the regional multiplier. A critical view of the value of such calculations is expressed in Wilson, T., *The Regional Multiplier—a critique*, Oxford Economic Papers (November, 1968).

36 *Economic Journal* (May, 1963).

37 See also Jay, D., *Board of Trade Journal* (July, 1965).

38 See Appendix to Chapter 8.

39 See p. 301.

40 Good surveys of events up to their publication dates may be found in *Midland Bank Review* (1964) Old and New Industrial Areas in Britain. Hemming, Mrs. M. F. W., *The Regional Problem*, N.I.E.R. (August, 1963), and Downie, Mrs. R., *Government Assistance to Industry*, University of Kent at Canterbury, Centre for Research in the Social Sciences, Ashford Study Paper 11 (February, 1968). An excellent article, from the standpoint of the planner, rather than the economist, is Self, P. J. O., *Region Planning in Britain. Analysis and Evaluation*, Regional Studies, Vol. 1, No. 1 (May, 1967).

41 In 1937 unemployment levels in the special areas were 18% compared to the average of U.K. as a whole of 10%. In 1945 the comparable figures were 1½% and 1%.

42 White Paper on Employment Policy, Cmnd. 6527, 1944.

43 Expanded in the *1952 Town Development Act.*

44 Rodwin, L. C., 'Choosing Regions for Development', Chapter 11 in Friedmann, J. and Alonso, W., *op. cit.*

45 As subsequently amended.

46 Offices were not included in these controls until 1965. See p. 288.

47 Covering approximately 17% of the working population of Great Britain.

48 Luttrell, W. F., *op. cit.*, pp. 68–9.

49 The first trading estate was Trafford Park, Manchester, 1896, and the first government sponsored one, the Team Valley Trading Estate, Gateshead 1936. Trading estates may be sponsored by the Board of Trade (through the English, Welsh and Scottish Industrial Estates Corporations) by local authorities (*) or be privately owned. In addition the Board of Trade may build single factories. New Town corporations and local authorities also provide factory accommodation. In 1968 250,000 jobs were provided in Board of Trade owned factories in Development Areas; of which a third were in Advance (and advance nest) factories—usually between 15,000–20,000 sq. ft.)—their distinguishing characteristic being that they were built and then offered to firms. (See article by Jay, D., in *Financial Times* (10/6/68) and *Financial Times* (3/7/68). Advance factories are an important technique of intervention since there is widespread evidence that firms are attracted by the availability of premises. This may outweigh the locational disadvantages of the area.

* See 'Arbroath for Growth', *The Courier* (27/12/68), Dundee.

50 See p. 291.

51 The L.O.B. has helped in the movement of over 50,000 office jobs out of London, compared to a total office employment of over ⅔ million. See Wabe, J. S., Office Decentralisation: An Empirical Study, pp. 35–55, *Urban Studies*, February, 1966). L.O.B. assisted moves have declined annually since 1968.

52 *Conditions Favourable to Faster Growth.*

53 Very roughly, these areas cover: all Scotland except Edinburgh, all Wales except the south coast and parts of the north, all England north of (approximately) York (i.e. the old North East Development Council Area) plus parts of Merseyside, Cornwall and Devon. Although considerably larger in geographical extent than Development Districts they covered 21% of the working population of Great Britain in 1966 compared with 16% for Development Districts in that year.

54 25% up to 31/12/68.

55 45% up to 31/12/68.

56 For an exhaustive summary of the aid available, presented as a package deal to the interested firm, see *Room to Expand*, a folder of booklets by the Board of Trade.

57 'In proportion to the number of male workers there are almost twice as many training places in Government Training Centres in Development Areas as in other parts of the country.' p. 7, D.E.A. Progress Report No. 35 (December 1967).

58 Self, P. J. O., Regional Planning in Britain. Analysis and Evaluation, *Regional Studies*, Vol. 1 (May 1967).

59 See Chapter 11, Part II in McClachlan, D. L. and Swann, D., *Competition Policy in the European Community*, Oxford University Press (1967). Measured in terms of income per head, regional variations in the E.E.C. ranged from the wealthiest province having over four times the income per head of the poorest province (Italy, 1963) to the wealthiest province having internal gross product at factor cost per habitant of 1·89 times the poorest (Belgium, 1959).

60 We are indebted in this section, and in the part of the chapter which deals with the causes of the regional problem, to material presented by Mr. F. Rendall at a staff seminar.

61 The *Ministry of Labour Gazette* (July, 1967), p. 552. 'Interregional migration of employees in Great Britain'. In the year 1965/66 705,000 changes of place of work between regions (*not residents*) are estimated to have taken place.

62 Oliver, J. L., 'Interregional Migration and Unemployment 1951/61', *Journal of the Royal Statistical Society*, Series A, Vol. 1217, Part 1 (1964).

63 See p. 282.

64 See p. 284.

65 See 'Regional employee activity rates', *Ministry of Labour Gazette* (July, 1967), p. 550.

66 Brown, A. J., 'Regional Problems and Regional Policy', *National Institute Economic Review* (November, 1968).

67 Coates, D. E. and Rawstron, E. N., 'Regional Variations in Income', *Westminster Bank Review* (February, 1966), Pullen, M. J., 'Unemployment and Regional Income per Head', *Manchester School* (January, 1966)—who states (p. 30) 'the aggregated regional data does not indicate a clear relationship between unemployment and the relative regional earnings' he argues that the criterion for regional policy should be income rather than unemployment.

68 Brown, A. J., N.I.E.R. (November, 1968), *op. cit.*

69 Humphrys, G., 'Growth Industries and the Regional Economies of Britain', *District Bank Review* (1962).

70 Stilwell, F. J. B., 'Location of Industry and Business Efficiency', *Business Ratios* (Winter, 1968).

71 Brown, A. J., Lind, H. and Bowers, J., *The Green Paper on the Development Areas*, N.I.E.R. (May, 1967).

72 Thirwall, A. P., 'Regional Unemployment as a Cyclical Problem', *Scottish Journal of Political Economy*, p. 205 (1966).

73 Richardson, H. W. and West, E. G., 'Must We Always Take Work to the Workers?', *Lloyds Bank Review* (January, 1964). West, E. G., 'Regional Planning: Fact and Fallacy', *Lloyds Bank Review* (April,

1966). See also Kahn, H. R., 'Labour Mobility: Some Critical Reflections', *District Bank Review* (March, 1966) and Thirwall, A. P., 'Migration and Regional Unemployment: Some Lessons for Regional Planning', *Westminster Bank Review* (November, 1966).

74 See p. 295.

75 Needleman, L. and Scott, B., 'Regional Problems and Location of Industry Policy in Britain', *Journal of Urban Studies* (November, 1964).

76 Seventy-six of the 203 said they would accept a job in another area at the same rate of pay, 29 of the 76 were married compared with 109 of the 203 sample. Only 29 of the sample could be classed as definitely immobile. Married men said that accommodation was the main problem, single men said that attachment to the area was the major problem.

77 Luttrell, W. F., *op. cit.*, p. 79, 'We should have liked to have given an example of a classic case of location choice in which operating cost estimates were made for two or more possible places, all imponderables or non-cost factors assessed and then a way found comparing the good and bad points of one place with those of another. Unfortunately we have not been able to find such a case.' Mr. Luttrell has pointed in correspondence that the use of consultants in this field is now widespread.

78 Luttrell, *op. cit.*, p. 39.

79 Quoted in Needleman, L. and Scott, D., 'Regional Problems and Location of Industry Policy in Britain', *Urban Studies* (November, 1964).

80 By Hart and MacBeen quoted in Fisher, G., 'Further Calculations on Regional Differences in Profitability and Growth', *Scottish Journal of Political Economy*, Vol. IX (1962) (reprinted in Needleman, L., *Regional Analysis*, op. cit.).

81 Holman, A. E., 'Industrial Development Certificates and Control of the Growth of Employment in South East England', *Urban Studies*, Vol. 1, No. 2 (November, 1964).

82 Needleman, L., 'What are we to do about the Regional Problem?', *Lloyds Bank Review* (January, 1965).

83 Brown, A. J., op. cit.

84 See account of cost benefit analysis in Chapter 8.

85 Howard, R. S., *The Movement of Manufacturing Industry in the United Kingdom 1945–65*, H.M.S.O. (1968). Howard shows how labour movement in terms of jobs has been

373,000 in the 7 years 1945–51
280,000 in the 8 years 1952–9
275,000 in the 6 years 1960–5

corresponding to periods of vigorous, less vigorous and more vigorous intervention. Over the whole period over half of the employment created has been in the peripheral areas.

86 Lipsey, R. G., *An Introduction to Positive Economics*, 1st Edition, p. xiii, 'Economic theory cannot, of course, ever show us what we ought to do, but only what will happen if we do certain things.'

87 See p. 289.

88 Sargent, J. R., 'Regional Economic Planning', in Prest, A. R. (Ed.), *Public Sector Economics*, Manchester University Press (1968).

89 Hunt, Sir J., *The Intermediate Areas*, Cmnd. 3998 (1969).

90 Robertson, D. J., 'A Nation of Regions?', *Urban Studies* (November, 1965).

91 See Brown, A. J., *op. cit.* See also Sargent, *op. cit.*

92 Clark, C., 'The Location of Industries and Population', *The Town Planning Review* (October, 1964).

Bibliography

Apart from specialised books in regional analysis, most of the rest of the material is in article form.

THEORY OF REGIONAL ANALYSIS

RICHARDSON, W. R., *Regional Economic Development: Location Theory, Urban Structure and Regional Change*, Wiedenfield and Nicholson, 1969

FRIEDMANN, J., *Regional Development Policy*, The M.I.T. Press, 1966

FRIEDMANN, J. and ALONSO, W., *Regional Development and Planning*, The M.I.T. Press, 1964

The parts of both books which are referred to in the text, will be helpful to the economist.

NEEDLEMAN, L. (Ed.), *Regional Analysis*, Penguin Modern Economics, 1968

BRITISH EXPERIENCE

DOWNIE, Mrs., 'Government Assistance to Industry', *University of Kent at Canterbury. Centre for Research in the Social Sciences. Ashford Study Paper II*, 1968

MCCRONE, G., 'Regional Policy in Britain', Allen and Unwin, 1969

Three recent articles dealing with current research in this field are:

BROWN, A. J., 'Regional Problems and Regional Policy', *N.I.E.R.*, November, 1968

STILLWELL, F. J. B., Location of Industry and Business Efficiency, *Business Ratios*, Winter, 1968

BROWN, A. J., 'Regional Economics, with Special Reference to the United Kingdom', *Economic Journal*, Vol. LXXIX, December, 1969

Authors and Works Cited

( ): footnote number; B: Bibliography

Index

For Product Safety Concerns and Information please contact our EU representative GPSR@taylorandfrancis.com
Taylor & Francis Verlag GmbH, Kaufingerstraße 24, 80331 München, Germany

www.ingramcontent.com/pod-product-compliance
Lightning Source LLC
LaVergne TN
LVHW020001031026
849161LV00023B/799
* 9 7 8 1 0 4 1 0 8 4 2 1 1 *